M. Wiens

D1473746

DATE DUE

DEC 7 1981	
APR 11 1988	
MAR 20 1989	
DEC 11 1989	
APR 26 2004	

TABOR COLLEGE LIBRARY
Hillsboro. Kansas 67063

TABOR COLLEGE LIBRARY
Hillsboro, Kansas 67063

Early Childhood Education

An Individualized Approach to Developmental Instruction

372.19
L729e

Early Childhood Education

An Individualized Approach to Developmental Instruction

David L. Lillie

University of North Carolina, Chapel Hill

 SCIENCE RESEARCH ASSOCIATES, INC.
Chicago, Palo Alto, Toronto, Henley-on-Thames, Sydney, Paris

A Subsidiary of IBM

810118

TABOR COLLEGE LIBRARY
HILLSBORO, KANSAS 67063

Acknowledgments

We would like to thank the following sources for material used in the text.

Figure 3-1 was adapted from material in the *P.M.A. Readiness Level*, copyright 1974, T. G. Thurstone; it is reproduced with the permission of the author and publisher (Science Research Associates). Figures 8-1, 8-2, 8-3, 8-4, 8-5, 8-6, 8-7, 8-8, and 8-9 are reprinted from *Learning to Think*, copyright 1972, T. G. Thurstone, with the permission of the author and publisher (Science Research Associates). The appendix art was supplied by, and is reprinted with the permission of, T. G. Thurstone.

Material for figures 4-3, 4-4, 4-5, 6-2, 6-3, 7-1, 7-2, 7-3, 7-4, 7-5, 7-6, 7-7, 7-8, 7-9, and 7-10 was supplied by T. G. Thurstone and D. L. Lillie and is reproduced with their permission.

Figures 4-1, 4-2, 6-5, 6-6, 6-7, and 6-8 are reprinted with permission from T. G. Thurstone and D. L. Lillie, *Beginning to Learn: Perceptual Skills*, copyright 1972, Science Research Associates.

Figures 5-2, 5-3, 5-4, 5-5, 5-6, 5-7, 5-8, and 5-9 are reprinted with permission from T. G. Thurstone and D. L. Lillie, *Beginning to Learn: Fine Motor Skills*, copyright 1970, Science Research Associates.

© 1975, Science Research Associates, Inc.
All rights reserved.
Printed in the United States of America

Library of Congress Catalog Card Number: 74-29042

ISBN 0-574-18602-6

Dedication

For a number of years now, I have had the extreme good fortune to work closely with Thelma Gwinn Thurstone. Without access to Mrs. T's wealth of information on curriculum development and research procedures, this book would have been much more difficult to write.

So it is fitting that this book be dedicated to Dr. Thurstone, whose wisdom has been a source of inspiration to all of us who are concerned with early childhood education.

Preface

This book on early childhood education is different. It addresses in specific terms what to teach young children (content) and how to teach young children (method). Early childhood education, as the term is used in this text, refers to an organized series of learning experiences for children from three to six years of age. (The curriculum can, of course, also be used with children who are slightly younger or older.)

This text does not present an exhaustive review of the history of early childhood education or of research efforts in child development. A brief historical overview is provided to establish a perspective for the instructional system presented here, and theory and research efforts are cited to establish its authoritative base. The emphasis of this book is on the development of instructional skills and the application of those skills to a specific method for individualizing instruction: the Developmental Task Instructional System.

The content of the Developmental Task Instructional System grew out of the research efforts described in the works of T. G. and L. L. Thurstone. The method evolved over a period of several years of working with young children and their teachers at the University of North Carolina.

Early Childhood Education provides, for both novice and experienced teachers, the tools necessary to help young children develop and strengthen the skills they must possess to function successfully in a learning environment. No teacher who has read this text should find herself, on that first Monday morning in September, looking down at a room full of young active children and wondering desperately: What do I do now?

The pronoun *we* is used throughout this text. This usage is particularly appropriate here because the thoughts expressed on the following pages are the result of an accumulation of experiences and contributions of many individuals. Foremost among the contributors is Dr. Thelma Gwinn Thurstone: her creative work in curriculum development for young children is the foundation on which the Developmental Task Instructional System is based. Dr. Mary Margaret Wood, the author of the chapter on social and emotional development, also made an important contribution to this work.

In addition, I am indebted to several generations of bright graduate students in our program at The University of North Carolina. In particular I would like to thank Gale Swann, Gloria Harbin, John Swetnam, Rusty Gray, Bud Moore, Roxie Smith, Don Bailey, Jane Findley, Paul Woods, and Ellen Nash. I would also like to express appreciation to Lorraine McNally and Sadie Briggs for typing numerous drafts and the final manuscript.

Chapel Hill, 1975

Contents

Early Childhood Education

An Individualized Approach to Developmental Instruction

Chapter 1

An Introduction to Early Childhood Curriculum

Objectives

After you have completed this chapter, you should be able to:

1. List the differences between the "open classroom," "structured task analysis," and the "eclectic" curricula approaches to early childhood education.

2. Cite several reasons why interest in early childhood education has increased tremendously over the last several years.

3. List at least four difficult-to-control variables that make curriculum research "messy."

4. Cite the results of two studies comparing different curriculum approaches for the preschool child.

5. Cite three implications for early childhood curricula as a result of recent research. Explain how teachers and other curriculum developers can make use of such research results.

Each September, all over the United States, children under six are introduced to what must seem to most of them an exotic new environment. The names attached to the new environments vary: the San Jose Day Care Center for Working Mothers, the Happy Tots Nursery School, Kalamazoo Public Schools Kindergarten, KLM's Day Care for Employees' Children, the Graham Child Development Center.

The children letting go of mother's hand also differ: some are self-confident, others shy; some are agile, others clumsy; some are laughing, others crying.

The teachers on the other side of the door also vary: many like children, some don't; some are confident of their abilities, others lack confidence; some are well trained, others have had no training at all.

But what skills and what knowledge about children should they have? Is there such a thing as a "curriculum" for early childhood education? The author believes that there should be such a curriculum, and in this text will present a specific system for organizing it. As the term is used here, *curriculum refers to systematic procedures for organizing educational activities; the procedures include both content (what to teach) and method (how to teach).*

There is a core curriculum for elementary school students (the three R's); the author believes that there should also be a core curriculum for preschool children. It should be based on a knowledge of child development and designed to revolve around a series of central topics, or "subjects." In addition, there should be a systematic methodology based on educational technology and knowledge about how young children learn.

Early Childhood Education: Pioneering Studies

In 1969 the President of the United States, in his State of the Nation message to Congress, indicated that there is little doubt that early learning experiences are crucial for optimal growth and development in the young child. Not long after these remarks were made, the U.S. Office of Child Development was constituted to coordinate the development and administration of federally funded programs for young children. The Office of Child Development was not the first government agency set up to provide services for young children, but its establishment at that time indicated the coming of age of the recognition of the role of experience in child development.

Coming of age was not easy. In the nineteenth century there were two quite different attitudes toward early childhood education. Many child psychologists and educators believed that the child's task experiences made little difference in his eventual intellectual development. These individuals believed that such experiences might be beneficial for the physical development of the child, but that early education programs were basically a convenience for adults. Other professionals, however, believed that future intellectual deficiencies could be prevented by early experience, particularly early sensual experience.

In this century one of the most persuasive arguments advocating the importance of early childhood education was presented by J. McV. Hunt in *Intelligence and Experience* (1961).* Hunt surveys the literature on the influence of experience on intelligence, and finds convincing evidence that challenges the belief in fixed intelligence and predetermined development.

---

*Unless otherwise indicated, complete publication data for all text citations is given in the references, pages 213–19.

In his concluding remarks, Hunt issues a challenge based on his findings:

In the light of these considerations, it appears that the counsel from experts on child-rearing during the third and much of the fourth decades of the twentieth century to let children be while they grow and to avoid excessive stimulation was highly unfortunate. The problem for the management of child development is to find out how to groom the encounters that children have with their environments to foster both an optimally rapid rate of intellectual development and a satisfying life. Further . . . it might be feasible to discover ways to govern the encounters that children have with their environments, especially during the early years of their development, to achieve a substantially faster rate of intellectual capacity . . . . It is one of the major challenges of our time. (p. 363.)

Benjamin Bloom's (1964) work also supports the importance of the role of experience in child growth and development. Bloom's review of the literature of child-development studies indicates that experience has a greater impact during the period in which a particular behavior characteristic is undergoing relatively rapid change. Since most behavior characteristics change more rapidly during infancy and early childhood, Bloom concludes that manipulation of experiences has the greatest effect during the first years of life.

It is interesting to note that the two best-known research studies supporting the need for early educational intervention dealt with children who were not developing normally. Kirk (1958, 1965) in a series of studies on young mentally retarded children found support for the positive effect of early education. One study compared institutionalized children: fifteen were given preschool education and twelve (of similar ages and I.Q.'s) were not. In follow-up studies, the preschool group was found to have gained substantially in intelligence and social maturity, whereas the nonschool group declined.

In a similar study of community-based normal children, twelve children from "inadequate" homes attending an experimental preschool were compared with siblings and twins living in the same home but not attending school. In addition, four children who had been taken out of inadequate homes and placed in foster homes, and who also attended the experimental preschool, were compared to the first two groups. Kirk found that all four foster-home children and eight of the twelve home-based preschool children gained in rate of mental development. In comparison, only one-seventh of the twins and siblings in the control group gained in rate of mental development. The implication of Kirk's efforts is that preschool programs for these children tend to intervene and reverse subnormal functioning by increasing the rate of development.

Perhaps Harold Skeels, more than any other individual, can be credited with the awakening of interest in the importance of early intervention. In 1939 Skeels and Dye discovered that two severely retarded young girls who had been placed in a ward of a state institution with a group of older girls showed dramatic gains in I.Q. This discovery prompted a formal investigation in which the investigators transferred thirteen mentally retarded young children (all under three years of age) from an orphanage to an institution for the retarded. The thirteen children received intensive mothering from a group of older retarded girls. Through the years it was noted that the intellectual abilities of these children increased significantly more than did the intellectual abilities of a similar group of children who had tested normal at the time of admission to an orphanage (Skeels and Dye, 1939).

The full impact of the Skeels studies, however, was not evident for thirty years. In a follow-up study (1966), Skeels finds remarkable differences between the two groups. All thirteen children in the experimental group are self-supporting. Four attended one or more years of college, and one had graduate training. In the normal control group, four persons are still wards of institutions.

Studies of this nature give a great deal of support to the argument that we need to provide stimulating experiences during early childhood, particularly if there is reason to believe that educational or experimental intervention is needed to enable a child to reach the maximum (or at least a higher) level of functioning.

To be sure, there are other important factors behind the surge of interest in early childhood education. More and more mothers and housewives are asserting their right to develop an identity outside the home. As a result, a greater proportion of the population of preschool-age children will be placed in substitute-care situations. Then, too, there are the women who cannot afford the luxury of a full-time role as housewife and mother; they are forced to work because of the need for a second salary in a low-income family or, as is the case in many families, the only salary.

Current Curriculum Approaches

Contemporary early education practices have been influenced by the recent emphasis on interventionist strategy. That is, within the last decade the focus of many programs has changed from one of supporting and nurturing the young child to one of providing for specific educational or developmental needs.

One curriculum dimension that varies quite noticeably from program to program is the degree of formality or structure in the curriculum. Many educators believe that early education programs should be primarily informal and child-directed; that is, that the child should be allowed to decide what activities he will be involved in. These educators usually believe that social and emotional development are the most important tasks of any preschool program. Other educators, however, believe that the curriculum should be very formal, stressing the cognitive development of the child.

Most educational technologists are in the second group; they believe that structure is necessary if one is going to provide meaningful intervention during the early ages. In the first group are the child-development specialists who, in the tradition of Froebel (1895), place emphasis on child-oriented play. The contemporary "humanist" focus on child-oriented activities suggests that structure may deprive a child of his learning potential.

Perhaps a great deal of the controversy about structure is due to a lack of communication between educators, child-development specialists, and other child workers. The term *structure* has many definitions. To some it means controlling impulsivity, establishing a consistent routine, and providing an inflexible physical room arrangement. To others it means specific goals and activities for each child and a teacher-directed instructional focus. To still others, it means all these things and more.

Actually, all programs have some degree of structure. Even the most flexible programs usually have a time format for the day. And most teachers have some idea about what they want their children to accomplish during the day or year. An unstructured program, such as the traditional play nursery, may provide a wide variety of materials, toys, and equipment for children, but these materials have been selected with specific purposes in mind.

Any person trained in child development knows that there is a sequential pattern of intellectual and physical development in children. The widely accepted intellectual-development theories of Guilford (1967), Piaget (Flavell, 1963), and Thurstone and Thurstone (1941) spell out this pattern in great detail. To be sure, there are individual differences in the quality or speed of development. Appropriate educational experiences during the preschool years may improve the quality and hasten the speed of various aspects of the child's development.

Present-Day Programs: An Overview

A number of different curricula have been developed in response to the need to provide meaningful educational experiences for young children. Figure 1-1 shows the curricula that will be discussed in this chapter on a continuum of diversity from informal to formal. We use the terms *formal-informal*, rather than *structured-non-structured* because, as we have already pointed out, the word *structure* means different things to different persons. The informal-formal continuum is based on the degree of directiveness in the daily

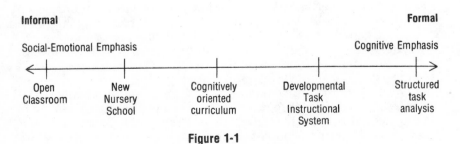

Figure 1-1

curriculum activities. *Informal*, as used here, refers to a very flexible child-planned and child-directed day, whereas *formal* refers to a fairly inflexible teacher-planned and teacher-directed day. In this sense, the continuum does not take into account the physical arrangement of the room and the amount of child movement around the room. These two factors can be, and often are, independent of the formal-informal classification.

In general, informal programs emphasize goals in social and emotional development, and formal programs emphasize goals in cognitive development. Although many educators and child-development specialists discuss these two important areas of child development as separate entities, they are intricately interrelated. (This interrelationship is discussed in detail in chapter 9.) Therefore, although figure 1-1 appears to suggest that one entity has to be emphasized at the expense of the other, educators should be warned against thinking in terms of a social-emotional/cognitive dichotomy when planning curricula.

The Open Classroom
Within the last several years there has been a mounting interest in an informal classroom structure for young children. The curriculum of the British Infant School, which is equivalent to kindergarten through grade three in the United States, has had a great deal to do with the stimulation of this interest. The Plowden report (1967) is generally pointed to as evidence for the effectiveness of the informal approach.

There are many open-classroom programs operating in the United States today. In general, the goals in such programs are similar: social, emotional, and intellectual development. Depending on the specific program, the age of the children will vary. Many have a wide age range, often combining four-, five-, and six-year-olds, in an attempt to provide some continuity between preschool and formal school activities.

The two significant features of the open-classroom programs are the *integrated day* and *vertical grouping.* The integrated day is closely tied to the concept of a child-oriented curriculum. Interest centers are provided in various parts of the classroom, and no time schedules are used. Rather, the child is permitted to seek his area of interest from the various activities going on in the room. He may choose to take part in a science or mathematics activity or in a more socially oriented activity such as adult-role playing. A basic assumption underlying the application of the open-classroom system is that children will accept the responsibility of organizing their own learning experiences in a systematic and beneficial manner. The teacher's role is one of a subtle facilitator: he helps the children develop various concepts but does not direct them in their choice of activities.

The concept of vertical (non-age-level) grouping goes hand in hand with open-classroom programs. It is also a predominant feature of ungraded schools in the United States. For example, one elementary school class might be composed of children varying in age from five to eight, all of whom share some of the same learning activities.

The rationale for vertical grouping is a straightforward one: chronological age grouping does not necessarily provide homogeneity of learning needs or abilities, nor does it facilitate viewing children as individuals.

One feature of the British Infant School approach that is often overlooked when it is transported to America is the age of the children in the British schools. We mentioned earlier that the British programs include children from five through eight. Many American educators, however, are applying this approach to preschool children, ages three through five.

Another factor often overlooked is that British society is more homogeneous than American society. It may be quite possible that "middle stream" children, who constitute a large majority of the children in a socialistic economy such as Great Britain's, are better equipped to take advantage of the open classroom than are children from outside the middle stream. This difference may be related to the respect for education and authority systems (schools) learned in British homes. Some educators have asked themselves if the American lower-class child can be expected to progress as quickly in the open classroom as the American middle-stream child. In spite of such questions, the open classroom has become quite popular in the United States today. Independence and self-direction have a long history in this country, and both of these concepts are clearly visible in the open-classroom approach.

At the opposite end of the philosophical continuum from the open-classroom approach is the structured task-analysis approach. The structured task-analysis approach to early childhood education grew out of the stimulus-response learning theories championed by Skinner (1938), and reflect the recent proliferation of research efforts in the changing of behavior by means of specific conditioning procedures.

Structured Task Analysis

Bereiter and Engelmann (1966a and 1966b) combined the stimulus-response approach to learning with the concept of behavioral objectives, as discussed by Bloom (1964) and Mager (1962), to establish their rather unique method for early educational intervention. This approach grew out of a basic concern for the lack of identifiable uniform goals for the disadvantaged children enrolled in federally funded Head Start programs. They argue that if programs such as Head Start are going to enable "culturally" disadvantaged preschool children to catch up with middle-class children, they must be rigidly structured to develop specific cognitive abilities. Bereiter and Engelmann believe that time is an important factor: a child who is a year or two behind his middle-class age mates in language and conceptual development cannot be expected to catch up unless he develops these skills twice as fast as the middle-class child.

Bereiter and Engelmann's approach does not distinguish between developmental skills and academic skills, and rejects the concept of school readiness. Priorities are established in areas of language development and academic-skill development. In establishing specific behavioral objectives the question is asked: what skills must the child entering first grade possess if he is to have an adequate chance of succeeding in school?

In answering this question Bereiter and Engelmann establish fifteen minimum goals for children in preschool programs. Three examples of these are: (1) the ability to name the primary colors, plus white, black, and brown; (2) the ability to count to 20 aloud without help and to 100 with help at decade points (30, 40, and so forth); and (3) a sight-reading vocabulary of at least four words in addition to proper names, with evidence that the printed word has the same meaning for them as the corresponding spoken word. "What word is this?" "Cat." "Is this a thing that goes 'woof-woof'?" "No, it goes 'meow'." (Bereiter and Engelmann, 1966b, pp. 48-49.) It should be noted that the Bereiter-Engelmann curriculum programs, although developed for so-called disadvantaged children at the preschool level, appear to be aimed more at six- and seven-year-old children than at three-, four-, and five-year-olds.

This curriculum approach is controversial. It is criticized not so much for what is taught as for the methods used in the teaching. The program is highly teacher-oriented, with heavy emphasis on "canned routine."

The instructional system of the Bereiter-Englemann program was initially divided into areas of language, arithmetic, and reading. Each of these areas is represented in an instructional program subsequently developed by Englemann and his colleagues and published by Science Research Associates under the trade name *Distar.*® These programs are designed to be used with a homogeneous group of from five to ten children.

In the language program, 22 fundamental concepts are presented: included are identity statements, action statements, part-whole relationships, polars (long-short), prepositions, and categories. The reading and arithmetic *Distar* programs concentrate on development of specific academic skills in those areas.

Unlike many early childhood curriculum approaches, this program has been extensively researched by the authors. Engelmann, as well as other independent investigators, has conducted a number of well-controlled studies to determine the effectiveness of the program. Some of these results are discussed under "Research Procedures" (see page 10).

The New Nursery School   The New Nursery School developed by Nimnicht, McAfee, and Meier (1969) combines elements of the Montessori curriculum with the more contemporary principles of compensatory education championed by Martin Deutsch. The program was initiated in Colorado in 1964, with three-, four-, and five-year-old disadvantaged children. The major goals of the program are the development of a positive self-image and an increase in the intellectual abilities of perceptual acuity, language-concept formation, and problem solving.

These goals are seen as necessary in preparing children for future successful learning experiences. In order to accomplish these goals, learning must take place within a carefully planned climate that is both active and responsive. Furthermore, Nimnicht believes that the child should participate in activities which are self-directed and autotelic. *Autotelic activities* are activities like game playing which are rewarding in themselves and do not depend upon unrelated rewards and punishments.

There are two adults for each group of fifteen children. One adult is a nonprofessional volunteer or assistant; the other is a trained teacher. Thoughtful and careful planning by both teacher and assistant is necessary to determine the appropriate time and manner to introduce a child to a particular skill. When planning, the teacher considers the school's objectives, the school's resources, her evaluation of a particular child, and time.

The program has six learning activities booklets that contain behavioral objectives and activities sequenced in ascending order of difficulty. The activities are planned in such a way that the child spends most of the day in self-directed activities. About fifteen minutes a day is devoted to group activities or planned learning episodes. The children are invited but not required to participate in these. Each day there are many choices of learning activities, none of which is mandatory. For the development of cognitive skills, each day's learning situation must provide: informal learning experiences in a wide variety of situations; some teacher-child interaction, either individually or in a group; a group time to consolidate, evaluate, and reinforce the concepts the child is learning; and additional informal experience to maintain and extend learning.

The cognitively oriented curriculum was developed by David Weikart and his associates over a period of years as part of the Perry Preschool Project in Ypsilanti, Michigan. This program is one of the few attempts to adapt Piaget's developmental theory directly to a preschool curriculum. The program, which stresses language usage and cognitive development, is aimed primarily at children three to six years old from low-income families. The general goals of the curriculum are to increase cognitive functioning at the formal operations level as defined by Piaget and to develop social and emotional maturity. The content in this approach is well specified and divided into four main areas: classification, seriation, temporal relations, and spatial relations. These four content areas relate closely to the reasoning area of the Development Task Instructional System, which is discussed in detail in chapter 7.

Although the content of the program is established by the teacher, the child chooses activities from a group set up beforehand. The teacher is mainly a facilitator of learning, encouraging the child to make judgments, evaluate, and experiment.

The classroom is divided into four distinct areas; the materials in each are arranged so that the child will progress sequentially from

The Cognitively Oriented Curriculum

simple to more complex tasks. The areas are large motor, small motor, housekeeping, and art. In addition to the classroom program, the Perry Preschool Project includes a teacher home-visitation program.

Research in Curriculum Methods

If education at any level is going to develop credibility as a social science, there must be a direct relationship between educational research and educational practice.

Until fairly recently there have been few objective research efforts investigating the efficacy of various early childhood curriculum approaches. (In fact, there were no studies to determine if early education had any value at all until the Skeels findings aroused interest.) The increase in studies investigating educational intervention at an early age has been primarily due to recent interest in specific subgroups of the early childhood population: the disadvantaged or the handicapped. Although there has been an increase in scientific inquiry, many current curriculum practices are based on "expert" opinion, testimonials, and anecdotal reports reflecting the opinionated beliefs of the proponent.

For the most part, educators and child workers, especially those in face-to-face situations with children, have little need for training in research methodology. However, if one is involved in curriculum organization, it is very desirable to have some knowledge of research findings on the relative effectiveness of various approaches to educating young children. This is not easy. Many research efforts are not directly applicable to practical situations. Some researchers present their results and arguments in such a manner that they are often uninterpretable by the practitioner. Nevertheless, a knowledge of what is happening in research is helpful in (1) making decisions about curriculum organization, (2) purchasing materials and supplies, (3) understanding what classroom methods can and cannot do for children, and (4) presenting and supporting an early childhood program to parents, administration, and the public.

Curriculum research at its best is thought of as "messy" research by the pure scientist. Many hard-to-control variables affect changes in children's behavior. It is extremely difficult to equalize differences in teachers, differences between groups of children, the prior experience of children, and classroom environmental differences. Nevertheless, well-controlled studies can and do provide information that can be useful in developing curriculum strategies.

Research Procedures

Just as there has been an evolution of curriculum practices, there has also been an evolution of educational research practices. Until recently, most studies of the effects of various curriculum approaches on the learning of young children have been what we would call a one-group study; that is, a reporting of the gains in development, intelligence, or achievement of children enrolled in a particular program without comparing these gains to gains of children enrolled in some other type of program.

Another frequently used research procedure is the comparison of an experimental group with a control group. The progress of both groups is usually measured by giving the children pre- and post-tests; that is, testing them at the beginning and end of the program with the same test. The progress of each group is then compared. Again, the implications that can be drawn from the results of this procedure are limited. We already have good evidence, discussed earlier, that children enrolled in a preschool gain significantly more in intellectual abilities than comparable groups of children who stay home. What we cannot find out from this procedure is what specifically determined the differences. Usually the experiences of the control groups go unrecorded. Therefore, the variable being manipulated—the experiences of the home-based children—cannot be defined.

Curriculum research in early childhood education has evolved to the point of trying to determine the extent of the "superiority" of one approach over another. Within the last decade a number of investigations have been conducted using a *treatment-comparison design*. Instead of employing one experimental group and one control group, these studies use several experimental treatment groups. Studies by Hodges, McCandless, and Spicker (1971), Weikart (1970), Bereiter and Engelmann (1966a), Karnes, Teska, and Hodgins (1969), and Miller (1970) are all examples of the treatment-comparison design. Although these attempts are commendable and perhaps even a necessary step in the evolution of educational-research practices, the comparison of total curriculum approaches is extremely complex if not impossible. Different teachers using the same set of daily lessons or activities will not necessarily be providing the same experiences for the children in their respective classes. The effects of interaction between teacher, physical environment, materials, time of day, and children, to name just a few of the variables, will vary even though each teacher is following precisely the same written curriculum program.

Typical of the treatment-comparison studies is the work of Karnes, Teska, and Hodgins (1969), who compared several curriculum approaches over a two-year period. In this study five different curriculum approaches were compared: (1) The Traditional Program—the goal was to foster acquisition of social skills through incidental informal learning; (2) Amelioration of Deficits Program—this curriculum was designed to develop language and teach specific content in areas of math, language arts, social studies, and science, and is described in some detail in chapter 8; (3) Direct Verbal Program—the task-analysis curriculum using *Distar* materials, described earlier; (4) Montessori Program—a program administered by qualified Montessori teachers using Montessori materials; and, (5) Community Integrated Program—a traditional nursery school program at four neighborhood centers conducted by four professional preschool teachers.

Findings at the end of one year of preschool suggested that the more structured programs, the direct-verbal and amelioration approach, had a greater effect on intellectual development than the other three programs. At the end of the second year of the study, only three approaches were compared; again, the children in the direct-verbal program showed greater gains in language development and intelligence. The results of educational achievement testing of the three groups indicated that the Karnes ameliorative program and the Engelmann direct-verbal program were more effective.

David Weikart, who, along with his colleagues, developed the cognitively oriented curriculum (Weikart et al., 1971), which was briefly discussed earlier, ran a similar treatment-comparison study over a period of several years. Compared were the cognitively oriented curriculum approach, the Engelmann program, and a traditional child-development program. All three programs had clearly defined week-by-week goals and carefully planned daily lessons and activities designed by the teachers in each program.

Weikart indicated that gains in intelligence were unusually high in all three programs. However, he could find no differences in effectiveness between the three programs (Weikart, 1970).

At first glance, Weikart's findings seem incompatible with the results of Karnes's study, which suggests that well-structured programs such as the Engelmann program are more effective with young children. However, in discussing these differences, Mayer (1971) points to the fact that in Weikart's study the child-development model included more deliberately planned activities than are usual in traditional child-development programs. All three programs in Weikart's investigation concentrated on getting the children to focus and sustain attention, and to inhibit random, purposeless activity in favor of deliberate and planned action (Mayer, 1971). The organization of goal-directed activities is a basic factor in the philosophy of the structured task-analysis approach (Bereiter and Engelmann, 1966b) and the cognitively oriented curriculum (Weikart et al., 1971), and is purposely avoided in the traditional child-development approach.

Mayer (1971) believes that the success of these preschool programs is due more to the planning and organizing of curriculum activities than to the philosphy and content of the programs. In supporting this conclusion he states that "the evaluations are based on program labels with little descriptive information or observational research documenting how children and teachers actually spend their time. Consequently, attempts to explain results as a function of differences in program models are still premature." (p. 133.) This point is extremely important because the variations within the programs labeled open classroom, Montessori, or structured task analysis may be as great as the variations between them.

Weikart's more recent conclusions concur: "I expected to find immediate differences on most measures among the three curriculum models. Instead I found that during the time I was able to maintain equal momentum and staff commitment for the three programs, we obtained equal results on most measures from standardized intelligence tests to classroom observations and teacher ratings . . . . From this situation, two essential points emerge regarding the operation of effective preschools: (1) planning . . . and (2) supervision." (Weikart, 1972, pp. 53-54.)

As a result of the efforts to determine the most effective curriculum approach in early childhood education, the following conclusions can be made.

1. Planning and organization of the curriculum are crucial elements in determining the effectiveness of early childhood education. Determine educational objectives for children and select curriculum strategies and activities that will facilitate reaching these objectives.

2. Attempts to prove the superiority of one curriculum approach over others are futile in the face of the inability to control important contributing factors and their interaction effects. It is irrational to believe that there is a one best curriculum approach for the early education of children. Much depends on the match between the strengths and weaknesses of the teacher, the environmental limitations, the curriculum strategies selected, and, of course, the characteristics of the children.

3. Labeling curriculum approaches is an extremely precarious pastime because of the inability to replicate a learning environment. If you select a curriculum system based on the results of this type of research, remember that the children, the classroom, and the interaction between the teacher, the classroom environment, and the children will be a unique situation that cannot be duplicated. Because a curriculum approach proved superior in one situation does not mean that it will work in another. Combining your knowledge of curriculum-research results with your knowledge of your children and your learning environment, you should then select and develop an instructional system that works for you.

4. More precise and perhaps more rewarding studies will begin to emerge as research practices evolve to the point of looking at distinct features of various curriculum approaches and their effect on behavior of individual children within groups. Curriculum research should focus on a specific program within a particular approach, such as a fifteen-minute-per-day segment of creative play that has spelled-out objectives for the children and a corresponding set of activities that can be repeated in different situations. How various children respond to a particular sequence of events is the kind of information that is most helpful to a curriculum organizer. Using this kind of data, he or she can create from a number of smaller curriculum components, a program and classroom environment for specific children.

What teaching skills and knowledge about children should an early childhood educator have? Should there be a core curriculum in early childhood education? The discussion so far has given us some clues to the answer.

The Curriculum Needs of Early Childhood Education

1. In view of past and present practices, the use of educational and scientific technology, as well as the child-oriented, humanistic teachings of

Froebel, are necessary in a viable curriculum approach. Both formality and informality have their place in the curriculum. The social-emotional development of the child and the cognitive development of the child are equally important, and perhaps inseparable.

2. Planning and organization on the part of the teacher are extremely important factors. The teacher or child worker needs to be well organized, using systematic curriculum procedures to ensure the success of his program.

Checkpoint
What Have You Learned?

Facts[*]

1. Three trends supporting the establishment of day-care, early childhood, public school, and child-development programs can be identified as: (1) _____: a growing awareness of the right of women to develop an independent identity. (2) Economic: a growing need for many women to work to supplement low incomes. (3) Educational: _____ strongly indicates that early _____ promotes greater intellectual development.

2. The _____ approach to early childhood curriculum is characterized by the integrated day and vertical grouping.

3. The integrated day refers to interest areas set up around the room where _____ involvement is based on his own interest(s) and motivation.

4. _____ is an example of a structural task-analysis curriculum approach.

5. The longitudinal study of young retarded children by _____ dramatically demonstrated large differences between individuals who received early _____ and those who did not.

6. Weikart's studies indicate that _____ and _____ are the most important factors in the operation of an effective preschool.

7. List two studies addressing the question of the relative effectiveness of early childhood curriculum approaches. (Identify names of investigators and approximate year of study.)

8. Instead of employing one experimental group and one control group, the _____ curriculum-research design uses several experimental treatment groups.

9. List four independent variables that need to be considered in early childhood curriculum research.

10. Briefly present two results of early childhood research that have implications for teacher-training programs.

[*]An answer key is provided on pages 242–43.

1. You have been asked to prepare a statement pointing out the recent increases in programs for preschool-age children. Organize your statement to integrate several reasons for this trend.

2. As a preschool teacher you have agreed to allow an educational researcher from a local university to run an experiment in your classroom. The researcher wants to investigate the relative effectiveness of four expressive-language programs. The researcher sits down with you to explain the tactics of the proposed research. List the variables he might say are difficult to control. Identify a research design that he might choose to minimize the effects of these variables.

3. A new school superintendent has just been hired and is doing a thorough investigation of all programs. He notices that the two preschool programs in his district are dramatically different in structure. One is traditional and nonstructured. The second program, which is yours, follows a structured, carefully prescribed curriculum. The superintendent, wishing to know more about preschool education, asks both you and the teacher in charge of the other program to prepare reports that contain a rationale for, and description of, your particular approaches. Develop an outline for your report. It should contain: (1) the results of studies, (2) the conclusions that can be drawn from these studies, and (3) the implications of these studies.

1. Visit and observe several early childhood classrooms. Which curriculum approach does each appear to be using: open classroom, structured task analysis, or an eclectic approach?

2. Secure a copy of the original Karnes (1969) and Weikart (1967, 1971) reports, and read the authors' accounts of their studies.

3. Visit a nonstructured traditional nursery school and a structured preschool, and ask each director to explain the rationale for his approach. Which director is applying curriculum-research results?

Chapter 2

The Developmental Task Instructional System

Objectives

After you have completed this chapter, you should be able to:

1. Define and draw a diagram illustrating the Developmental Task Instructional System.

2. Compare the common elements in Thurstone's and Piaget's theories in terms of developmental tasks.

3. Discuss the acquisition and performance of learning skills in both the structured task-analysis approach and the open-classroom approach.

4. Define the terms *invariance* and *cumulative development* as used by Piaget.

5. Name at least two of the underlying principles of (or supporting reasons for) the Developmental Task Instructional System.

6. Identify and define the six developmental areas of the Developmental Task Instructional System.

A Basis for Developmental Instruction

The Developmental Task Instructional System is based on current knowledge of child growth and development patterns. The study of age trends for various aspects of behavior provides sets of averages or norms that can be used to assess a particular child's development. Does he begin to climb stairs, one foot at a time, within the same age range as the average child? Does he follow simple two-part directions at the appropriate age? Is his vocabulary similar in quantity and quality to that of the average child? Because the development of academic abilities in later childhood appears to be related to the development of certain abilities in early childhood, it is extremely important that we understand normal child growth and developmental patterns.

Various researchers have attempted to define and organize developmental abilities. Gesell (1940) divided his developmental schedules into five main areas: language, motor, personal, social, and adaptive. Thurstone (1941) and Guilford (1967) employed the procedure of factor analysis to arrive at specific areas of intellectual functioning. The Thurstones concentrated on content as well as process, and identified primary mental abilities as verbal meaning, word fluency, quantitative thinking, reasoning, perceptual speed, spatial relations, motor abilities, and memory. Using similar methods, Guilford identified specific intellectual processes as memory, convergent thinking, divergent thinking, and evaluation.

Is there actually continuity and sequence in specific areas of development? Empirically, continuity is difficult to establish beyond a doubt; nevertheless, there is evidence that a great many professionals believe that such continuity exists. For example, most textbooks in child development are organized on an age-sequence basis. But perhaps the most noteworthy support for the concept of sequential stages of development is the highly creative work of Jean Piaget. Piaget's theories of child development have held a central position in developmental psychology for the last several years.

As pointed out by Evans (1971) two characteristics are basic to the Piaget theory: invariance and cumulative development. *Invariance* refers to the fixed sequence of development: to reach point Z the child must start from point A, and proceed through all the intermediary points along the way. The order is the same for all children; however—and this is the most relevant characteristic of the theory for the practitioner—individual children can and will differ in the time it takes to go from one step to the next.

Cumulative development refers to the quality of a child's performance of various tasks in a specific sequence. The quality of a child's performance at a higher level of functioning depends on the quality of underlying, prerequisite tasks.

Piaget organizes cognitive development into three main stages: Stage I—Sensorimotor; Stage II—Concrete Operations; and Stage III—Formal Operations.

The first two stages, sensorimotor (birth to two years) and concrete operations (two to eleven years) incorporate the intellectual abilities that we focus on in the Developmental Task Instructional System. In comparing the elements in Thurstone's work with the characteristics of Piaget's stages of development, we find a great deal of commonality between Piaget's sensorimotor stage and Thurstone's motor factor. As Piaget breaks down his second stage, concrete operations, into two major phases: preconceptual (two to four) and intuitive thought (four to seven), the comparison is even more striking. The elements in Thurstone's perceptual factor overlap with elements in Piaget's preconceptual phase, and the language and reasoning factors overlap with the intuitive-thought phase. Table 2-1 lists the common elements in Piaget's analysis of developmental stages and in the curriculum content derived from Thurstone's

TABLE 2-1 Common Elements in Thurstone's and Piaget's Theories

Piaget	Thurstone	Piaget	Thurstone	Piaget	Thurstone
Sensorimotor Stage	Motor Factor	Pre-conceptual Phase	Perceptual Factor	Intuitive-Thought Phase	Reasoning Language
Hand and Finger Dexterity		Auditory Discrimination		Analogies	
Arm and Hand Precision		Perceptual Flexibility		Figure Grouping	
Body Coordination		Visual Closure		Time Sequencing	
		Figure Ground		Associations	
		Perceptual Accuracy		Space Sequencing	
				Classification	
				Word Fluency	

primary mental abilities (P.M.A.) studies. The Developmental Task Instructional System is based, in part, on the primary mental abilities theory.

It is significant to note that the same developmental tasks fit logically into both Thurstone's P.M.A. structure and Piaget's stages. The main difference between the two theories is that Piaget's theory is a developmental theory stressing time sequence, whereas Thurstone's is an analysis of the components of intelligence based on empirical evidence. In other words, Piaget concentrated on how the child develops intellectual competency as he matures, whereas Thurstone analyzed what elements or components exist in the intellectual functioning of the competent child.

The Developmental Task Instructional System is based on the assumption that motor development, perceptual development, reasoning development, and language development all take place in an irreversible sequence. To be sure, many investigators can point to exceptions to this rule, but in general, child-development literature supports this position. In addition, we do have empirical evidence that a uniform sequence of ability development does, in fact, take place very similarly in all children (Gesell, 1940; Bayley, 1936).

The Developmental Task Instructional System

The primary purpose of the Developmental Task Instructional System is to prepare three-, four-, and five-year-old children to cope successfully with the demands of society. For the young child successful coping means that he must acquire the skills that will permit him to master the tasks that lie ahead in the early years of elementary school. In elementary school, the child must master certain tasks (for example, developing reading, writing, and problem-solving skills) before he can realize fuller success as an

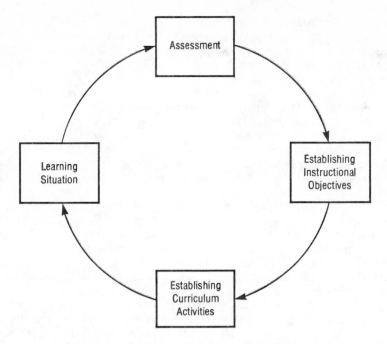

Figure 2-1   The Developmental Task Instructional System

adult. To be sure, a child must have other attributes to cope successfully: he must develop a positive feeling about himself, and acquire both socialization and creative problem-solving skills. We believe that a child's intellectual and social development are closely related, and that both can be increased by developmental instruction.

The Developmental Task Instructional System is a systematic plan for developing the activities that you, as a teacher, will emphasize with each child enrolled in your early education program. The teacher or child worker begins by determining the present functioning level of each child in the room. This assessment is for the purpose of determining the child's point of entry into the instructional system; in other words, what skills does the child need to learn? The next step is to establish individual objectives for each child in your classroom.

It is inconceivable that a teacher can be successful in planning his daily curriculum activities without establishing objectives. Without objectives, the teacher or child worker is admitting that he literally doesn't know where he is going.

Once objectives have been established, the appropriate curriculum activities can be chosen. The establishment of daily activities, in turn, leads to that interaction of child, teacher, and environment which we refer to as an instructional, or learning, situation. With the process of reassessment, the cycle begins again. Figure 2-1 illustrates the Developmental Task Instructional System cycle.

Assessment   There are at least three different purposes for assessing a child. School evaluations are concerned mainly with assessing the student's level of academic achievement—information that is useful in determining the effectiveness of teaching methods. Often, however, teachers think of achievement-test results, not as a measure of their ability to teach but of the student's ability to learn.

Another widely accepted purpose for assessing children is to obtain a differential diagnosis. This type of assessment usually takes place after a child has demonstrated an inability to function either academically, developmentally, or socially within "normal limits." The assumption behind this type of assessment is that once you have diagnosed a child as mentally retarded, brain injured, emotionally disturbed, or minimal brain dysfunction, to name a few of the more popular diagnostic labels, you can place him in a specific program that will meet his needs. This assumption has been seriously challenged in recent years.

Although related to the first two kinds of assessment, assessment within the Developmental Task Instructional System pertains directly to the teaching process. Identifying the level of developmental abilities is a continuing process involving a constant observation of each child's specific abilities. Assessment in this manner is undertaken for the purpose of establishing a continuing series of developmental curriculum experiences that will meet the specified objectives.

As the school year begins, or a new child enters the group, you will need to establish at once what it is that each child can and cannot do. The developmental assessment provides a profile of age-appropriate abilities for each child. From this beginning, the teacher is able to establish teaching-objectives priorities.

On pages 22–23 we show a two-page excerpt from an assessment instrument.* As can be seen from the summarized information on the cover, Johnny, who is four years and five months old, is developing his reasoning and receptive language skills somewhat in advance of his age. Gross-motor development and perceptual development suggest an approximately normal rate of development. However, Johnny's assessment suggests that he is behind in the development of fine-motor skills (note specific tasks on checklist) and in the ability to express himself verbally. Initial objectives for Johnny, then, should give priority to fine-motor and expressive-language skills.

Establishing Instructional   A vital step in any curriculum activity is the determination of
Objectives   objectives. Plowman (1971) defines an objective as "a quantifiable and/or observable achievement accomplished under specifiable conditions." (p. xxii.) In other words, an objective must be defined in such a way that you can measure whether or not you have obtained it.

---

*An expanded version of the *Carolina Developmental Profile,* which includes instructions for administering the various tasks, is reproduced on pages 220–40.

This differs quite markedly from a goal statement. In education "goals" and "objectives" often become confused. A goal is a general statement revealing the direction, philosophy, and rationale of your program. An objective is a statement of a specific achievement that is to take place within the framework of the program goals.

Identifying the developmental objectives is a natural outcome of assessment activities. If objectives are not spelled out, the relevancy of planned curriculum activities can be questioned. If you don't know where you are going, how can you get there? In order to identify your curriculum activities, then, you must know what you want to achieve.

Nowhere in education is the lack of objectives more apparent than in early childhood curriculum. Goals are vague: educating the whole child, providing for emotional and social growth, developing a feeling of self-worth, providing a child-oriented curriculum, and developing creativity and independence are phrases often cited by early childhood educators as objectives for preschool, day-care, or nursery school programs. Although these are all important educational goals, they do not clarify the instructional tasks ahead for the teacher.

The age-old adage of teaching the "whole child," that is, taking into consideration his emotional and social growth, is often held as the general objective of early childhood and day-care endeavors. The difficulty with this "objective" is the inability to determine when you have accomplished it. What is acceptable social adjustment for a four-year-old child? How do you determine when a child is socially adjusted?

A developmental objective must be specific enough to enable the teacher to establish criteria for achieving it. For example, which of the following might be a more usable objective: (1) the development of reasoning skills to a four-and-one-half year level, or (2) the ability to sort 30 pictures into classification groupings of food, animals, furniture, and people, with no more than four errors? The first, of course, is more general, although measurable. The second is much more specific and easily measured. A number of specific objectives like the second could very well constitute what is needed to achieve the first, more general, long-range objective. When we refer to a "long-range objective" we are talking about an objective that may take several months to a year to meet. "Short-range objective" refers to more specific objectives that could be met in a period of a few days or a few weeks.

We believe that a series of general statements like the one above can serve as the basis for establishing short-range objectives. In the example above, you, as a teacher, should know what specific abilities indicate a four-and-one-half-year-old level of reasoning. You then can proceed to establish a sequential series of short-range objectives to reach your long-range objectives. In the next chapter we discuss assessment procedures in detail; we will talk more about establishing long- and short-range objectives in chapter 12.

The information on the cover of Johnny's developmental profile (see below) indicates that he is doing fine in areas of reasoning and

Carolina Developmental Profile

A Criterion-Referenced Checklist for
Planning Early Childhood Education

Name _Jonathan Jenkins_

Date of Birth _5/9/70_

Date _10/25/74_

Developmental Age Level	Gross Motor	Fine Motor	Visual Perception	Reasoning	Receptive Language	Expressive Language
5	(20) (19) (18) (17) ~~16~~	(15) (14) (13) (12)	(12) (11) (10)	(12) (11) ~~10~~ (9) ~~8~~ ~~7~~	(12) (11) ~~10~~	(12) (11)
4	(15) ~~14~~ (13) ~~12~~ ~~11~~	(11) (10) ~~9~~ (8)	(9) ~~8~~ ~~7~~	~~6~~ ~~5~~ ~~4~~	(9) ~~8~~ ~~7~~	(10) ~~9~~ (8) ~~7~~
3	~~10~~ ~~9~~ ~~8~~ ~~7~~ ~~6~~	~~7~~ ~~6~~ ~~5~~	~~6~~ ~~5~~ ~~4~~	~~3~~ ~~2~~ ~~1~~	~~6~~ ~~5~~ ~~4~~	~~6~~ (5) ~~4~~
2	5 4 3 2 1	4 3 2 1	3 2 1		3 2 1	3 2 1

Priority Long-Range Objectives (by area and task number): _Fine motor tasks 8, 10, 11, 12, 13, 14, 15. Expressive language tasks 5, 8, 10, 11, 12._

FINE MOTOR

Task Number	Description	Developmental Age	Can Do	Cannot Do
1	Turns a few pages in a child's storybook one at a time	2		
2	Builds tower of six to eight one-inch cubes	2	O.K.	
3	Strings at least two beads in no more than two minutes	2		
4	Unwraps piece of twisted-end wrapped candy	2		
5	Builds three-block bridge	3	✓	
6	Copies circle from sample	3	✓	
7	Cuts paper in two pieces with scissors	3	✓	
8	Traces diamond shape with primary pencil or crayon	4		✓
9	Copies cross (+) from sample	4	✓	
10	Catches eight- to ten-inch ball from five feet	4		✓
11	Places ten pennies in box one at a time	4		✓
12	Copies square from sample	5		
13	Crumples piece of tissue paper to form a ball	5		
14	Places matchsticks in box with both hands simultaneously	5		
15	Folds six-inch paper square to make triangle	5		

Developmental Age Ceiling (highest age level at which child can do three or more tasks): _3_

Tasks that child cannot do *at* and *below* Developmental Age Ceiling: _____

Long-Range Objectives (by task number): *8, 10, 11, 12, 13, 14, 15.*

Notes and Comments: _____

receptive language. Gross-motor and perceptual development also appear to be adequate. However, his fine-motor skills are lagging behind at a three-and-one-half-year level of development. Expressive-language skills are also below age level, although this lag is not as great as the one in fine-motor development.

In establishing developmental objectives for this child, emphasis should be placed on the below-age-level areas. However, the remaining areas of development should not be neglected. A simple method of selecting specific objectives that would meet Johnny's long-range developmental needs would be to make a list of the next age level of developmental abilities (see, for example, the developmental checklist of fine-motor skills illustrated above). It must be emphasized, however, that the tasks listed in the profile represent only a few of the tasks that are appropriate for each age level; you will need to establish additional ones.

Additional objectives can be established by referring to developmental data compiled by such researchers as Gesell (1940) and Bayley (1936), and to the program goals of your own particular program. Additional objectives for each developmental area are also listed in subsequent chapters of this text.

Establishing Curriculum Areas

Only after instructional or developmental objectives have been determined can curriculum activities be selected. In other words, after the teacher has decided what he wants each child to accomplish, he is now ready to choose the curriculum activities that will help the children reach these objectives.

The curriculum of the Developmental Task Instructional System is organized around the following developmental areas.

Gross-motor development: Large-muscle coordination; includes factors of balance, agility, strength, and general body coordination.

Fine-motor development: Small-muscle coordination; includes factors of finger dexterity, wrist flexibility, arm and hand steadiness, and finger speed.

Perceptual development: The quality of visual perception; includes discrimination between likes and differences, figure-ground, visual closure, and perceptual flexibility.

Development of reasoning processes: Cognitive processes of association, classification, part-whole relationships, sequencing, and analogies.

Receptive-language development: The meaningful interpretation of what is heard.

Expressive-language development: The meaningful expression of ideas and thoughts through the spoken word.

Social-emotional development: The ability to cope effectively with daily demands, with a reasonable degree of balance between the child's own values, concerns, and needs and those of the cultural group of which he is a part.

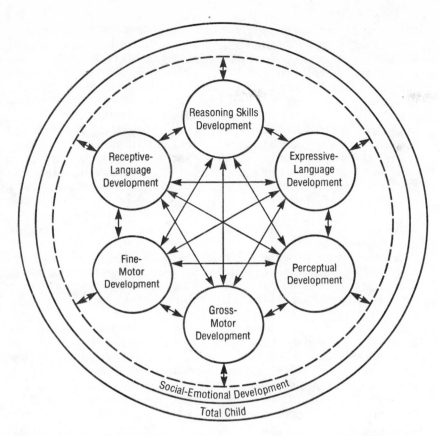

Figure 2-2 The Developmental Task Instructional System: Curriculum Areas

Figure 2-2 illustrates the interrelationship of the various instructional areas. We can see that growth in one area affects growth
in all the others. The purpose of dividing developmental behaviors
into seven precise areas is to make our task as educators easier; it is
not to dissect the various components of a child's development. If
instructional systems were devised to provide for the development of
the whole child without taking into consideration the component parts of that development, the task of individualizing the
instructional process would be impossible to complete with
any degree of success.

In figure 2-2, social and emotional development is represented by a
ring around the other six areas of development. This was done to
indicate that social and emotional development is a constant
curriculum factor and is attended to simultaneously with the other
six areas of development. Later, in chapter 9, Mary M. Wood
identifies various stages of social and emotional development and

points out how they interrelate with other areas of development.

Some educators separate social and emotional development from other areas of development by assigning it to an affective domain, and putting all other areas into either a cognitive or psychomotor domain (Bloom, 1956). However, this kind of classification sets up a false dichotomy between social and emotional development and other areas of development. We believe that development in social and emotional abilities can occur as a result of lessons highly focused on cognitive development if the social and emotional aspects of the learning situation are attended to by the teacher. Thus, development of reasoning processes or fine-motor skills, for example, can contribute to the development of positive social and emotional abilities and attitudes.

The Learning Situation   Any instructional activity is made up of two basic elements: *content* and *method.*

Content refers to what is actually being learned: what is being learned could be a specific task, such as writing your first name so that it is recognizable by others, or it could be a more complex, generalized task, such as acquiring the reasoning skills needed for classification.

It is very helpful to think of the learning situation as a two-step process: the *acquisition stage* and the *practice/generalization stage.* Some teachers fail to make this distinction. For example, the teacher who teaches beginning reading by asking each child in his class to take turns reading aloud is operating at the second-stage level; he has not given his students an opportunity to acquire word-attack skills. There is often a significant difference in the method used in the acquiring of a skill or thinking process and the practicing of that skill or process in a performance situation.

In looking at the example in table 2-2 the content of the learning situation, classification of pictures, remains the same across the two stages. However, in the practice/generalization stage the content is generalized to additional types of applications of the classification ability. In this manner the skill or process that has been acquired can be built into part of the child's reasoning mechanism, and can be applied to numerous problem-solving situations.

Method refers to how the content is presented and reinforced. Does the teacher provide a structured modeling situation, does he use visual aids such as films and transparencies, are primary reinforcements used as the children respond acceptably? In the classification example, the method for the acquisition stage is modeling; the teacher, with the use of visual aids, explains the task and demonstrates the classification process. In the practice/generalization stage, the child's interest takes him to a particular problem-solving activity that requires the use of classification processes for completion.

There are many techniques and methods used in various learning situations, and it must be kept in mind that method is a dimension of the learning situation that must be considered apart from the

TABLE 2-2 The Learning Situation

Stages of Learning	
Acquisition	**Practice/Generalization**
Content: Classifying various pictures—animals, people, food, and furniture.	**Content:** Generalizing the use of classification skills to playing games, solving problems, and other real-life situations.
Method: Use of transparencies for modeling and explanation; trial and reinforcement activities.	**Method:** Free choice of activity centers where child is confronted with a number of problem-solving situations.

content. This is true regardless of whether the learning is task-oriented, skill-oriented, or process-oriented.

This two-stage concept of the learning situation relates directly to the discussion in chapter 1 concerning the various early childhood curriculum philosophies. One can clearly identify the structured task-analysis approach with the acquisition of specified skills and processes. It is difficult, however, to see how the structured approach would facilitate the practice and generalization of these skills or processes. It is also quite clear that the reverse is true when considering the application of the open-classroom philosophy. It is difficult to explain how specific skills or processes are acquired or developed in this informal setting. However, the open classroom can clearly provide for a variety of excellent settings for the practice and generalization of skills and/or processes.

Is it possible to pronounce a happy union between these opposite views of early childhood curriculum? It is not only possible, but probably very necessary, if we are to plan and carry out an effective total curriculum for young children.

Checkpoint
What Have You Learned?

1. The Developmental Task Instructional System is based on child _____ and _____ normative data and the _____ studies isolating the primary mental abilities at an early age.

Facts

2. _____ is the developmental area that refers to large-muscle coordination. Name the other five developmental areas.

3. During a learning situation, open classrooms may provide only for the _____ of skills, whereas completely structured (or programmed) classrooms usually provide for the _____ of skills and/or processes.

4. Assessment is the _____ step in the Developmental Task Instructional System.

5. Assessment activities are undertaken for the primary purpose of _____ instructional _____, which is the second step in the Developmental Task Instructional System.

Simulation

1. You are to plan a series of workshops for a group of kindergarten teachers who have had very little training in early education. Outline the topics you would cover and in what sequence.

2. You want to teach the concepts of "over" and "under" to a group of three- and four-year-olds. Discuss how you might set up learning situations both for acquisition and for practice/generalization.

3. Cite three classroom activities for five-year-olds that would include experiences in two or more of the developmental task areas.

Application

1. Write three instructional objectives for a five-year-old child that meet the requirements for well-written instructional objectives.

2. Select a young child in a classroom program to observe for approximately one hour. Count the frequency of the child's involvement in fine-motor activities, receptive-language experiences, and expressive-language experiences.

3. Visit an early childhood education program and observe the children and teacher. What appears to be occurring more frequently: acquisition of new skills or practice and generalization of skills already acquired?

Chapter 3　Assessing Children

Objectives

After you have completed this chapter, you should be able to:

1. Cite the differences between assessment and evaluation as they apply to preschool education.
2. Explain the various purposes of child assessment.
3. Point out the difference between normative-referenced and criterion-referenced measures.
4. Identify the six developmental areas assessed by the *Carolina Developmental Profile*.
5. List five additional tests that are frequently used in educational programs for young children.

Child-assessment activities aid the teacher or day-care worker in determining the appropriate instructional objectives for his or her children. Therefore we believe that the teacher should play a vital part in the assessment process. It is common practice for psychologists, guidance counselors, and others with professional training in testing and measurement to administer various forms of standardized tests to school children. Assessment information from such tests has been used to establish homogeneous grouping by intellectual or academic ability. It has also been used to provide the teacher with more "insight" about the child, with the anticipation that this will enable him or her to identify instructional activities for that child.

Unfortunately, the value of using test results in this manner is becoming more and more questionable. Much of the testing children undergo today has little relevance to their educational needs because of both the manner in which the testing is conducted and the manner in which the results are used. Many diagnostic procedures currently employed continue to emphasize as their goal an etiological or clinical-symptom classification, which enables the school or community sytem to group the child with other children who have been similarly classified as needing a particular kind of treatment or training. This practice widely persists in the face of increasing evidence that homogeneous grouping by intellectual ability has little relevance to the educational progress or needs of the children. For example, low-ability children grouped homogeneously in special classes on the basis of traditional diagnostic classifications progress educationally at a slower rate than low-ability children remaining in regular grade placements (Kirk, 1972; Goldstein, Moss, and Jordan, 1965; Dunn, 1968; Guskin and Spicker, 1968).

If assessment for instructional purposes is to be meaningful, you as the teacher must be involved in the assessment process. Actually teachers are involved in observing and assessing children every day, although the chances are that the techniques used are quite subjective and nonsystematic. The teacher is familiar with the educational facilities at her disposal, the environment in which learning is to take place, the materials available, and, more important, her own teaching strengths and weaknesses. The psychologist or counselor, who comes from outside the classroom, has to assess in a relative vacuum, and therefore has a difficult time relating the recommendations he makes on the basis of test results to the environment in which the child is expected to learn.

The main departure in the assessment procedure used in our Developmental Task Instructional System from the usual procedures is our emphasis on determining specific developmental objectives. Most available assessment devices provide information that is only marginally related to the task-based developmental information needed to establish meaningful instructional objectives.

There is no one developmental scale that can provide a composite profile of the abilities we outlined earlier: gross-motor skills, fine-motor skills, perceptual skills, reasoning skills and processes, receptive-language skills, and expressive-language skills. To compensate for this lack, many workers use subtests from a variety of scales and tests. The annotated test bibliography at the end of this chapter provides a list of scales which have been developed to measure various developmental abilities.

Although we regard assessment as part of the total instructional system process, we must mention here that a recent trend in education has caused many to take a critical look at established measurement procedures at the preschool level. The public, and in turn the federal government, has become increasingly concerned about the failure of educators and other child workers to demonstrate the effectiveness of their procedures. As a result, federal and state governments now expect recipients of large sums of public funds to show that these funds have been efficiently used. This demand has fostered a frenzied search for effective assessment instruments and evaluation techniques.

Many workers in education confuse the process of assessment with the process of evaluation. Assessment, as we are using the term here, refers to the process of determining the child's strengths and weaknesses in specific areas of behavior. Evaluation refers to the process of determining how successful a teacher (or an instructional program) was in accomplishing a set of goals or objectives. For example, if you, as a project director or a principal of a school, establish three main program objectives for the year, your evaluation plan should be designed so that you can determine whether or not you met those objectives.

The need for establishing evaluation procedures for the Head Start program led to the development of an assessment instrument called the Preschool Inventory (Caldwell, 1967). Caldwell's task was to create an instrument that could assess the changes that took place in children as a result of intervention. Because of a lack of curriculum-development guidance in many of the Head Start classes, some Head Start teachers used the Preschool Inventory as a base, or a "curriculum guide," for their curriculum activities. Although many psychologists and educators frowned upon this practice, suggesting that the teachers were "teaching for the test," this use of the Preschool Inventory can be considered an early application of a criterion-referenced testing program.

Criterion-Referenced Measurements

Criterion-referenced measurement is a concept articulated by Glaser (1963) in an effort to develop a more relevant use of educational testing. *A criterion-referenced measurement is constructed to yield scores that are directly interpretable in terms of a specific standard of performance.* This performance standard could also be viewed as a desired outcome of an instructional objective.

The criterion-referenced measure is different from a normative-referenced test, the type of measure that most people think of when the word *test* is mentioned. *A normative-referenced test compares the child taking the test with the hundreds or thousands of children on whom the test was standardized; its purpose is to determine the relative standing of the child.* Normative-referenced tests, however, often do not provide the kind of information needed to make intelligent instructional decisions. In fact, the information derived from a normative-referenced test may often impede the development of good educational strategies; for example, when a teacher uses the results of an I.Q. test to determine where a child stands in language development or reading skills, his or her resultant decisions on instructional activities for that child will be based on faulty assumptions.

We advocate the use of a criterion-referenced approach for child assessment for two main reasons. The first is to provide assistance to the teacher in developing specific instructional objectives for each child in her program. As you begin the year, you can use the results of this type of assessment to establish a point of entry into the instructional system cycle. The second purpose for using a criterion-referenced approach is to provide some means for evaluating the effectiveness of the instructional activities used in reaching your instructional objectives. Many educators argue that failure to learn, in most cases, demonstrates the limitations, not of the learner, but of the instructional activities used to help him learn.

The Carolina
Developmental Profile—
A Criterion-Referenced
Checklist

To meet the need for a criterion-referenced measurement of developmental tasks in the primary mental abilities area we developed the *Carolina Developmental Profile.* The profile should not be considered a test, for it was not designed as one. Rather, it was designed and developed to help assess the abilities of young children (ages two to five) in the following developmental areas: gross-motor skills, fine-motor skills, visual-perception skills, reasoning processes, receptive-language skills, and expressive-language skills.

The items on the profile are similar to standardized items that can be found in a number of different developmental scales. Their inclusion in the profile was based on several criteria: (1) they are relevant to developmental and early education instruction, (2) they are easy to administer, and (3) they are precise and easy to measure, rather than vague and difficult to measure (or can be measured only by subjective criteria).

Sample pages from the *Carolina Developmental Profile* were shown in chapter 2. The complete contents of the profile, including instructions for administering the various tasks, are reproduced on pages 220–40.

Assessment of Children
Ages Five and Six

We have already learned that the pioneering work of L. L. Thurstone and Thelma Gwinn Thurstone produced the primary mental abilities theory, which in turn, provided a basic part of the rationale for the Developmental Task Instructional System.

The late Professor L. L. Thurstone was one of America's leading specialists in psychological measurement. His book, *Multiple-Factor Analysis* (1947), is a scientific explanation of the mathematical analysis and research techniques underlying the primary mental abilities theory.

We have successfully used the *Primary Mental Abilities K–1* test (Thurstone, 1963) to provide developmental profiles for five- and six-year-old children. Although the test does provide a measure for overall intellectual level, it also gives individual scores for the various primary mental ability levels. Therefore, the P.M.A. test* makes an excellent assessment instrument for five- and six-year-olds.

---

*The P.M.A.K—1 test was revised in 1974; the new edition, also published by SRA (Chicago), is called the *P.M.A. Readiness Level.*

The five primary mental abilities measured by these tests are briefly:

Verbal Meaning: The ability to understand ideas expressed in words. In later school years this is the most important single index of a child's academic potential.

Number Facility: The ability to work with numbers, to handle simple quantitative problems rapidly and accurately, and to understand and recognize quantitative differences. At the lower grade levels number-facility scores are determined by a pictorial test that requires no reading. Addition problems are also used. Arithmetical reasoning problems are substituted at the upper levels.

Reasoning: The ability to solve logical problems. Separate measures of this ability are not provided in the batteries designed for grades K through 4. In the 4–6 battery it is measured by word-grouping, letter-series, and number-series tests.

Perceptual Speed: The ability to recognize likeness and differences between objects or symbols quickly and accurately. This ability is important in acquiring reading skills, but tends to plateau at a relatively early age.

Spatial Relations: The ability to visualize objects and figures rotated in space and the relations between them. The test measuring this ability appears at every level of the P.M.A. and is important throughout the school years.

Figure 3-1 shows sample test items from each of the four primary mental abilities found in the *Readiness Level* test battery.

The five primary mental abilities measured in the P.M.A. test are not all-inclusive. Many more factors have been isolated through research. Nor are all abilities equally important at all ages: their relative importance shifts with age. The importance of verbal meaning, for instance, increases as a child advances through school, whereas perceptual speed becomes relatively less and less important.

A number of other tests are available to use with young children. Your criteria for selecting these tests should be based on how useful they are in assisting you in establishing objectives for your particular group of children. The annotated bibliography that follows describes a few tests that may help you develop your assessment procedures.

Informal Assessment

Many teachers devise their own series of assessment checklists, either to replace or to supplement information from more formal measures. This is often a desirable practice, especially for experienced teachers who have developed program goals that reflect the special character of the children in their program, the kind of home and community they come from, and their own philosophy of early education.

Before you can devise your own observational checklist, you must have a clear understanding of your long-range objectives. What should most of the children in your program be able to accomplish by

Verbal Meaning

Slide your marker down under the next row of pictures. Mark the picture that goes with this story. After he washed his face and ate his breakfast, Jack carried his book to school. Mark it.

Perceptual Speed

Look at the picture that is all by itself in the little box, and then mark the picture in the long box that is just like it. Go ahead—work as fast as you can. (A timed test.)

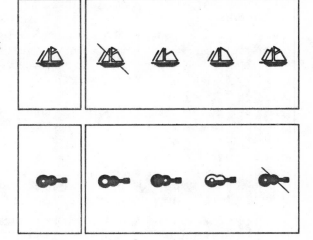

Number Facility

Now put your marker under the first row of pictures. James and Sandra want to dig in the yard. How many shovels do they need? Mark them.

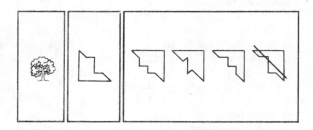

Spatial Relations

Put your finger on the tree. Look at the picture in the box right next to it. That is *part* of a square. Find the *rest* of the square and mark it.

Figure 3-1

34

the end of the year? Do you want them to be able to count to ten? Do you want them to be able to play cooperatively for long periods during the day? Spell out these objectives in clear, precise statements enabling you, or others, to tell by observing the child if that objective has been met. These items can be placed in a simple sequence on a page much like the items in the *Carolina Developmental Profile* booklet. How often should you use the checklist to review the abilities of your children? Practices vary: some teachers use a checklist daily; others, once every week or two.

Annotated
Test
Bibliography
for Children Under Six

California Preschool Social Competency Scale S. Levine, F. F. Elzey, and M. Lewis. Palo Alto, California: Consulting Psychologists Press, Inc., 1969.

The *California Preschool Social Competency Scale* proposes to measure independence, the adequacy of the preschool child's interpersonal behavior, and the degree to which he assumes social responsibility. It also covers such areas as task behavior, relationship to adults and peers, and response to new situations. It is designed for use in evaluating social competence of children aged two years six months through five years six months. Norms are based on teacher ratings of children who are attending preschool or nursery school programs. This scale relies on the judgments of a rater, usually the child's teacher, although another adult familiar with the child's behavior will do. The child's competence on each item is to be rated in terms of his habitual or typical performance. There are 30 items, each with four possible rating options. Percentile norms are available for four preschool age groups for males and for females of high and low occupational groups.

Cassel Developmental Record R. M. Cassel. Jacksonville, Illinois: Psychologists and Educators Press, Inc., 1954.

The *Cassel Developmental Record* is essentially a record form for plotting developmental profiles on the same individual at different ages. Profiles span the dimensions of chronological age, physiological development, emotional development, psychosexual development, intellectual development, social development, and educational development, providing an average total developmental age. Chronological ages are from birth to old age. The author suggests using objective test data (from such instruments as the Vineland and Gesell scales) when it is available. If it is not, the profiles do provide guidelines. The author also suggests that the profile be used for young children, where developmental factors may determine educational objectives, and that it become a part of the cumulative file.

Denver Developmental Screening Test W. K. Frankenburg and J. B. Dodds. Denver, Colorado: Ladoca Project and Publishing Foundation, Inc., 1970 (Revised Ed.)

The *Denver* is designed to assist in the early detection of serious developmental lags in children aged two weeks to six years. The test consists of 105 tasks, of which an individual child will be tested on about 20. Some items can be rated by report of someone who knows the child well, whereas other items must be individually administered. Areas covered are gross motor, fine motor adaptive (use of hands, ability to solve nonverbal problems), language (receptive and expressive) and personal-social (self-care, relating to others). The test must be administered by someone familiar with it, and some small props are needed. The test is designed for screening purposes, not for diagnosis or program evaluation. Task norms are available for boys, girls, and all children. They indicate the age at which 25, 50, 75 and 90 percent of testees can do each task. Cut-off points for indication of developmental lags that require further testing are given. The test has been clinically validated and found reliable.

Detroit Tests of Learning Aptitude H. J. Baker and B. Leland. Indianapolis: Bobbs-Merrill Company, Inc., 1967 (Revised Ed.)

The *Detroit Tests* are a series of nineteen subtests designed to measure abilities in reasoning and comprehension, practical judgment, verbal ability, time and space relationships, number ability, auditory attentive ability, visual attentive ability, and motor ability. The examiner selects a number of subtests (usually from nine to thirteen) appropriate to the subject. Guidelines are provided. The range of mental ages measured is three to nineteen years. Six subtests are recommended for the preschool-age level. The authors also suggest which subtests may be used for individuals who are visually impaired, partially deaf, cerebral palsied, speech impaired, or who have a foreign-language handicap. They report that the test is suitable for use with mentally retarded children. The tests yield a general mental age as well as subtest mental ages. It was standardized on pupils in the Detroit public schools, a population typical of large metropolitan cities.

Preprimary Profile H. J. Schiff and M. I. Friedman. Chicago: Science Research Associates, Inc., 1966.

The *Preprimary Profile* is a rating form on which the parent describes some areas of his child's behavior for the benefit of his first teacher before school begins. Areas (unnamed on the form) in which parents give the information are self-care, classroom management (behavior with peers), skill development (muscular coordination), language development (reading and arithmetic readiness), and previous experience. Ratings are designed to be informative and nonthreatening. For example, in the language-development area, the parent can rate items such as "tells colors of things" and "tells time," as "not yet," "just beginning," or "very well." Self-care items such as "washes his hands and face" are answerable as "not yet," "needs a lot of help," "needs a little help," and "needs no help." The rating form is called "Introduction to my Child." Also available is a letter to parents describing the scale. In addition to giving the teacher insight into a child she has not yet encountered, the *Preprimary Profile* might also provide a useful forum for discussion between teacher and parent. There are no norms, but a section on "How to Interpret and Utilize Profile Results" is included in the Teacher's Handbook.

Preschool Attainment Record E. D. Doll. Circle Pines, Minnesota: American Guidance Service, 1966.

The *Preschool Attainment Record* provides an assessment of physical, social, and intellectual functions in a global appraisal of young children from birth to age seven. The assessment is done by means of an interview with an informant familiar with the child. There is one item for each half-year period in each of the following areas: ambulation, manipulation, rapport, communication, responsibility, information, ideation, and creativity. The examiner can plot the child's profile of scores, and can obtain his attainment age and his attainment quotient. This is a research edition, and no reliability or validity data is yet available.

School Readiness Survey F. L. Jordan and J. Massey. Palo Alto, California: Consulting Psychologists Press, Inc., 1969 (Second Ed.)

The *School Readiness Survey* is designed to involve parents in the assessment of their child's readiness to begin school, so that each parent may better understand the child's abilities, the school's expectations, and areas in which the child might need further experiences. The test items require the child to choose the appropriate picture, figure, words, or symbol, or to answer orally. Subscales are number concepts, discrimination of form, color naming, symbol matching, speaking vocabulary, listening vocabulary, and general information. Instruction and tasks are presented simply for the non-professional parent, and the test booklet includes suggestions for improving skills in areas in which the child is weak. The test booklet classifies subtest scores for parents as "Ready for School"; "Borderline Readiness"; and "Needs to Develop." The Professional Manual includes cumulative percentage norms for each subtest and for the total score.

Stanford Early School Achievement Test R. Madden and E. F. Gardner. New York: Harcourt, Brace, Jovanovich, Inc., 1969.

The *Stanford Early School Achievement Test* measures cognitive abilities in several areas in order to assess the preschool child's learning and to help

TABOR COLLEGE LIBRARY
Hillsboro, Kansas 67063

establish a base line for beginning school experience. Norms are provided for prekindergarten and pre-first-grade testing. This group test is designed to be given in three sessions (a total of 90 minutes) to six to fifteen children (depending on age). The teacher reads directions and the child marks the picture that represents his answer in his booklet. There are four subtests: the environment (social studies and science); mathematics; letters and sounds (visual recognition and auditory perception); and oral comprehension (attention and logical operations). A percentile rank and stanine is available for each subtest and for the total test.

Valett Developmental Survey of Basic Learning Abilities R. E. Valett. Palo Alto, California: Consulting Psychologists Press, Inc., 1966

The *Valett Developmental Survey* is designed to aid in the evaluation of developmental abilities in children aged two to seven. It consists of 233 tasks, many selected or adapted from other developmental scales, that will give the teacher an estimate of the child's task proficiency and stimulate further investigation in areas where it seems to be needed. The areas covered include motor integration and physical development, tactile discrimination, auditory discrimination, visual motor coordination, visual discrimination, language development and verbal fluency, and conceptual development. The test is individually administered by someone who is familiar with it; some easily obtainable props are required. Age norms are provided for each task.

Checkpoint
What Have You Learned?

Facts

1. The process of determining a child's strengths and weaknesses across specific developmental areas is referred to as _____.

2. The purpose of child assessment should be to aid the _____ in determining instructional _____ for the children.

3. If assessment for instructional purposes is to be meaningful, the _____ must be involved in the assessment of the child.

4. The process of determining the extent to which you have been successful in meeting your stated objectives is referred to as _____.

5. Tests that compare an individual child to thousands of other children across the country to determine the child's relative standing are _____ referenced tests.

6. The major purpose of using the *Carolina Developmental Profile* is to assist the teacher in establishing _____.

7. Earlier factor-analysis studies led the author of this text to establish six developmental behavioral areas on the *Carolina Developmental Profile*. Name those developmental areas.

1. You have just been hired as a preschool teacher for a group of four- and five-year-old children, and your supervisor has appointed you to serve on a committee that will decide which assessment instruments to adopt. Identify three to five instruments and explain why you would propose that the committee adopt them.

2. You have just administered the *Carolina Developmental Profile* (see pages 220–40) to a four-year-old child with the following results:

Gross motor:	passed all items up to 9, missed 10, passed 11, missed 12 and 13, passed 14, and missed 15, 16, 17, 18, 19, and 20.
Fine motor:	passed through 5, missed 6, 7, 8, and 9, passed 10, and missed 11, 12, 13, 14, and 15.
Perceptual:	passed 1 through 8, missed 9, passed 10 and 11, missed 12.
Reasoning:	passed 1 through 6, missed 7, passed 8, missed 9, passed 10, missed 11 and 12.
Receptive language:	passed 1 through 10, missed 11 and 12.
Expressive language:	passed 1, 2, and 3, missed 4, 5, and 6, passed 7, missed 8, 9, 10, 11, and 12.

Identify the Developmental Age Ceiling in each developmental area, and select long-range objectives from the curriculum-guide pages at the back of the appropriate curriculum chapters for this child.

1. Visit and observe several preschool programs. When talking with the program staff ask them to explain the assessment procedures, and when observing instructional settings see if the teaching activities appear to relate to the assessment program.

2. Select a three- to five-year-old child, and using the *Carolina Developmental Profile*, identify and write four long-range objectives to meet the instructional needs of that child.

Chapter 4   Individualizing Instruction

Objectives

After you have completed this chapter, you should be able to:

1. Define individualized instruction in terms of teacher behavior.

2. Identify the relationship between identification of child needs and resultant instructional objectives.

3. Specify some of the most common obstacles to implementing an individualized-instruction system.

4. Identify the two learning phases that should be included in each teaching-learning session.

5. Specify the desired rate of correct response rate to allow for maximal learning.

6. List criteria for grouping children in small instruction units.

"Every child is different and should be treated differently!" "Individualized instruction is the only way to meet the needs of all our children!" "Our school system believes in individualized instruction!" How many times have you heard your colleagues and other educators citing the need for individualized instruction? Although on the surface a simple statement, individualized instruction means different things to different people.

For example, in a first-grade classroom in Pennsylvania, children are sitting in four different circles, one in each corner of the room. One child is reading aloud in each circle and the others are following along. The teacher, a staunch advocate of individualized instruction, has divided her class into beginning reading groups, and the children have been grouped according to oral reading abilities.

In a classroom in Illinois, children are scattered all over the room, some are reading or looking at books in one corner, others are playing with push toys in another area, and still others are playing with puppets. While all this is going on, the teacher is sitting with one child pointing out some words he is attempting to read on a bulletin board.

In both these instances, individual learning as well as individualized instruction may be taking place, even though the organization and atmosphere of the two settings are quite different.

Individualized instruction is most often viewed as a systematic approach to instruction focusing on the different learning needs of individual children. Content and methodology of instruction may vary from child to child within a class according to each child's individual needs. For example, one of the generally agreed upon goals of the Head Start program was to give the "disadvantaged" child the skills necessary to enable him to compete successfully with middle-class children in the first grade. To individualize instruction in a Head Start program, then, the teacher must translate that general goal into more specific objectives for each child in her room. These objectives might include developing the child's ability to name five different colors or to select a task independently and follow it through to completion.

Individualized instruction, then, indicates an organized attempt by the teacher or child worker to identify the needs of a specific child, and to provide a set of conditions for learning that meet those needs. The execution of the learning situation may take place with or without the teacher or child worker involved directly. However, the environmental situation must reflect planned organization to meet specific recognized needs of the child.

Our definition of individualized instruction should leave no doubt that the teacher or child worker must be actively involved in the process. Let's look again at the three elements of this definition.

1. *An organized attempt by the teacher.* This element of our definition refers to the role of the teacher or child worker in planning the individualized objectives, activities, and learning conditions for the child. Learning as a result of individualized instruction cannot "just happen." If it does, instruction did not take place.

2. *Identification of the child's need or set of needs.* These learning needs will certainly be influenced by the overall goals of your program. For example, if one of your goals is that the child, upon leaving your program, should be able to express himself fluently, an identified need might be a more frequent use of three-word phrases.

3. *A set of conditions that provide for learning.* This element of individualized instruction provides you with many options. The trick is, of course, to select the best options for a specific child: for example, use of an aide in a one-to-one situation, use of a workbook with minimal guidance, interaction in a small group, or a programmed teaching

machine. Many people think that individualized instruction always refers to a one-to-one adult-to-child learning situation. Although individualized instruction does occur in this manner, the one-to-one learning situation is probably used less frequently than any other method. This is due to cost constraints as well as to the fact that some objectives, particularly in the social and emotional areas of development, are best met through group activities.

Implementing Individualized Instruction

If individualized instruction is so wonderful why doesn't everyone use it? That question is rather easy to answer. Individualized instruction is easy to talk about and difficult to carry out.

There are several very real constraints operating to prevent large-scale individualization of instruction. Some of these are: (1) cost of reducing teacher-child ratio; (2) lack of instructional space; (3) tradition; (4) cost of materials and equipment; (5) lack of training; and (6) disagreement among "experts" on what is good individualized instruction.

As we mentioned above, the most obvious, and perhaps least used, type of individualized instruction is the one-to-one learning situation. With the cost of education skyrocketing today, it is becoming increasingly difficult to reduce the large teacher-child ratios that exist in many early childhood programs. To combat this problem many schools are hiring lower-paid nonprofessionals or encouraging volunteer participation. It has been found that under the guidance of a good teacher, the teacher aide and the adult or high-school-age volunteer can work successfully with children. To be sure, it is necessary to have each "lesson," or learning episode, well planned out for the aide or volunteer.

Although a one-to-one adult-to-child ratio is advantageous in many learning situations, there are many other situations where a small group of children is much more desirable. Children learn from one another, and if group instruction is planned appropriately, your objectives for each individual child may be achieved much quicker. Children are highly motivated by one another, and interaction in a small group will be quite rewarding for most young children.

If you are following a systematic instructional system and grouping children with similar needs, long-range objectives can be carried out quite easily. Later in this chapter we will discuss how you can individualize your program, even for groups of 30 or more children, by careful planning.

Individualized instruction can also be hampered by a lack of physical space. Some teachers have overcome this problem by judiciously arranging the limited space in their rooms. Bookcases are often used as partitions to make small learning and interest areas. We have also seen some improvising teachers set up small learning settings in the hallways adjacent to their rooms. In good weather outdoor patios often provide additional areas for individualized instruction.

Many of the educational innovations geared toward individualizing instruction involve the use of expensive electronic or mechanical teaching materials. Auditory and visual devices such as the Language Master and the Dukane Readers are often too costly for limited-budget programs. When available, however, such devices can be used very effectively to meet specific individual instructional needs. In general, individualized instruction involves the use of a great many educational materials. Therefore, if all your individualized activities require materials, particularly materials you must make yourself, you will find such activities possible only if you spend as much time planning and preparing materials as you do actually working with the children. Individualized instruction is less time-consuming when the teacher uses a combination of commercial and homemade instructional materials. These materials may vary from manipulative objects and toys for the very young to worksheets for older children.

As you are no doubt aware, worksheets are criticized by many educators. Actually, the criticism is aimed more often at how the worksheets are used than at the worksheets themselves. No one would disagree with the fact that worksheets should not be used as busy work for children. However, when used wisely and systematically, and no more than 15 or 20 minutes per day, worksheets can be a very effective individualized-instruction tool.

Many teachers and child workers do not use individualized instruction because they have not been trained to apply systematic instructional technology to the educational process. Being assured that every child is engaged in an activity certainly does not necessarily mean that the child's learning needs are being met.

Another obstacle that stands in the way of the acceptance of individualized instruction for children is that we have traditionally approached education in a "lockstep" manner. That is, we teach children of the same age as if they all had the same learning needs. This approach is no doubt the least expensive but it is also the least effective. Many professional experts disagree over what constitutes "good" instruction, and therefore it naturally follows that disagreement also prevails over successful procedures for individualizing instruction. Ofton the disagreements are philosophical in nature. For example, some educators might question our position that the first step in individualizing instruction is to determine the learning needs of the child. Some might advocate that the child should determine his own learning needs, and then, in turn, select his own avenues for meeting those needs. Our position, of course, is that you, the teacher, are a valuable leader in the learning process, and that if planned instruction does not take place, your goals and objectives will not be met in any reasonable fashion.

To be successful at individualizing instruction, you must plan and execute the procedures involved in a systematic fashion. Many teachers and child workers have developed a procedure and use it consistently, but do not realize they are following a particular system. Others have consciously worked out a system that they use with any child under their guidance. A successful system or

A Systematic Approach to Individualizing Instruction

procedure should not tell you "what to do" with each child, but rather "how to plan" what you are going to do.

The Developmental Task Instructional System outlines the steps involved in developing an individualized curriculum for children. To review briefly, you first determine the child's needs. This may be accomplished many different ways: observation of the child, behavior checklists, or formal and informal testing. Based on the observed needs, you then determine what objectives you want to establish. Determination of instructional objectives should reflect the philosophy and goals of your program. After instructional objectives have been established, you can plan your curriculum activities and strategies.

Earlier, we discussed the learning situation as a two-stage process: the acquisition stage and the practice/generalization stage. In any individualized-instruction situation, you should plan to have some of your children working at the practice/generalization stage; that is, doing some task (either independently or cooperatively as part of a small group) the child himself has selected. At the same time you should be working individually with a smaller group at the acquisition stage. Another group of children at this stage may be using programmed aids such as a Language Master or a Listening Post.

Recognizing the importance of individualizing instruction based on needs of children, we initiated a multilevel series of lessons for perceptual, reasoning, and language development in the *Beginning to Learn* series (Thurstone and Lillie, 1970, 1972). The programs are designed to make it possible for one teacher to work with a large group of children and still provide for individual differences within a specific area of development. The practice sheets in this series are designed for three levels of difficulty: easy, medium, and difficult. Although the same activity is undertaken by all children in the group, children demonstrating a lower level of development are provided with a practice sheet that is less difficult than the others. Two perceptual development lessons are illustrated on pages 45–46 (figures 4-1 and 4-2).

The lesson in figure 4-1 is designed to assist in the development of the perception of figure-ground relationships. Notice the gradual increase in difficulty from level 1 to level 3. Lesson 16 (figure 4-2) illustrates the difficulty-level progression on another perceptual development lesson. For example, the scribbly line drawing in level 1 has fewer scribbly lines obscuring the pictures than does level 2. Level 2, in turn, has fewer scribbly lines than level 3.

The same type of difficulty calibration is used for individualizing reasoning lessons. Figures 4-3, 4-4, and 4-5 (See pages 47–49) are examples of sequencing tasks. As you can see, the tasks at level 1 (figure 4-3) contain only "two event" sequencing; tasks at level 2 (figure 4-4) involve "three event" sequencing; and tasks at level 3 (figure 4-5) call for sequencing four events.

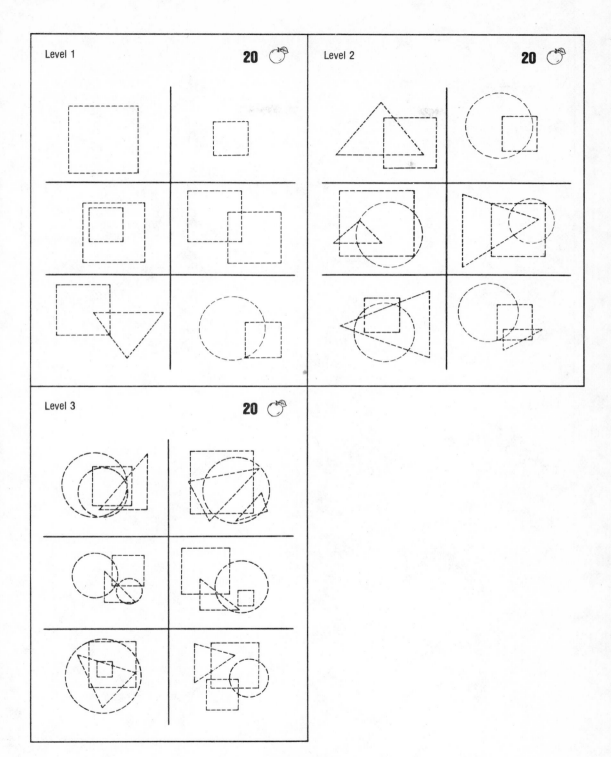

Figure 4-1

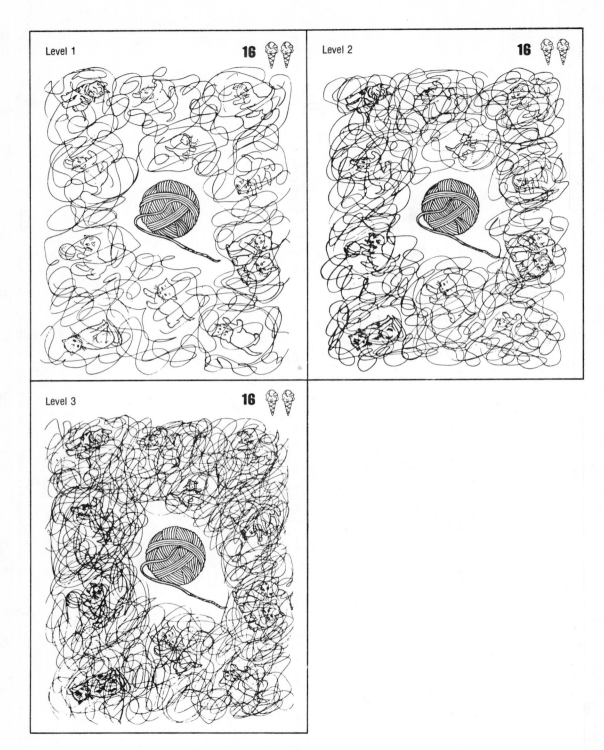

Figure 4-2

Figure 4-3 A Sequencing Task (Level 1)

47

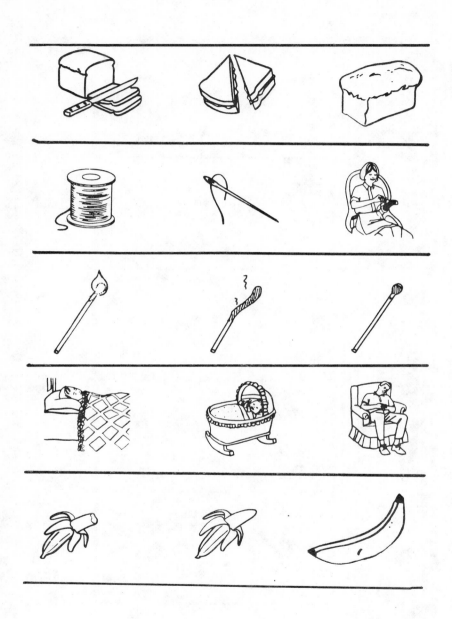

Figure 4-4 A Sequencing Task (Level 2)

Figure 4-5 A Sequencing Task (Level 3)

It is our belief that, for optimal learning to take place, a child should be able to perform successfully approximately 85 to 90 percent of the time. A higher percentage of error is likely to discourage the child, decreasing his motivation to undertake additional or new learning tasks. We encourage teachers to set up reasonably flexible standards for moving a child from one level of difficulty to another. We have found that most children move up at least one level during the course of the year, and that very few have to be moved to an easier level.

Individualizing instruction is not an easy undertaking. The more resources you have available to you in the form of helpers, equipment, and facilities, the more effectively you will be able to meet the needs of your children. Nevertheless, with all the resources in the world, you will find it difficult to implement a successful individualized-instruction program unless you have first established a systematic procedure for instruction.

Checkpoint

What Have You Learned?

Facts

1. Instruction implies that there are certain specific _____ that the teacher wants a child to reach.

2. _____ might be defined as "an organized attempt by the teacher or child worker to provide a set of conditions for learning that meet the needs of a specific child."

3. Before an organized plan for instruction is presented to a child, his individual _____ must be identified.

4. We hear a great deal about individualized instruction, but we don't see it occurring in all our schools. List three reasons why.

5. Although many classrooms are not ideally suited for individualized instruction, there are a number of ways a teacher can meet individual needs. List four of these.

6. The Developmental Task Instructional System is discussed again in this chapter. List the four sequential steps in this instructional system.

7. The process of learning may be viewed as occurring in two phases. It is important for a teacher to take both phases into account in each learning situation or activity. These phases are _____ or development and _____ and/or generalization.

8. It is the belief of the author that a child should be successful approximately _____ percent of the time for optimal learning to take place.

9. Identify three different ways to group children for instructional purposes.

1. You have been asked by the president of the local PTA to speak at the next meeting. Many of the parents believe that individualized instruction is nothing but placing a child on a "teaching machine" and are concerned that the machines will not know what is best for their child. The topic of your presentation will be "The Whys and Hows of Individualized Instruction." Develop an outline for a speech that will convince the parents that individualized instruction is essential and does not occur in a sterile environment.

2. You have been hired to teach a preschool class and are fortunate enough to have a full-time aide and more than enough materials. Briefly explain how you would go about implementing and maintaining an individualized-instructional system for the 20 preschool children in your class.

Establish some criteria for determining what constitutes an individualized-instructional system. Then visit two or three early childhood classrooms, and evaluate the degree to which each individualizes. After your observation and evaluation, elicit from the teachers their opinions on how well they individualize to meet specific needs of children.

Chapter 5

Developing Motor Skills

Objectives

After you have completed this chapter, you should be able to:

1. Identify activities that are primarily fine motor or gross motor in nature.
2. Discuss the relationship between motor proficiency and mental ability.
3. Present the major findings of the author's research on gross-motor and fine-motor education for young children.
4. List and define the factors found to be present in fine-motor development.
5. Cite two general rules for planning motor development activities to provide for maximum student involvement and learning.
6. Discuss what fine-motor skills should be developed in a child as he approaches school age.

Through the years we have come to recognize that some of the most important skills developed during early childhood are those that depend on the coordination of various sets of muscles. Development of proficiency in these motor skills is a prerequisite for future learning experiences.

When a child enters school, he is assumed to posses certain motor-skill competencies. Many children, however, do not perform at this assumed level, and as a result find themselves in increasing difficulty as time goes on. A comparatively low level of motor ability may affect a child's self-concept and his motivation to learn. Lack of motivation could, in turn, inhibit future motor development.

Early childhood educators generally break down motor skills into two major categories: fine motor (small muscle) and gross motor (large muscle). Fine-motor skills, which are sometimes called manual or manipulation skills, refer to such skills as finger dexterity, wrist flexibility, arm and hand steadiness, and finger speed.

On the other end of the motor-skills continuum are the gross-motor skills. Gross-motor skills refer to skills such as static and dynamic balance, strength and agility, and general body co-ordination.

In the Thurstones' original work (1941) on primary mental abilities, motor ability was one of the factors identified at the five-year age level. A survey of the research on motor development (Heath, 1942 and 1953; Sloan, 1951; Distefano et al., 1958; Howe, 1959; Francis and Rarick, 1959; Malpass, 1960; and Langan, 1965) reveals that a large majority of the investigators report positive relationships between motor proficiency and mental ability.

Motor Development Research

Very few attempts have been made to investigate the feasibility of motor-skill training prior to our work on the development of the *Beginning to Learn: Fine Motor Skills* program (Thurstone and Lillie, 1970). Researchers Helman (1932), Kephart (1960), Godfrey (1964), Oliver (1958), and Corder (1966) were among the few concerned with children's ability to learn motor skills in the classroom.

During the middle 1960s we (Lillie, 1968) investigated the effects of 65 lessons in motor development on the motor proficiency of culturally deprived, mentally retarded children of preschool age. An experimental preschool group, a kindergarten control group, and a home control group were pre- and post-tested with the *Lincoln-Oseretsky Motor Development Scale.* This scale provides only a total raw score; thus, gross-motor and fine-motor proficiency scores were obtained by categorizing each item in the test on the basis of previous studies in which motor development tasks had been factor analyzed.

The treatment variable (the lessons) for the experimental group consisted of a series of motor development lessons based on the pretest Lincoln-Oseretsky profiles of the children, Guilford's (1958) factor analysis of motor skills, and the performance of the children on previous motor development lessons. The kindergarten control children received a typical kindergarten curriculum that included such general areas of instruction as socialization, communication skills, and school-readiness activities. The home control group received no formal instruction. It was assumed that they engaged in the motor activities associated with free play in the neighborhood and home.

When we retested the children at the end of the year we found some surprising results. Although all groups gained, there were no differences between the three groups of children in gross-motor abilities. This surprised us because both school groups had regularly scheduled daily physical-education activities. We were forced to conclude that the children at home were developing gross-motor skills as effectively as the children in school. However, we did not find this to be the case in fine-motor development. The analysis of the fine-motor post-test scores demonstrated that the children in the experimental group, who received fine-motor lessons, showed a significantly higher level of fine-motor ability than the children in either control groups. Our conclusion was that the use of well-planned fine-motor lessons does make a positive difference in the development of motor skills.

Because we had extended and made changes in the fine-motor program used in this study, we decided to test the program again during the summer of 1968. This time we wanted to see if we could increase the fine-motor proficiency of disadvantaged children enrolled in a six-week summer Head Start program.

Four classes of approximately twenty children each were selected at random from the elementary Head Start classes in Chapel Hill, North Carolina. Two classes were randomly chosen to receive lessons for a 30-day period, and the remaining two were used for control.

This time we used the Eye-Motor Coordination subtest of the *Frostig Developmental Test of Visual Perception* (1964), administering it to all four classes in a pretest, post-test manner. The two experimental-class teachers were given instructions and materials for the daily lessons at the beginning of the study. This was the only time we had any contact with the teachers during the program. A post-test was administered by examiners who were unaware of which classes were experimental and which were control; we wanted to make sure that personal bias was not a factor in evaluating the children's performance. Because all the children were enrolled in a unique program and were experiencing a school-like atmosphere for the first time, we did not believe that motivational factors would bias our results. And because the groups were selected randomly, we assumed that there would be no significant difference in group mean intelligence.

Upon pretesting, we noted that the fine-motor-ability group means were slightly different, with the control group showing a slightly higher level of fine-motor skill. This difference and a small difference in group age means were statistically controlled by the employment of analysis of covariance, which nullified the effect the pretest differences in age and motor skills would have on the results of the study.

Upon analysis of the post-test data we found that the experimental group of children displayed a statistically significant (.01 level of confidence) higher level of fine-motor skill than the control group.

Even though 30 days is probably too short a period of time to develop long-lasting motor skills, the results of the investigation attest to the effectiveness of a specific fine-motor development program for short-term summer Head Start programs. Children with a higher level of fine-motor skills at the end of the summer will be in a much better position to participate successfully in the many manipulative activities that take place in a primary-level classroom.

Large-muscle coordination is one of the first skills acquired by the individual, and thus provides the basis for future, more complex learning. Therefore, gross-motor activities should be an essential component of any early childhood curriculum.

Gross-Motor Curriculum

Guilford (1958) identifies the main gross-motor factors as: static balance, dynamic balance, gross-body coordination, agility and endurance/strength. Static balance refers to nonmoving balance, such as balancing on one foot. Dynamic balance, on the other hand, refers to balance when the body is in motion, for example, walking a rail or riding a bicycle.

You should be aware of the various kinds of gross-motor functioning and choose activities that will develop these specific skills. The amount of time the child is actually engaged in gross-motor activities is extremely crucial. In many group games there is a great deal of waiting: waiting to be chosen, waiting to be tagged, standing in the team line, or just waiting for a turn. Within a 30-minute gross-motor activity period, then, it is very possible that each child will participate only five to ten minutes. In curriculum planning for preschool children it is essential that you plan activities that are designed to: (1) encourage development of each of the specific gross-motor factors and (2) permit all children to be physically engaged in the activities a large portion of the time allocated.

Examples of activities that we have used to meet these two criteria extremely well are very simple calisthenics (such as running, jumping, snow angels, jumping jacks, and sit-ups), trampoline activities, and tunnel crawling. Formal calisthenics such as jumping jacks are very difficult for most preschoolers to perform. However, accuracy of performance should be a secondary goal; the primary goal is to develop agility, endurance, and balance.

The developmental activities guide at the end of this chapter suggests some activities for gross-motor development; these activities correspond to the tasks listed in the developmental profile reproduced in the appendix. Activities are presented at each developmental age level, and all are designed to provide experiences that will lead to specific developmental accomplishments. In addition, the text *Perceptual Motor Efficiency in Children* (Cratty and Martin, 1969) is an excellent resource for gross-motor activity planning.

Fine-Motor Curriculum

If children under four are allowed to experiment with a large variety of manipulative objects, their fine-motor abilities will develop sequentially in a normal pattern. However, as the child approaches school age he must add to his repertory of general fine-motor skills, skills that will enable him to perform successfully in specific task situations. Therefore, our discussion of fine-motor curriculum activities focuses on the more "manipulative" types of activities for children from four to six years of age.

Fine-Motor Activities for Two- to Four-Year-Olds

As you can see in the fine-motor curriculum activities guide at the end of this chapter (pages 76–81), most of the manipulative activities

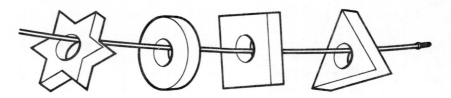

Figure 5-1 Shape Beads

at these ages are fairly standard: bead stringing, block play, sandbox play, water play, finger games, manipulation play with rubber or wooden animal and people figures, large stacking and nesting blocks, toy-vehicle play (trucks, trains, and cars), household and dramatic play, sewing-card activities, tool toys, simple puzzles, clay modeling, and finger painting.

Lessons built around the use of the shape beads (see figure 5-1) that we developed to use with Head Start children are an excellent way to develop fine-motor skills for the child at the two- to four-year-old level of development. The shape beads are flat, one and one-half inches in diameter and one-quarter inch thick. They come in four shapes (round, triangle, square, and star) and four colors (blue, red, yellow, and green). Each bead has a quarter-inch hole in its center. Large bead strings and dowels are also used in this series of lessons.

With these materials a series of lessons with high potential for fine-motor development can be carried out. For example, the following activities can be presented.

1. Stacking shape beads in stacks of five or six by color.
2. Stacking shape beads in stacks of five or six by shape.
3. Stacking shape beads by a pattern called out by the teacher.
4. Placing shape beads over like shapes predrawn on a sheet of paper.
5. Placing shape beads in the appropriate cut-out form on a form board.
6. Stringing shape beads by color.
7. Stringing shape beads by shape.
8. Stringing shape beads in a pattern called out or demonstrated by teacher.
9. Placing shape beads by color on a dowel held in other hand.
10. Placing shape beads by shape on a dowel held in other hand.
11. Placing shape beads on a dowel according to a pattern demonstrated or called out by teacher.
12. Placing shape beads on a dowel held by another child.

These types of activities not only foster development of such fine-motor skills as finger dexterity, arm and hand steadiness, and finger speed, but also provide skill development in areas of visual perception (shape and color), receptive language (following directions for patterns), and social cooperation (working together on same task).

As mentioned previously, we spent several years in creating a curriculum for the development of fine-motor skills in children four to six years old. These efforts resulted in publication of *Beginning to Learn: Fine Motor Skills* (Thurstone and Lillie, 1970). This program provides eight different types of fine-motor experiences. Activities within each area are sequenced in increasing order of difficulty to provide for a smooth and sequential development of fine-motor skills. In addition, the subject matter is designed to motivate children and provide familiar content that the children can identify with and talk about with the teacher.

Lessons are sequenced by difficulty and type of task, and include such activities as tracing a path, connecting dots, drawing lines, aiming, using templates, cutting, following a maze, and completing a figure. In addition, they expose the children to such concepts as front, back, bottom, left, right, up, down, straight line, circle, square, triangle, oval, star, and parts of the body. The program also gives the children training in following directions and left-to-right and top-to-bottom orientation to a page.

On pages 59–66 you will find an example of each of the eight types of individualized lessons in the fine-motor skills program. The corresponding lesson instructions appear beside each sample worksheet.

Following Paths. In this series of exercises the child's task is to draw a line along the path without crossing the path boundaries. As the series progresses, the paths become narrower and longer. The development of arm steadiness and arm and hand precision is the primary purpose of these path-tracing activities. An example of this kind of lesson is presented in figure 5-2.

Connecting Dots. This type of exercise, shown in figure 5-3, develops arm steadiness, arm and hand precision, as well as hand and finger dexterity. As the program progresses the dot-connecting activities are designed to provide a higher level of proficiency.

Drawing Horizontal Lines. As can be seen by our example in figure 5-4, these lessons are designed to present both a highly stimulating activity for young children and needed experience in drawing short, straight, horizontal lines from a definite starting point to ending point. This type of activity assists in developing arm and hand precision.

Drawing Vertical Lines. Figure 5-5 shows an example of the type of activity that can be designed for increasing arm and hand precision, and still provide a high level of interest.

Tracing Dotted Lines. Nursery rhymes such as "Little Bo Peep" and "Wee Willie Winkie" are used as themes for interest building in several lessons designed to promote a higher level of arm steadiness, arm and hand precision, and hand and finger dexterity. (Note figure

5-6.) The paths the child is asked to trace become longer and more complex as the lessons proceed.

Cutting and Pasting. Many of the fine-motor activities that the child must cope with in first grade involve cutting and pasting exercises. The series of lessons provides specific training for children in simple cutting and pasting. As you see by the example in figure 5-7, these lessons are designed to be self-motivating for the child. Again, as this type of lesson progresses, the skill level increases.

Drawing Circles, Squares, Triangles, Ovals, and Stars. Figure 5-8 provides an example of lessons in drawing shapes with templates. These lessons are sequenced by shape as well as by complexity of the task. Lessons for drawing circles are presented first, followed, respectively, by lessons for squares, triangles, ovals, and stars. First, the children are asked to use the template to draw circles on the chalkboard and on paper. Next they use a template to draw circles around pictures. As you can see by the example, they are then asked to draw circles by tracing dotted line circles. Finally, the children draw free-hand circles around pictures. This sequence is repeated for each shape.

Completing Figures. This series of activities is designed to continue the development of hand and finger dexterity and precision, as well as developing the child's body awareness. As can be seen in figure 5-9, a series of drawings of a person are presented with a part missing in each drawing. The children add on the missing parts, which become increasingly numerous as the series proceeds.

The learning theory of *motor chaining* discussed by Gagne (1965) was used in developing the fine-motor tasks found in the lessons. Motor chaining takes place when a number of movements are connected in a close time succession. Many athletic skills are learned through a process of motor chaining, such as hitting a tennis ball or pitching a baseball. One of the main conditions for the successful establishment of a chain is getting the child to sequence properly each fine-motor movement involved in a task. As we mentioned earlier, activities selected for the development of motor skills should help children sequence fine-motor movements as they develop proficiency in finger speed, arm steadiness, arm and hand precision, and hand and finger dexterity.

The subject matter of your lessons should be designed to interest children in the tasks and provide familiar objects and situations that they can talk about with you. As we mentioned, several of our motor lessons are based on nursery rhymes. In addition, the program contains enough plastic templates so that many children can be actively involved in template lessons at the same time.

A fine-motor lesson should be a regularly scheduled part of the class's daily routine. Young children are reassured and motivated by routines they expect and look forward to. Routine and structure are particularly important for educationally disadvantaged children and children with learning difficulties.

Lesson 43

Objectives

To develop arm steadiness
To develop arm-and-hand precision
To develop hand-and-finger
    dexterity

Materials

For each child
Pages 75 and 76 of the *Fine Motor
    Skills* Children's Book
Primary pencil

For the teacher
Fine Motor Skills Children's Book
Nursery rhyme
    "Pussycat, Pussycat"

Procedure

1. Read or recite the nursery rhyme "Pussycat, Pussycat" to the children.

> *Pussycat, pussycat, where have you been?*
> *I've been to London to visit the queen.*
> *Pussycat, pussycat, what did you there?*
> *I frighten'd a little mouse under her chair.*

If you have a nursery-rhyme book, discuss the picture accompanying this rhyme. Have some of the children act out the poem while the class chants the rhyme.

2. Pass out the Children's Books and have the children open them to the first page, page 75. Have them tear out the page and locate its front by finding the picture of the front of the dog. Point to this picture in your book. Check to see that the children have positioned their pages so that the dog is in the upper left-hand corner.

3. Tell the children that they are going to help the pussycat get to London to visit the queen. Point to the cat, the queen, the chair and mouse, and the path in your book.

> *Take your pencil and start at the pussycat and mark along the path so the pussycat can find the queen and her chair. Be careful, and don't go off the path.*

Move around the room and encourage the children.

4. Have the children turn their page over. Point out the cat, queen, chair and mouse, and path. Have the children mark along the path with their pencil. Then have them put their names on their page.

Figure 5-2 Following Paths

Lesson 13

Objectives

To develop arm steadiness
To develop arm-and-hand precision
To develop hand-and-finger
   dexterity

Materials

For each child
Pages 23 and 24 of the *Fine Motor
   Skills* Children's Book
Primary pencil
Crayons

For the teacher
Fine Motor Skills Children's Book
Pencil

Procedure

1. Pass out the Children's Books, pencils, and crayons. Have the children open their books to the first page, page 23. Have them tear out the page and close the books. Have the children locate the front of their page by finding the picture of the front of the baby. Point to this picture in your book.

2. Demonstrate with page 23 in your book.

> *Look at the broken line on your page. It makes a picture. Can you guess what it is?* (When the picture is identified as an umbrella, discuss uses and types of umbrellas.) *We are going to finish this umbrella by making a line over the broken line. Watch how I do it.* (Make a solid line over the dotted lines in your book.) *Now you go ahead and finish your picture of the umbrella.*

Praise each child's drawing when it is completed.

3. Have the children turn their page over. Have them guess what picture the broken line makes. Talk about different ways whistles are used. Have the children complete the drawing by marking along the dotted line with their pencil.

4. As the children finish, have them choose one of their drawings to color. Then have them put their names on their page.

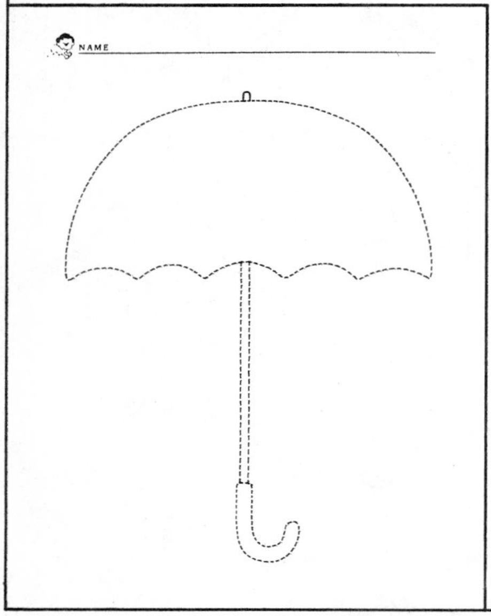

Figure 5-3 Connecting Dots

60

Lesson 34

Objectives

To develop arm steadiness
To develop arm-and-hand precision

Materials

For each child
Pages 59 and 60 of the *Fine Motor Skills* Children's Book
Primary pencil
Crayons

For the teacher
Fine Motor Skills Children's Book
Pencil

Procedure

1. Pass out the Children's Books and have the children open them to the first page, page 59. Have them tear out the page and locate its front by finding the picture of the front of the jacket. Point to this picture in your book.

2. Have the children describe what is going on in the picture on page 59.

> *Yes, the little boy is crying because his cat is stuck up on the roof of his house. Why can't the boy climb the ladder to get his cat down?* (Bring out that some of the steps of the ladder are missing.) *We're going to fix the ladder by drawing straight lines between its two sides. See, the three bottom steps have been done for you.* (In your book, point to the bottom three steps.) *Watch me.* (Demonstrate by drawing in the steps. Start at the bottom of the ladder.) *Now you go ahead and put steps in your ladder. Start at the bottom and go all the way to the top. Don't skip any of the steps.*

Move around the room, giving additional instructions where needed.

3. Have the children turn their page over.

> *Look, we have some monkeys in a cage. But there's something wrong with the cage.* (Bring out that the bars of the cage are missing.) *We're going to put the bars back on the cage by drawing straight lines from the little lines at the top of the cage to the little lines at the bottom of the cage, like this.* (Demonstrate in your book by drawing lines down to form the cage's bars.) *Work carefully and draw the lines as straight as you can.*

4. Have the children take a crayon and go over their pencil lines on one of the pages. Then have them put their names on their page.

Figure 5-4 Drawing Horizontal Lines

Lesson 49

Objectives

To develop arm steadiness
To develop arm-and-hand precision
To review the concepts
left, right, down, bottom

Materials

For each child
Pages 87 and 88 of the *Fine Motor Skills* Children's Book
Primary pencil
Crayons

For the teacher
Fine Motor Skills Children's Book
Pencil

Procedure

1. Pass out the Children's Books and have the children open them to the first page, page 87. Have them tear out the page and locate its front by finding the picture of the front of the squirrel. Point to this picture in your book. Check to see that the children have positioned their page so that the squirrel is in the upper left-hand corner.

2. Have the children identify the Indian and arrows on the page.

Yes, this is an Indian. He's shooting arrows at the targets over here. (Point to the targets in your book.) *We're going to take our pencils and draw straight lines from the arrows to the targets to show where the arrows will go. Start here with this arrow and draw a straight line to this target.* (Demonstrate in your book by drawing a line from the first arrow to the first target.) *Now, you do it. Make sure your line is straight. When you finish the first line, go ahead and draw lines for all the arrows.*

Move around the room and give help where needed.

3. Have the children turn their page over. Have them identify the picture on page 88.

Yes, it's a lion. See, the bars on its cage are gone. The lion might get out if we don't put in the bars. Take your pencil and start at the top of the cage and draw lines down to the bottom to put in each bar, like this. (Demonstrate by drawing lines down to form each of the cage's bars.)

4. Have the children choose a crayon and go over the pencil lines they made for the bars.

5. Have the children color the feathers on the arrows. Then have them put their names on their page.

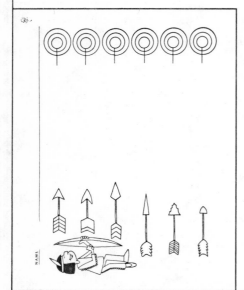

Figure 5-5 Drawing Vertical Lines

Lesson 10

Objectives

To develop arm steadiness
To develop arm-and-hand precision
To develop hand-and-finger
  dexterity

Materials

For each child
Pages 17 and 18 of the *Fine Motor Skills* Children's Book
Primary pencil
Crayons

For the teacher
Overhead projector
Transparency 6
Grease pencil
Fine Motor Skills Children's Book

Procedure

1. Read or recite the rhyme "Wee Willie Winkie."

   Wee Willie Winkie runs through the town,
   Upstairs and downstairs in his nightgown,
   Rapping at the windows, crying at the locks,
   Are the children all in bed, for now it's eight o'clock?

If you have a nursery-rhyme book, discuss the pictures accompanying this poem. Have the children act out the rhyme.

2. Pass out the Children's Books. Have the children open them to the first page, page 17. Have them tear out the page and close the books. Tell them that they are going to help Wee Willie go through the town. Project the transparency. Tell them that this picture is the same as their page. Have the children locate the front of their page by finding the picture of the front of the truck. Point to the picture on the transparency. Check to make sure that the children turn their page so that the truck is in the upper left-hand corner. Demonstrate on the transparency.

   Look, here is a picture of Wee Willie running through the town. (Point.) *Down here is one of the houses he is going to.* (Point.) *And this broken line shows the path he must take to get to the house. Take your pencil and start here on Wee Willie and follow the line to the house, like this.* (Trace over the broken line on the transparency.) *Now you do it. Be careful to stay on the line with your pencil.*

Move around the room giving help when needed.

3. Have the children turn the page over. In your book, point out the truck. Make sure the children position their page so that the truck is in the upper left-hand corner. Point out Wee Willie, the house, and the path. Have the children mark the path with their pencil.

4. Have the children choose a crayon and go over the pencil line they make on the path on one or both sides. Then have them put their names on their page.

Figure 5-6 Tracing Dotted Lines

Lesson 32

Objectives

To develop finger speed

To develop hand-and-finger
dexterity

Materials

For each child

Page 55 in the *Fine Motor Skills*
Children's Book

Scissors

Paste

Crayons

For the teacher

Fine Motor Skills Children's Book

Scissors

Procedure

1. Pass out the Children's Books, scissors, and crayons. Have the children open the books to the first page, page 55. Have them tear out the page and close the books.

2. Have the children identify the picture on page 55.

   Yes, it's a ship. This is a pirate ship. But there is something missing. The ship can't move. Why not? (Bring out that the ship's sails are missing.) *We're going to cut out the sails and paste them on the ship so the pirate can sail again. But first let's color the sails.* (Point to the two sails at the top of the page.)

3. When the children finish coloring, continue.

   First cut along this dotted line on your page. (Point to the line separating the sails from the picture.) *Now, cut out the sails you colored.*

4. Pass out the paste.

   Now paste the sails on the ship. See, the small sail goes here and the big sail goes here. (Demonstrate by positioning the cutout sails within the outline in the picture. Move around the room. Some children will need **help** placing the sails in the correct place.)

5. Have the children put their names on their page.

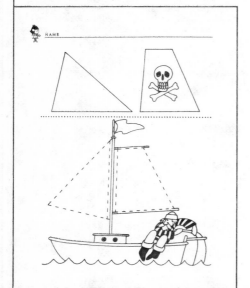

Figure 5-7 Cutting and Pasting

Lesson 35

Objectives

To develop arm steadiness

To develop arm-and-hand precision

To review the concepts
circle, square, triangle, oval

Materials

For each child

Pages 61 and 62 of the *Fine Motor Skills* Children's Book

A circle, a square, a triangle, and an oval template

Primary pencil

For the teacher

A circle, a square, a triangle, and an oval template

Procedure

1. Pass out the circle, square, triangle, and oval templates. Remind the children of how they used the templates to draw shapes in their books. Using the templates, draw each shape on the chalkboard. Have the shapes identified.

2. Pass out the Children's Books and have the children open them to the first page, page 61. Have them tear out the page and locate its front by finding the picture of the front of the clown. All the pictures in lesson 35 are clothing items. Have the children identify and talk about the clothing on page 61.

3. Tell the children that they are going to draw each shape.

   On this page we're going to draw circles and squares. Take your circle pattern and draw a circle around the parka. (Do not demonstrate.)

   Move around the room and give help where needed. When the children finish, have them draw a circle around the dress by marking over the broken line, without the template.

4. Continue by having the children use the template to draw a square around the shirt. Then have them make a square around the jeans by marking over the broken line, without the template.

5. Have the children turn their page over. Have the pictures identified.

   Now we're going to draw more shapes. This time we're going to draw triangles and ovals. First take your triangle pattern and draw a triangle around the hat. Then, without your pattern, make a triangle around the boots by drawing over the broken line.

6. Continue by having the children draw an oval around the shoe, using the template. Then have them draw an oval around the mittens by going over the broken line, without the template.

7. Have the children put their names on their page.

Figure 5-8 Drawing Shapes

Lesson 53

Objectives

To develop arm-and-hand precision
To develop hand-and-finger
    dexterity
To develop body awareness

Materials

For each child
Pages 93 and 94 of the *Fine Motor
    Skills* Children's Book
Primary pencil
Crayons

For the teacher
Fine Motor Skills Children's Book

Procedure

1. Pass out the Children's Books and have the children open them to the first page, page 93. Have them tear out the page and locate its front by finding the picture of the front of the rabbit. Point to this picture in your book.

2. Tell the children that they are going to do something with all the men on this page.

> *Look at the man up here.* (Point to the man in the upper left-hand corner. Point to the figure's head, arms, hands, legs, feet, trunk and have the children identify the parts.) *This man is finished; all his parts are here. But the other men on this page are not finished. Look at the next man.* (Point to the man in the upper right-hand corner.) *He's not finished, is he? What part is missing? Yes, his hand is missing. Take your pencil and draw his hand where it belongs. Draw the hand just like the hand in the first picture over here.* (Point to the hand on the complete man.)

3. When the children finish, continue.

> *Now look at this man.* (Point to the man in the lower left-hand corner.) *What part is missing? Yes, his foot is missing, isn't it? Go ahead and finish this man and the man next to him.*

4. Have the children turn their page over. Have them identify the figures' missing parts and then have them complete each figure.

5. Have the children choose and then color one of the men in the lesson. Then have them put their names on their page.

Figure 5-9 Completing Figures

The types of lessons presented here have been developed primarily as aids in the young child's acquisition of new fine-motor skills. During the practice/generalization activity phases discussed earlier, more emphasis should be placed on child-initiated activities. Art activities and craft activities are excellent vehicles for providing children with follow-through activities for generalizing the fine-motor skills they have acquired through the more structured lessons. Some of these activities can be found in the developmental activity guide at the end of this chapter.

As you develop your fine-motor program you will no doubt add procedures that you find particularly successful with your children. The richer the teacher's contribution to the curriculum, the greater will be the children's improvement in fine-motor skills, paying attention, and learning to follow oral directions. Children enjoy learning to do serious tasks; this attitude is an important factor in their motivation, since it is in effect a reward for their efforts. Capitalize on this built-in motivation by being very generous in your praise of each child's efforts. Praise will encourage children to help themselves as they work to develop fine-motor skills.

Generalization of Motor Skills

The type of motor lessons and activities that have been discussed so far apply primarily to the acquisition of new skills. During the practice/generalization phase of learning, the emphasis is on child-initiated activities that generally take place in what we call "interest centers." Following are examples of interest centers that can be used for the generalization of motor skills.

Arts and Crafts Center

Arts and crafts are sometimes combined in one interest center; sometimes they are treated as separate interest areas. The equipment and materials that are selected for the center determine the kinds of activities that will be undertaken there. Therefore, even though the activities are child-initiated, the teacher is able to plan the activity range. In most art activities there is an extremely large range for practice of motor skills. In painting activities, for example, at one extreme we see a child splashing different colors of paint onto his paper with a brush; at the other extreme, we see a child executing detailed line paintings with subtle shading. At both ends of this activity range the child is generalizing his fine-motor skills in an appropriate manner for his level of ability. In an arts and crafts interest center, a child can:

1. paint, draw, and color.
2. finger-paint.
3. tear, cut, paste, and fold.
4. model with clay and play dough.
5. do simple macrame projects.
6. do simple woodworking and work with tools.

7. participate in various craft activities, making use of such materials as buttons, spools, bottle caps, corks, towel and toilet paper cores, wire, nuts, macaroni, pipe cleaners.

Object Manipulation and Blocks Center

It is important to establish one or more interest centers that permit the child to manipulate objects in a creative and imaginative way. This type of interest center may be referred to as a play center, a self-directed learning center, a wheel-toy center, or a manipulation and construction center. Again, the kinds of activities that go on are determined by the materials and equipment within the center. In an object manipulation and blocks center, gross-motor as well as fine-motor skills are practiced and generalized to other applications. In this kind of center, the child can:

1. manipulate building blocks of various sizes, shapes, and weight, including parquetry blocks.
2. manipulate wheel toys such as Kiddie Kars, wheelbarrows, large ride-on dump trucks.
3. handle and use balls, beanbags, marbles, and other materials for tossing, rolling, and stacking activities.
4. place objects in large and small containers.
5. put together children's puzzles.
6. manipulate doll house materials, including dolls, dolls' clothing, and sturdy doll furniture, and play cooking and cleaning utensils.
7. manipulate farm-yard animal sets and play farm sets.
8. place pegs in pegboards.
9. manipulate push-pull floor toys such as cars, airplanes, buses, trains.

Water and Sand Center

A water and sand center could be established either indoors or outdoors depending on your physical facilities. Many activities in this type of center will provide children with opportunities to generalize their fine-motor skills. In this interest center the child can:

1. use funnels, trays, and other containers to transport water from one place to another, or pour it from one container to another.
2. manipulate an array of floating objects.
3. use sand trays, molds, and other containers to shape and carry sand.
4. manipulate small push-pull toys in the sand.

There are a number of other types of interest centers that can be used for the practice/generalization of motor skills, such as game centers, music centers, and housekeeping centers. It is extremely important to provide an array of centers that will allow for the generalization of all developmental skills and processes. To a certain degree, there is an overlapping of skill generalization in almost any interest center. We have stressed the motor-development aspects of the centers mentioned above, but all provide a desirable and necessary interaction between the various developmental skill areas.

Developmental Activity Guide

Motor Development: Gross Motor, Fine Motor

In this guide, the task number refers to the corresponding item on the *Carolina Developmental Profile* (See pages 220–40). The objective states the behavior to be learned. In the instructional activities column, we suggest several activities that will give your children the experience necessary to accomplish the stated objective. (Note: the activities do not have to be presented in the sequence given below.) As you gain more experience working with children, you will no doubt add additional activities that will increase the usefulness of the guide.

GROSS MOTOR

Developmental Objective *(by task no.)*	Instructional Activities
1. Seats self in small chair without loss of balance *Materials for Activities* 1. *Chairs* 2. *Chairs* 3. *Chairs; record player; record* 4. *Chairs*	1. Teacher writes song using lines "sit down fast, stand up tall, laugh out loud, one and all"—to be acted out as a song. 2. Teacher tells a story including the action "sit down." Child performs action. Example: "Freddie sat down [child sits down]. He was all alone. He waved to a bird, etc." 3. Musical chairs (very simplified version). Do not remove chairs. 4. "Fruit basket turn over." Divide class into three groups: apples, oranges, and grapes. All children are seated. Teacher is caller. Caller names fruit and members of that group exchange seats. More advanced versions: (a) Name more than one fruit at a time. (b) Remove one chair each time. (c) Have one child be the caller. He also tries to seat himself, and the remaining child becomes caller.
2. Stands with heels together without falling for about five seconds. *Materials for Activities* 2. *Chalk, tape, or 8 x 8 inch paper squares* 3. *Whistle or bell* 4. *Bell*	1. Copycat game. Teacher stands against the wall and has children do the same thing. 2. Standing on a square. Mark small (8 x 8 inch) squares on floor for children to stand on; play a game in which every time the teacher says "Change," children run to another square to stand on. 3. Who can be a good statue? Use bell or whistle to start and stop being a statue. Increase length of time that child is a statue. 4. Children stand sideways on wide walking beam with heels together. "Who can stand like this without falling until I ring the bell?"

Developmental Objective *(by task no.)*	Instructional Activities

5. *Paper footprints; tape; record player; record*

5. Tape to floor a pair of paper footprints with heels together. Have a child stand on footprints. You may assist him if necessary. Advanced activity: children walk around room with music playing; when music stops children must position themselves on footprints.

6. Teacher and assistant act out story of Hansel and Gretel. Children act as trees standing with heels together while Hansel and Gretel are lost in forest. Children stand same way to form witch's cage to hold Hansel, as called for in the story.

3. Tosses tennis ball forward

Materials for Activities

1. *Ball*
2. *Small soft objects; box*
3. *Balls; tub of water; plastic sheet*
4. *Beanbags; hoops; cartons; inner tubes; etc.*
5. *Paper snowman; Styrofoam balls*
6. *Ball; bell or timer*

1. Seat children in a circle and practice rolling the ball to different players. Progress to bouncing and then throwing.

2. Throw small soft objects into large box.

3. Throw rubber balls into a tub of water (protect floor).

4. Toss beanbags through hoops or inner tubes, or into different size containers, or at cartons.

5. Mount a large snowman on a wall or bulletin board. Have children take turns throwing styrofoam balls at the snowman.

6. Hot potato. Children stand in circle, toss ball quickly to each other. Teacher may set timer, ring bell, or stop music; child caught with ball is "It."

4. Picks up one-inch cube from floor while standing, without falling

Materials for Activities

1. *Wagon; articles*
2. *Objects; bricks*
3. *Handkerchief*
4. *Small objects; pail or other container*
5. *Container*

1. Child is asked to load wagon with articles. Examples: "moving day" or "construction worker."

2. Ask child to pick up objects placed on top of a sturdy waist-high stack of bricks. Periodically remove one brick at a time until there are no more bricks, and the child is picking up objects from the floor.

3. Squatting games: ring around the rosie, stoop or squat tag, drop the handkerchief, etc.

4. Set pail or box in middle of floor, and have children pick up blocks or toy objects and place in box. Provide game atmosphere.

5. Squirrel and nut. Children pick up as many objects (nuts) as they can and place in a container in a specified time.

Developmental Objective *(by task no.)*	Instructional Activities

5. Walks up and down three steps without support, using alternating or nonalternating steps

Materials for Activities

1. *Jungle gym*
2. *Sliding board*
4. *Ladder; blocks*
5. *Auto tires*
6. *Record player; record*
7. *Sliding board*
9. *Markers; ribbons*

1. Jungle gym experience; free climbing experiences.

2. Climbing up sliding board.

3. Obstacle course requiring climbing.

4. Ladder walking. Ladder is placed horizontally on floor and elevated one to three inches from floor with blocks. Child steps through spaces between rungs.

5. Stepping in and out of auto tires spaced at intervals. Child steps from one tire to another.

6. Marching to music with exaggerated knee lift.

7. Climbing down sliding board ladder.

8. Experiences on stairs, beginning with very low heights.

9. Tape or draw black and red squares on steps. Tie a black ribbon to one foot, a red ribbon to the other. Have child stop on squares with the correct foot.

6. Throws six-inch to ten-inch diameter ball at least five feet, without losing balance.

Materials for Activities

2. *Ball; target*
3. *Blocks*
4. *Ball*
5. *Ball*

1. See activities for task 3 and adapt for size of ball.

2. Child throws ball at large target or into container.

3. Build tower of blocks; from an assigned distance have children try to knock down tower.

4. Child throws ball to adult.

5. Child tosses ball against wall.

6. Angels in the snow.

7. Jumps from an elevation of approximately six inches

Materials for Activities

1. *Sliding board*
3. *Record player; record*

1. Child walks up slight incline and jumps to ground.

2. Jumps from bottom step.

3. Imitates hopping animals, to music.

4. Jumps over rope or other objects on ground; gradually raise rope.

5. Teacher attaches large ball to a string, and hangs or holds it out of reach of child. Child must jump up to touch.

Developmental Objective *(by task no.)*	Instructional Activities
4. *Rope* 5. *Large ball; string* 7. *Hoops*	6. Teacher has children line up on steps and play jump-to-the-fireman (teacher) from the bottom step. The children may pretend to be kittens in a tree. 7. Place three or four hoops flat on the floor, several feet apart. Have the child walk in and out of them. Then have him jump in and out.
8. Walks straight line one inch wide and ten feet long without stepping off more than three times *Materials for Activities* 1. *Wrapping paper; tape* 2. *Rope* 3. *Maze on floor* 5. *String* 7. *Paper footprints; tape*	1. Child walks on wide wrapping paper taped to floor. "Follow the yellow brick road." 2. Practices walking straight line by holding onto rope. 3. Walks mazes laid out on floor with chalk or tape. 4. Teacher draws lines on the floor and sets up a game of follow the leader. 5. Teacher places string on the floor. Child walks on string to find "hidden treasure." 6. Have child walk barefooted across surfaces that offer a variety of tactile stimulation: wet grass, gravel, concrete, wet sand, wood floors, asphalt. Have child discuss how each area feels on his bare feet. 7. Tape footprints on floor in straight line. Have children walk on footprints forward and backward.
9. Walks backward for ten feet along line *Materials for Activities* 3. *Walking board* 4. *Record player; record*	1. Organize walking backward relays. 2. Organize a game of "Mother may I." Have children take normal, giant, and baby backward steps. 3. Walking board exercises. (a) Walk length of board backward pretending it is a bridge. (b) Walk to end, turn, come back. (c) Walk holding object in hand. 4. Walk around in a circle to music, and on signal walk backward. 5. See activities from task 8.

Developmental Objective *(by task no.)*	Instructional Activities
10. Walks up and down three steps without support, alternating the forward foot in climbing and descending	1. Use activities for task 5 and encourage alternating steps.
11. Throws tennis ball using overhand throw with little torso participation *Materials for Activities* *1, 2, and 3. Tennis balls*	1. Modified baseball game. Pitcher throws tennis ball to batter; batter catches ball, throws overhand, and runs bases. 2. Child throws ball over a barrier. 3. Teacher has children do arm exercises, starting with simple lead-up drills: first, leg-weight shifts only; then arm-and-leg weight shifts, with and without ball. 4. See activities for tasks 3 and 6.
12. Balances on one foot without support for five seconds *Materials for Activities* *2. Paper squares of different sizes* *6. Record player; record*	1. Hold onto child's arm to help him balance while he is standing on one foot. After a few times suggest a game in which you will let go of child's arm for one second and gradually increase time. 2. Place squares of different sizes on floor. Child stands on one foot in large square, then progresses to smaller squares. 3. Song: "You Can Do What I Do." 4. Follow the leader. 5. Song: "If You're Happy and You Know It, Stand on One Foot." 6. Play Freeze. March around the room to music. When music stops, or teacher calls "freeze," child must stop and stand on one foot until he is told to melt.
13. Hops at least twice on one foot without support, either in place or not *Materials for Activities* *2. Hopscotch squares drawn on ground*	1. Hopping relays. 2. Hopscotch. 3. Hop into squares chalked on the floor. 4. Follow the leader. 5. Imitate hopping animals: rabbits, frogs, kangaroos. Emphasize being on toes.

Developmental Objective *(by task no.)*	Instructional Activities
	6. Require that all movements from one activity area in the classroom to another be accomplished only by hopping on one foot.

14. Jumps at least two inches high from crouched position

Materials for Activities

2. This is Music
4. *Large squares on paper*
5. *Small object*
6. *Mexican jumping beans*

1. Imitate hopping animals: rabbits, frogs, kangaroos.

2. Pretend to be jack-in-the-boxes while singing the jack-in-the-boxes song from *This is Music*, Adeline McCall (Boston, Allyn and Bacon, Inc., 1965, p. 112).

3. Pretend to be popcorn popping.

4. Stepping stones. Place large squares of paper on floor. Child leaps without stepping off paper.

5. Play "Jack jump over the candlestick." Place small object on floor, and have children say rhyme and jump over object from crouched position.

6. Bring Mexican jumping beans to class. Have students imitate jumping beans and jump in a prescribed manner.

15. Makes running broad jump of at least 23 inches

Materials for Activities

1. *Chalk or tape*
3. *Stick; tape*

1. Make two parallel lines on the floor. Lines should be about 18 inches apart. Child tries to jump across both lines (a make-believe river).

2. Jump over low objects.

3. Place stick on ground and have children run to jump over it. Gradually move the stick farther away from starting point. Children back up to get a running start.

4. Obstacle course.

5. Play "jumping horses" on playground.

16. Balances on one foot without support for ten seconds

Materials for Activities

1. *Timer or clock; whistle*
3. *Large paper squares; record player; record*

1. Teacher sets timer or watches clock, and blows whistle after a few seconds, gradually increasing time.

2. Tag. Any child is "safe" if he is balanced on one foot.

3. Tape large paper squares on floor. Have each child hop in square while music is playing. When music stops, he must balance in square until music begins.

Developmental Objective *(by task no.)*	Instructional Activities

4. *Rope; tape or balance beam*

5. *Bricks*

4. Play circus. Some children can be tightrope walkers who must stop in middle of rope and balance on one foot; others, trained dogs that stand on one foot, etc. (Use balance beam or tape on floor.)

5. Set up bricks as stepping stones one step apart; bricks can be placed in several short lines, one long line, or in a circle.

---

17. Balances on toes with feet together and heels off the ground for ten seconds, without support

1. Use activities for tasks 12 and 16.

2. Change from balance on one foot to balance on toes.

3. Pretend to reach for imaginary objects.

4. Teacher acts as dog trainer, children as dogs. Teacher trains dogs to stand on toes and beg for a bone. Use as game or with circus unit.

---

18. Makes running broad jump of at least 28 inches

1. See activities for task 15.

---

19. Kicks an eight-inch to ten-inch diameter ball, either from floor or using drop kick, at least eight feet in air

Materials for Activities

1. *Kickball*

2. *Kickball*

3. *Tags; pillow*

4. *String; kickball*

5. *Record player; record; beanbags; kickball*

1. Have children play a modified version of kickball.

2. Kick ball at target.

3. Determine foot dominance. Then place tags on dominant foot and have child swing foot at soft object (pillow) while standing still.

4. Have child kick at a ball suspended on a string held by the teacher.

5. Have child stand and practice swinging leg back and forth to music. Practice aiming by kicking at a large beanbag, then kickball.

Developmental Objective *(by task no.)*	Instructional Activities
20. Skips smoothly *Materials for Activities* 1. *Record player; record* 2. *Chalk or tape* 3. *Drum* 4. *Stick horse*	1. Have child step and hop on same foot to 6/8-time music; alternate pattern. 2. Crossing the road. Using chalk or tape, make two five-foot lines twenty feet apart; child skips, hops, runs, crawls, etc., at teacher's direction. 3. Indian war dance. Pretend children are Indians doing dance. Beat cadence with drum. Children hop two times on one foot and then switch. 4. Have child gallop on a stick horse.

FINE MOTOR

1. Turns a few pages in a child's storybook, one at a time with definite control and ease *Materials for Activities* 1. *Playing cards* 2. *Jars with lids* 3. *Plastic nuts and bolts* 4. *Newspaper* 5. *Shirt cardboard; ring binders; pictures* 6. *Spools; thread; yarn* 7. *Clay*	1. Places playing cards of different colors in different piles. 2. Unscrews jar lids and screws them on again. 3. Screws and unscrews large plastic nuts and bolts. 4. Teacher has children tear newspaper by grasping the paper with the thumb and forefinger of each hand. Grasp, move the left hand toward the body; move the right hand away from the body. Stress tearing the paper in long, thin strips. 5. Put together with ring binders three pieces of shirt cardboard with pictures pasted on each piece. The children should tell what is happening on each "page" of their "book," turning each page as the teacher says to. 6. Winds yarn onto spool. More difficult: thread onto spool. 7. Pinches clay.
2. Builds a standing tower of six to eight one-inch cubes *Materials for Activities* 1. *Cartons; boxes; cans* 2. *Cubes; blocks* 3. *Cubes*	1. Stacks large cartons, books, cans. 2. Builds structures in block corner. 3. See if the child can stack two cubes. After success, gradually increase the number of cubes.

Developmental Objective *(by task no.)*	Instructional Activities

3. Strings at least two beads in no more than two minutes

Materials for Activities

1. *Commercial or homemade sewing cards; needles; yarn*
2. *Paper plates; pictures; paste*
3. *Pegboard*
4. *Threader*
5. *Thread spools; shoestrings*

1. Give child large needle threaded with yarn, and show him how to sew up and down through holes. Same activity can be done with valentines, greeting cards, tree ornaments.

2. Have child cut out picture and paste in center of paper plate.

3. Pegboard activities.

4. Creative Playthings' Threader.

5. Make a necklace from spools. Let children string 12 spools on a 30-inch shoestring. Children can decorate the spools with crayons.

4. Unwraps piece of twisted-end wrapped candy without any help

Materials for Activities

1. *Paper*
2. *Plastic nuts and bolts*
3. *Button board*
4. *Large packages*
5. *Bananas*

1. Have children tear paper into the smallest pieces possible.

2. Children should screw nuts and bolts using both hands, one hand turning the bolt toward the body, the other turning the screw away from it.

3. The child buttons and unbuttons his own coat or works with button board.

4. Unwraps large packages.

5. Peels banana.

5. Builds three-block bridge

Materials for Activities

2. *Blocks*
3. *Cloth or cardboard blocks*
4. *Blocks*
5. *Plastic animal; blocks*
6. *Blocks*

1. See activities for task 2.

2. Makes imaginary train with blocks.

3. Uses large light blocks (12-inch cubes) to build bridges.

4. Builds forts or houses with blocks.

5. The teacher tells a story about a cow (use plastic cow or other animal) who wandered away from the barn. "It started to rain, and the cow, who was wet, looked for shelter under a bridge." The teacher should demonstrate building a bridge with small blocks, and then point out to

the children that the bridge is too small for the cow to fit under. "Can you build the cow a big bridge? Try using the big cardboard blocks."

6. The teacher constructs simple bridges with large blocks. Let children duplicate the bridges and then demolish them. Have children rebuild the bridges and then use them in creative play. The children may use bridges as overpasses (on model roads) or drawbridges.

---

6. Copies circle from sample

Materials for Activities

2. *Sandbox or sandpaper*

3. *Finger paints*

4. *Template; chalk; newsprint; crayons; tempera paints; magic markers*

1. Teacher demonstrates making large circle in air. Teacher and child may want to put index fingertips together.

2. Traces circle in sandbox or over sandpaper symbol.

3. Finger painting. Child makes circular motions.

4. Make a template of a circle (6 inches in diameter) and have children use it to draw circles. First let them draw the circle on the blackboard with chalk. Have them follow the same procedure using, first, newsprint and primary crayons, then, newsprint and tempera paint or magic markers. Always be careful to discuss the quality of their work when it is completed.

---

7. Cuts paper in two pieces with scissors

Materials for Activities

1. *Clothespins; box*

2. *Paper; paste; scissors; cards; cartons*

3. *Straws*

4. *Construction paper; scissors; paste*

5. *Play Dough; clay*

1. Have child make "fence" by clipping clothespins around open box.

2. Child snips irregular shapes to be used as leaves to paste on tree drawn on paper or to decorate cards and cartons.

3. Cuts straws into short pieces.

4. Have children cut different colors of construction paper into small pieces. When the children are finished cutting, have them paste pieces together to form a collage.

5. Have children snip Play Dough or clay.

---

8. Traces diamond pattern with primary pencil or crayon

Materials for Activities

1. *Paper; pencil or*

1. Make a straight wide path and have child trace it. Put a picture of a mouse at the top and a picture of cheese at the bottom. Say "Help the mouse get the cheese."

2. Make a wide path that is shaped like half a diamond. Follow the procedure outlined in activity 1 above.

Developmental Objective *(by task no.)*	Instructional Activities

crayon; picture of mouse; picture of cheese

4. Paper; pencil; plastic animal or truck

5. Sand; finger paint; sandpaper

3. Make a narrower path that is shaped like three-quarters of a diamond. Follow the same procedure as above.

4. Make a diamond shape, and have child guide a plastic animal, truck, etc., around the shape.

5. Make a diamond shape in the sand (or make one with finger paint or sandpaper), and have child move finger over shape.

---

9. Copies cross (+) from sample

Materials for Activities

1. *Chalkboard; chalk; paper; crayons*

2. *Crayons*

1. Teacher places four dots on chalkboard arranged like this: ∴ The two side dots should be the same color, and the top and bottom dots the same color. Children make crosses by connecting the same color dots. Repeat as a paper and crayon task.

2. Present a worksheet constructed of dots that will form several rows of crosses when connected. Have children connect the dots, using different colors of crayons for each row of crosses.

3. See activities for task 6.

---

10. Catches an eight-inch to ten-inch diameter ball, thrown from approximately five feet away, with arms flexed

Materials for Activities

1. *Beanbags*

2. *Large ball*

1. Catches beanbags. Start close together, move farther apart.

2. "Pass the ball" relay. Two lines, stride position; each leader given large ball. At signal ball is passed between legs. First team to get ball to end wins.

---

11. Places ten pennies in box one at a time (using preferred hand) within fifteen seconds

Materials for Activities

1. *Marbles; box*

2. *Marbles*

1. Child picks up and drops marbles in small box.

2. Marble games.

3. Places checkers into large box.

4. Child picks up a penny from the floor, runs and puts it in a box three yards away, runs back, picks up another penny, etc. The first child to get five pennies in his box wins the race.

5. Sorts buttons by color. Give each child a box or egg carton divided into

Developmental Objective *(by task no.)*	Instructional Activities

3. *Checkers; box*

4. *Pennies; box*

5. *Buttons; egg cartons; envelopes; boxes*

four sections, and an envelope containing 40 buttons the size of a penny, ten each of blue, red, yellow, and green. Show the children how to sort the buttons according to color.

---

12. Copies square from sample

Materials for Activities

1. *Templates*

2. *Sandbox*

3. *Sandpaper squares*

4. *Dot-to-dot pictures*

1. Using square templates, organize activities similar to those in task 6.

2. Child traces with finger square-shaped pathways in sandbox.

3. With finger, traces sandpaper squares.

4. Completes dot-to-dot picture to make a square.

---

13. Crumples piece of tissue paper (4½ inch by 4½ inch) to form a ball

Materials for Activities

1. *Modeling clay or Play Dough*

2. *Puppets*

3. *Glue*

4. *Squares of colored tissue paper; paper; paste*

1. Modeling clay or Play Dough. Child makes simple round small objects. Example: snowman.

2. Puppet play. Manipulates head and arms.

3. The teacher should squirt a dab of Elmer's glue on one of each child's thumbs. The children should let the glue dry for a few seconds and then try to rub it off by rubbing the thumb against the other four fingers. The opposite hand should be held behind the children's backs or under the table.

4. Teacher has children make an animal collage out of colored tissue-paper balls. Give each child a number of four-inch tissue squares of various colors. Have him roll the tissue squares into small balls. When children are finished give them an outline drawing and let them paste the balls to the drawing to make a collage.

---

14. Places matchsticks in box with both hands simultaneously

Materials for Activities

1. *Pegboard and pegs*

2. *Paper bags; matchsticks*

1. Pegboard activities: (a) every hole; (b) "fence" around outside; (c) simple design.

2. Pick-up sticks. Two children make a team. The teacher is the judge. Each team has two paper bags. On the floor the teacher has placed about 20 matchsticks per team. When she says "Go," the children pick up all the matchsticks in front of them, placing them in the bags. The first team to pick all matchsticks wins.

3. Child sorts macaroni according to shape. Give each child a box divided

3. *Different kinds of macaroni; box; bowl*

into four sections and a bowl containing different kinds of macaroni (elbow, spaghetti in small pieces, shell, etc.), and ask child to sort according to shape.

---

15. Folds six-inch paper square to make triangle

Materials for Activities

1. *Napkins*

2. *Newspaper*

3. *Construction paper; pins*

4. *Paper; paper reinforcers*

1. Fold napkins for table setting.

2. Children make hats by folding a double sheet of newspaper in half lengthwise, then folding upper left- and right-hand corners down to center mark. Fold edges to make brim.

3. Child makes a simple pinwheel. Takes a six-inch square of construction paper, folds the square into a triangle so that opposite corners are superimposed. Open and refold so that the remaining two corners are superimposed. Cut in heavy lines and pin corners a, b, c, and d to center. Thrust pin in end of rod.

4. A six-inch square piece of paper should have a red reinforcer pasted in the upper right-hand corner and a green reinforcer in the lower left corner. Children should play "match the rings."

Checkpoint

What Have You Learned?

Facts

1. Why is the work of J. P. Guilford and L. L. Thurstone important to anyone involved in organizing motor development activities for young children?

2. _____ refers to skills that require small-muscle coordination. Factor-analysis research has identified four skill factors in the area. Name those four factors.

3. Which of the following are primarily fine-motor activities?

    a) Walking a balance beam

    b) Drawing straight horizontal lines.

    c) Telling all about a picture just drawn.

    d) Matching pictures

    e) Building block towers

    f) Cutting and pasting

    g) Following paths with a pencil

    h) Placing blocks into groups of large and small blocks

    i) Stacking pennies

    j) Using templates

    k) Tossing a ball

4. A large majority of those who have done research in motor development report a positive _____ between motor proficiency and mental ability.

5. The author's study of the effects of treatment (that is, daily lessons) on gross- and fine-motor skill development failed to show significant effects in the _____ motor area, but did show that _____ motor skills may be significantly altered through such treatment.

6. In planning motor development activities, you should design the activities so that each specific _____ of gross-motor development is frequently engaged and that all children _____ during a large portion of the activity time.

7. Several activities presented in this chapter allow for total group involvement at the same time that specific gross-motor factors are engaged. Name five such activities.

8. As a child approaches school age, fine-motor skills must be developed to allow the child to perform successfully in specific _____ situations involving motor behavior.

1. You have been assigned the topic of "Gross- and Fine-Motor Development" in a curriculum-methods course at a university. You want to demonstrate how to teach specific skills to children by showing that skills should be taught in sequential steps and that the children must be kept interested. Outline a weekly motor program (in both the fine and the gross areas) that meets these sequential and motivational specifications. **Simulation**

2. An irate parent who sees no need for motor development programs has requested an interview with you. Briefly outline what you will say to the parent in favor of such programs, citing sources to support your position.

Visit an early childhood classroom and observe the program. With the help of the daily schedule, determine the number of minutes per day that the children are actually engaged in fine-motor development and gross-motor development. Determine the ratio of gross- to fine-motor activity. **Application**

Chapter 6   Developing Visual Perception Skills

Objectives

After you have completed this chapter, you should be able to:

1. Identify the two sensory modes through which learning most frequently takes place in an educational environment.

2. Define perceptual selection, perceptual flexibility, perceptual accuracy and speed, and perceptual structuring.

3. Discuss the importance of breaking tasks down and providing motivation for learning in teaching young children.

4. List three academic habits (skills) that may be developed through systematic perceptual lessons.

5. Discuss the results and implications of the author and Dr. Thurstone's 1969 and 1970 research in visual perception.

6. List two interest centers that can be established to provide for the practice/generalization of perceptual skills, and give examples of the types of activities that could be made available in each.

Because more and more educators have become aware that intellectual development in young children is the result of an interaction between maturation and experience, many early childhood programs have modified their curricula to include activities specifically designed to further cognitive development. The television program "Sesame Street," with its structured "lessons" in perceptual and reasoning skills, is perhaps the best-known illustration of this trend.

Thurstone and Thurstone (1941) identified perception as one of the specific mental abilities present at the five-year-old level. In general terms, perception refers to the ability to attach meaning to incoming stimuli. Incoming stimuli can be perceived through any of the senses: vision, touch, smell, taste, or hearing. In the development of our early childhood curriculum, we have focused on visual-perception skills because of their importance as a foundation for later learning. Auditory perception, also an extremely important area of early development, is discussed later as a part of language development (chapter 8).

Visual perception can be defined as the dynamic process of attaching meaning or order to incoming visual stimuli. Visual perception is usually discussed as a specific concept. Experimental evidence, however, indicates that the visual-perception process is made up of a number of separate and specific measurable factors (Thurstone, 1944; Roff, 1953). Most researchers agree that there are four major visual-perception factors: *perceptual selection, perceptual flexibility, perceptual accuracy and speed, and perceptual structuring* (Cratty, 1970).

Visual-perception abilities have long been recognized as important prerequisites for all school learning, particularly reading. Interpreting the reading symbol code depends on the learner's ability to focus on visual stimuli quickly without distorting or changing the structure of that perception.

Visual-Perception Development Research

Papp (1964), in analyzing the results of a carefully controlled study, suggests that letter rotations and reversals are the result of a lack of experience rather than the result of poor or slow physiological maturation. Studies by Kahn and Birch (1968) and Gill, Herdtner, and Lough (1968) support Papp's findings.

For a number of years we have been engaged in the development and field testing of visual-perception materials for young children. (These efforts led to the development of the *Learning to Think Series* [Thurstone, 1972] and *Beginning to Learn: Perceptual Skills* [Thurstone and Lillie, 1972].) In the summer of 1969, we investigated the effectiveness of our materials on five-year-old children selected at random from four Head Start classes in Chapel Hill and Durham, North Carolina. Control groups consisted of four other Head Start classes randomly selected from the same area. The *Frosting Developmental Test of Visual Perception* (1964) was given to the children in all eight classes in a pretest, post-test manner. At the beginning of the summer we held a half-day training session with the four Head Start teachers who would be using our program. Each teacher was given a series of 30 lessons to be used over a six-week period. One lesson was to be given each day; the time allotted for each lesson was approximately 20 minutes.

When we retested the children at the end of the six-week period we found that the children in the experimental classes gained significantly more in perceptual development than did the children in the control classes.

The program was tested again in the spring of 1970 with approximately 100 five- and six-year-old children enrolled in an ungraded public school program at Saxapahaw, North Carolina.

For a three-month period all children received daily 20-minute lessons. Using the *Primary Mental Abilities* test in a pre- and post-test fashion, we found that the five-year-olds had gained, on the average, ten months in primary mental abilities, and that the six-year-olds had gained six months.

As you can see from the results of these studies, visual-perception ability can be dramatically increased in preschool children. It is not our intent, however, to suggest that an increase in visual-perception ability alone has a direct influence on a child's ability to learn to read. It is our belief, rather, that higher levels of competence in all areas of the primary mental abilities, including perception, affect such intervening variables as self-confidence, willingness to attack new tasks, and feelings of success and well being. In addition, the child develops habits and skills that will have a direct effect on later academic success: for example, attending to a specific task, listening to and following directions, and acquiring left to right page orientation.

Perception Curriculum Activities for Two- and Three-Year-Olds

Two important features of planning cognitive curriculum activities for children under four are: (1) breaking down large and difficult tasks into a series of small and simple tasks (When the child is able to do each of the small tasks, he can then be asked to accomplish the larger, more difficult task.); and (2) presenting each task in a format that is motivating, stimulating, and suitable for the child's level of manipulative and organizational skills.

To illustrate these curriculum-planning concepts, examples of two lesson activities—Katy the Kangaroo and Cognitive Cubes—are presented here. These lessons were developed by Thelma Thurstone for use with two- and three-year-old children at the Frank Porter Graham Child Development Center in Chapel Hill.

Katy the Kangaroo

The eight activities presented here involve the use of a large mat-board figure of a kangaroo. Katy (see figure 6-1) wears a bright-colored plastic apron with nine transparent plastic pockets; she is three feet tall, and is supported by a firm tail that enables her to stand on the floor or on a low table. The lessons, which are structured in arrangement and purpose, may be used with individual children or with small groups. Some lessons may take only a few minutes; no lesson should ever take longer than 20 minutes.

The first five Katy lessons are designed to develop perceptual accuracy and the concepts of shape, color, number, arrangement, and size.

Lesson 1 As shown in figure 6-1, four cards, each displaying a different shape, but all of the same color, are placed in the top row of four pockets. The single pocket on Katy's chest contains additional cards, five to match each of the four shapes displayed in the row below. Note that only the backs of the cards can be seen through the single plastic pocket. The child (or children) draws one card at a time from the pack of 20, and places it in the pocket that is directly under

Figure 6-1   Katy the Kangaroo

the one that contains the corresponding sample card. In the illustration, the children have drawn and correctly matched the circle, square, and triangle.

Lesson 2   The four colored cards used for lesson 2 (see figure 6-2, page 88) are placed in any order in the first row of four pockets. The task is to draw additional cards one at a time from the top pocket, and place them in the second row of pockets so that they match the color of the card directly above them.

Lesson 3   Note the four cards showing one, two, three, and four candy canes. The task is to match cards on the basis of number. With very young children, only three, and sometimes only two, numbers are used.

Lesson 4   The four cards shown for lesson 4 all have four dots, but the arrangement of the dots varies. The task is to match the patterns.

Lesson 5   The four cards shown for this lesson have pictures of four jack-o'-lanterns, varying in size only. The task is to match other cards with varying size pictures to the sample sizes. For very young children two pictures, the largest and the smallest, are used.

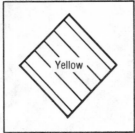 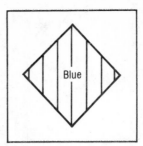 
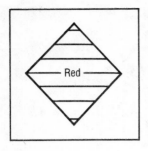

Lesson 2

Lesson 3

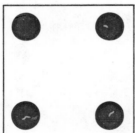 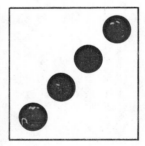 

Lesson 4

Lesson 5

Figure 6-2

Lesson 6

Lesson 7

Lesson 8

Figure 6-3

89

Lessons 6, 7, and 8 (see page 89) are designed to develop perceptual precision or accuracy. The difficulty of the lessons covers a wide range.

Lesson 6   The four cards used in this lesson show pictures of four persons: a man, baby, woman, and girl. The child's task is to find the pictures in the top pocket that match the four pictures presented.

Lesson 7   The four cards presented show pictures of four kinds of fruit. The procedure is similar to that of lesson 6.

Lesson 8   The four cards presented show pictures of four elephants. The procedure is similar to lesson 6. Greater perceptual precision is required in this lesson.

Cognitive Cubes

The cognitive-cube lessons presented here (see figure 6-4) involve the use of four one-and-three-quarter-inch cubes. The cubes, which are of clear plastic, are designed so that they can be taken apart for the insertion of slightly smaller cardboard cubes. The cardboard cubes are covered with a variety of matching pictures and shapes.

Cognitive-cube lessons can be used with individual children or with small groups. Again, no lesson should last longer than 20 minutes per day. The child's task is to manipulate each cube until all the pictures or shapes in a set are turned up in the same direction. In some cases, this means that the child must examine all six sides of each of the four cubes. Following are examples of four lessons used at the Frank Porter Graham Child Development Center.

Lesson 1   "Show me the pictures on each block that look just alike." If the child finds two alike and stops, say, "That's right, can you find any more just like these?"

Lesson 2   "Show me the animals on each block that look just alike." Again, prompt the child if he stops before finding four animals that are alike.

Lesson 3   "Show me the birds on each block that look just alike." In this series, the perceptual discrimination becomes increasingly difficult as the child progresses from lesson 1 to lesson 3.

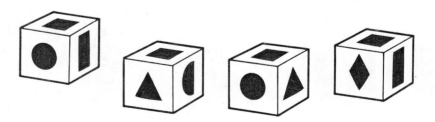

Figure 6-4   Cognitive Cubes

To make sure that perceptual activities designed for older pre-school-age children are related to actual perceptual functioning in the child, we selected specific perceptual factors to use as a logical base for the development of our training activities. These factors, as mentioned earlier, were identified as perceptual selection, perceptual flexibility, perceptual accuracy and speed, and perceptual structuring.

Perceptual selection referes to the ability to perceive figure-ground relationships; that is to distinguish between foreground and background visual stimuli. An illustration of this type of task is shown in figure 6-5. (See pages 92-99 for illustrations of various perceptual tasks.) Most of the activities in the perceptual-selection area deal with locating and tracing dotted outlines of overlapping geometric shapes, and locating and identifying two overlapping object or animal shapes.

Perceptual flexibility refers to the ability to recognize similarities (and, inversely, differences) in size. (Note figure 6-6.) Another aspect of perceptual flexibility is the ability to recognize similarities in direction orientation. (See figure 6-7.)

Perceptual accuracy and speed, the factor most people think of when visual perception is mentioned, refers to the ability to recognize likeness and differences in pictured objects. Figure 6-7 shows a lesson for developing perceptual-accuracy ability.

The fourth factor, *perceptual structuring,* deals with an ability more commonly known as *visual closure.* Visual closure refers to the ability to draw visual inferences or conclusions from partial visual information. Many lessons in perceptual structuring involve finding partially hidden objects, animals, or people. (Note the example in figure 6-8.)

The perceptual skills program provides fifteen different types of perceptual-training activities. They are: matching two out of three pictures, matching scattered pictures, finding hidden pictures, finding scattered pictures, discriminating dots in circles, finding geometric designs, matching two out of four pictures in picture squares, finding overlapping geometric shapes, recognizing similarities in size, matching to sample, finding scribbled pictures, discriminating picture reversals, discriminating design reversals, matching faces, and discriminating overlapping figures.

Our perceptual activities program is sequenced according to difficulty level. In addition each individual lesson has three levels of difficulty. Thus, the teacher is able to place each child at the level of perceptual training that is commensurate with his ability. The strong point of this program is the fact that individualized instruction can be managed by one teacher with a large group of preschool children. Lesson activities should include visual media if possible. The perceptual program discussed here contains sets of children's worksheets on spirit duplicator masters, filmstrips, and overhead-projector transparencies.

A sequential perceptual development program should be a

9   Tracing Shapes (Circles)

Objective: To develop perceptual selection

Task: To find and trace every circle on the page

Materials

For the children

Spirit master sheets:
Lesson 9 – pages 1 and 2 (1 pear;
2 pears) for level 1 (circle), level
2 (square), and level 3 (triangle)
Kindergarten pencils
Markers (approximately 8×4)

For the teacher

Spirit masters:
Lesson 9 – page 1 (1 pear) and
page 2 (2 pears) for levels 1, 2,
and 3
Overhead projector
Screen
Transparency:
Lesson 9 – Tracing Shapes
(Circles)
Grease pencil
Soft cloth
(for erasing marks from the
transparency)
Marker
(approximately 8½×11)

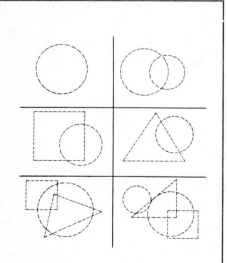

Procedure

NOTE: If your class has not had experience identifying circles or objects with round shapes, delay using this lesson for a few days. Before using it, expose the children to the concept of "circle" by having them trace around round objects such as lids, checkers, plates, and coins. Have them identify the shapes as circles. Have them find and name round things in the classroom and at home. When they understand the meaning of *round* or *circle*, introduce this lesson.

Run off pages 1 and 2 of lesson 9 spirit masters for each level. Keep the spirit master sheets in reserve.

Group Lesson (Transparency)

Project the transparency for lesson 9 onto a screen or chalkboard with an overhead projector. Place your marker under the top two pictures of circles. Cover the rest of the transparency with your marker.

Review with the children some objects in the classroom that are shaped like circles. Examples: checkers, coins, cooky cutters, bottle caps, lids.

Have the children identify the shapes shown on the transparency. Say: *We are going to trace some circles. Watch me trace this dotted-line circle. I am going to take my pencil and slowly trace the circle.* Trace the first circle on the left. *Each time we see a circle, we're going to trace it.* Call attention to the circles on the right. *I see two circles here.* Have one of the children trace both circles on the screen with a finger while you simultaneously trace them on the transparency. Follow this procedure for the rest of the transparency.

Individual Lesson (Spirit Masters)

Pass out the spirit master sheets for all three levels. You should have two pages for each child. Have the children write their names on each page.

Tell the children: *Find the page with one pear in the top corner and mark it with an X. You're going to trace some more circles. Trace only the circles, no other shapes. When you've finished tracing the circles on this page, go on to the second page and trace every circle on that page.*

Group Lesson

Figure 6-5 A Perceptual Selection Task

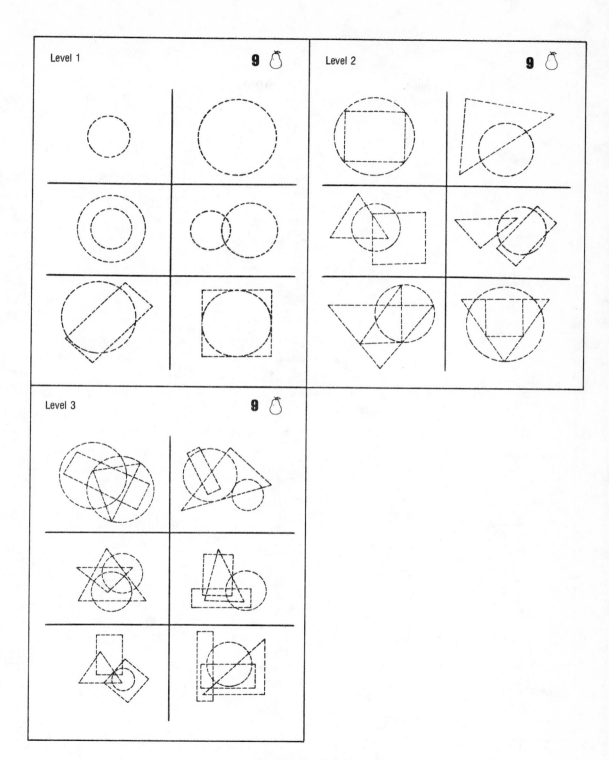

Figure 6-5 (cont'd)

32 Making Size Comparisons

Objective: To develop perceptual flexibility

Task: To look at the first picture in each row and mark the other picture in the row that is the same size

Materials

For the children

Spirit master sheets:
   Lesson 32—pages 1 and 2
   (1 boat; 2 boats) for level 1
   (circle), level 2 (square), and
   level 3 (triangle)
Kindergarten pencils
Markers (approximately 8×4)

For the teacher

Spirit masters:
   Lesson 32—page 1 (1 boat) and
   page 2 (2 boats) for levels 1, 2,
   and 3
Overhead projector
Screen
Transparency:
   Lesson 32—Making Size
            Comparisons
Grease pencil
Soft cloth
Marker
   (approximately 8½×11)

Procedure

Run off pages 1 and 2 from lesson 32 spirit masters for each level. Keep the spirit master sheets in reserve.

Use blocks or small toys to review matching objects of like size. When the children understand the process, introduce the lesson.

Group Lesson (Transparency)

Project the transparency for lesson 32. Cover all but the first row with your marker.

Say: *Look at the first picture in this row. It's a picture of a chair. Point to it. Now look at the other chairs in the row. Let's take a close look at the first chair and see if we can find another one in the row that is the same size. Pause. I'm going to mark this picture because it is the same size as the first chair in the row. Mark the fourth chair with an X. Follow the same procedure for the other rows.*

Individual Lesson (Spirit Masters)

Pass out the spirit master sheets for all three levels. Be sure that the children have two pages. Have them write their names on each page.

Say: *Find the page with one sailboat in the top corner and mark it with an X. Slide your marker under the first row of pictures. Look at the first picture in the row and see if you can find another one in the row that is the same size. When you find it, mark it with an X. When you finish this page, go on to the second page. Have the children follow the same procedure for the second page.*

Group Lesson

Figure 6-6 A Perceptual Flexibility Task

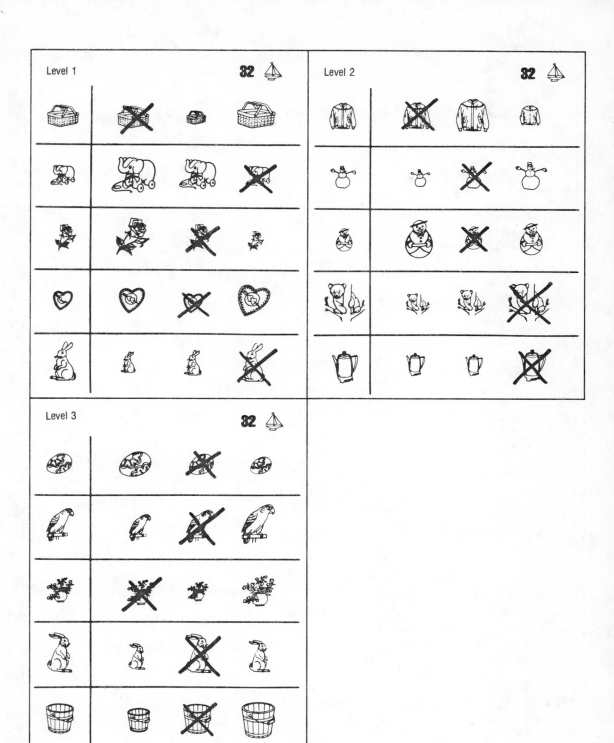

Figure 6-6 (cont'd)

95

15 Making Picture Comparisons

Objective: To develop perceptual accuracy and flexibility

Task: To look at the first picture in each row and mark the other picture in the row that looks just like it

Materials

For the children

Spirit master sheets:
Lesson 15 – pages 1 and 2
(1 goat; 2 goats) for level 1
(circle), level 2 (square), **and**
level 3 (triangle)
Kindergarten pencils
Markers (approximately 8×4)

For the teacher

Spirit masters:
Lesson 15 – page 1 (1 goat) and
page 2 (2 goats) for levels 1, 2,
and 3
Overhead projector
Screen
Transparency:
Lesson 15 – Making Picture
Comparisons
Grease pencil
Soft cloth
Marker
(approximately 8½×11)

Procedure

Run off pages 1 and 2 of lesson 15 spirit masters for each level. Keep the spirit master sheets in reserve.

Group Lesson (Transparency)

Project the transparency for lesson 15 onto a screen or chalkboard with an overhead projector. Place your marker under the first row of pictures. Cover all rows except the first.

Say: *Look at the first picture in the row.* Point to it. *Now look at the other three pictures in the row.* Point to each one. *One of these pictures is exactly like the first picture in the row. I'm going to mark the scissors* (point to them), *because they're exactly like the first picture in the row.* Point to the first pair of scissors. Mark the scissors. For the other rows, have a different child point to the answer in each row on the screen while you mark it on the transparency.

Individual Lesson (spirit masters)

Pass out the individual lessons for all three levels. Be sure that the children have two pages. Have them write their names on each page.

Say: *Find the page with one goat in the top corner and mark it with an X. Slide your marker under the first row of pictures. Look at the first picture in the row. Then look at the other pictures in the row. Mark the picture that is just like the first picture. Finish this page and go on to the second page.* Tell the children to mark the second page like the first.

Group Lesson

Figure 6-7 A Perceptual Accuracy Task

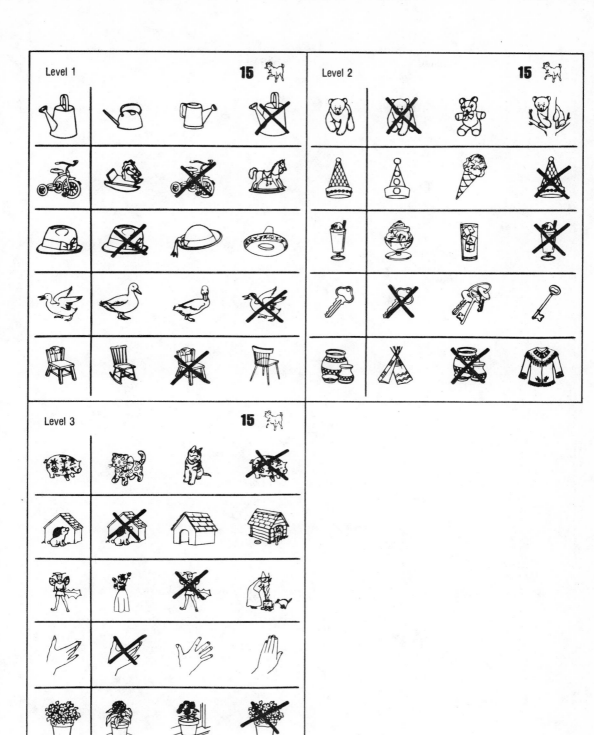

Figure 6-7 (cont'd)

12 Hunting Pictures

Objective: To develop perceptual structuring

Task: To find and mark the specific object asked for in each picture

Procedure

Project the transparency "Hunting Picture I—Looking for Elephants" onto a screen or chalkboard with an overhead projector and tell the following story:

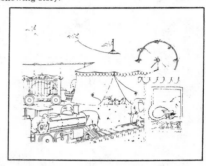

Six old men who were very smart and blind decided to write a book for people who wanted to know about animals. When they began writing about elephants, they didn't know what to say, because none of them knew anything about them. They heard that a circus was in town and would have many elephants.

At the circus, the first blind man touched the side of one elephant. "An elephant feels like a wall," he said.

The second blind man found an elephant's tusk and said, "An elephant feels like a spear."

An elephant's trunk curled around the third man's arm and he said, "An elephant is like a snake."

The fourth blind man felt an elephant's knee. "The elephant is like a tree," he said.

The fifth blind man felt an elephant's ear and said, "The elephant is like a fan."

The sixth blind man grasped the tail and thought that the elephant was like a rope.

Each blind man described the elephant in a different way. Which blind man was right? Let's describe an elephant.

Now we're going to hunt for some elephants in this picture. Some are hiding and some aren't. Have the children point to the elephants they find in the picture. Each time a child points to an elephant, mark it with an X on the transparency. When all have been found, ask the children to count to see how many elephants there are. (There are nine.)

Materials

Overhead projector
Screen
Transparencies:
    Lesson 12—Hunting
    Pictures I, II, and III
Grease pencil
Soft cloth

Figure 6-8 A Perceptual Structuring Task

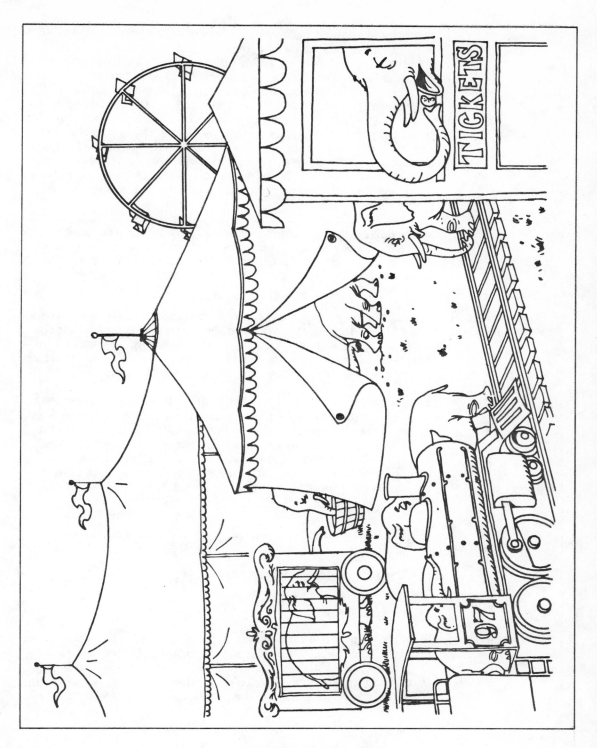

Figure 6-8 (cont'd)

regularly scheduled part of the children's daily routine. The perceptual lessons take only fifteen to 20 minutes a day and constitute a relatively small part of the children's total program.

You may have noted the lead-in activities in the sample lessons. We believe that such activities help to develop motivation and interest in the instructional tasks that follow. In many lessons, we make suggestions for a lead-in discussion. If time is available, you should expand, or alter, these sessions to fit your own teaching style and your own particular group of children. When the children have finished their worksheets, or other kinds of work materials, the work should be sent home. Going over these activities with parents is a good way for children to review the activity and to gain (we hope) praise for their efforts.

As mentioned previously, if you are using a prepared program such as the *Beginning to Learn* series, you should add procedures that you find useful with your own group of children. The richer your contribution as a teacher, the greater the children's improvement in perceptual skills, paying attention, and learning to follow oral directions.

Generalization of Perceptual Skills

Because visual perception is so integrated and interrelated with other areas of development, most learning centers will provide for some generalization of these skills. The learning centers discussed in chapters 5, 7, and 8 will, for the most part, provide suitable practice activities. In addition the following centers can be established.

Book Center

The book center can be established by itself or in combination with a language-arts center. Again, the materials and supplies that are found in this center determine the range of activities. This center should be comfortable, attractive, and quiet. Even though most preschool children are not reading, noise is distracting to almost any kind of focused attention, particularly visual and auditory attention. Children in a book center may participate in the following activities.

1. storybooks with pictures
2. information books with pictures, such as picture dictionaries
3. photographs
4. filmstrips (perhaps with assistance)
5. panorama/activity scapes
6. paintings and drawings

Self-Directed Learning Center

In this center you may place an array of games and activities that promote generalization of visual-perception as well as other developmental skills. Puzzle games, as well as simple card and matching games, can be played either individually or in small groups. Children may participate in the following activities.

1. picture dominoes and regular dominoes

2. chalkboard activities

3. bingo and lotto

4. complete the picture

5. sorting and matching letter symbols

6. sorting and matching number symbols

Developmental Activity Guide
Visual-Perception Skills

In this guide, the task number refers to the corresponding item on the *Carolina Developmental Profile.* The objective defines the behavior to be learned. In the instructional activities column, we suggest several activities that will give your children the experience necessary to accomplish the stated objective. As you gain experience working with children, you will no doubt want to add additional activities that will increase the usefulness of the guide.

Developmental Objective *(by task no.)*	Instructional Activities
1. Matches color to sample *Materials for Activities* *1. Colored blocks* *2. Color-matching book* *3. Burlap; colored yarn; large needles*	1. Teacher places a pile of different colored blocks in center of room and has children sort by color. Large beads, colored shapes, and colored squares can also be used as a variation. 2. Color-matching book. Pocket on one page contains given color. Child selects from various colors on the facing page the one that matches color in pocket. 3. Simple design drawn in color on light-colored burlap. Child chooses same color yarn and sews over design.

Developmental Objective *(by task no.)*	Instructional Activities

4. Crayons

4. Coloring. Small portion colored by teacher to indicate colors.

5. Paste; construction paper

5. Child pastes correct color of construction paper over simple design. Small portion colored by teacher to indicate colors.

6. Parquetry blocks

6. Parquetry designs.

7. Colored beads

7. Sorting box. Child sorts different color beads by color.

2. Groups things together by color, form, or size

1. Sorting games and activities. You can use egg and soft-drink cartons as sorting boxes. It is sometimes helpful to begin with objects of the same size and form and vary the color. Gradually you can introduce different sizes and forms.

Materials for Activities

1. Egg and soft-drink cartons; objects of different sizes, colors, and shapes, such as paper pegs, beads, buttons, measuring cups and spoons, blocks and logs.

2. Have children string beads. Demonstrate stringing all one color or one shape.

3. Provide different colored paper either cut or torn into pieces and let children make pictures. In the beginning provide no more than three colors. Notice if children choose all one color or different colors in clusters.

2. Beads; laces

3. Large construction paper; glue; small pieces of colored construction paper

4. Have children make macaroni art pictures using macaroni of different sizes and shapes.

4. Macaroni; paper; glue

5. Dye macaroni different colors and use in pictures.

5. Food coloring; macaroni; paper, glue

6. Sort macaroni or buttons into different shapes and sizes.

6. Macaroni; buttons

3. Stacks five rings on a peg in order

1. Using two building blocks, have the child stack the smallest on top of the largest. Use different combinations of blocks for large and small. Then add a third, a fourth, and a fifth.

Materials for Activities

1. Building blocks

2. Have children stack small paper plates on top of large paper plates.

2. Paper plates of varied sizes

3. Stack plastic measuring cups and spoons.

3. Plastic measuring cups

4. Stack pots and pot lids.

4. Pots and pot lids

Developmental Objective *(by task no.)*	**Instructional Activities**

4. Matches to sample circle, square, and triangle

Materials for Activities

1. *Ten circles; ten squares; ten triangles*

2. *Blocks; masking tape*

3. *Cardboard cutouts*

4. *Object-matching book*

5. *Frame or box with geometric shapes; cardboard cutouts; beanbag*

1. Have children sit in a circle on the floor. In the center of the circle are cardboard cutouts of circles, squares, triangles. The teacher also has the same cutouts. Hold up a form and ask children to find one like it.

2. Place a pile of block squares, circles, and triangles in center of room. Using masking tape make a large circle, square, and triangle on the floor in different parts of the room. Have children select a block from the pile and place it inside the corresponding taped outline.

3. Place cardboard cutouts around the room. Teacher holds up a shape and children are to find another like it in the room.

4. Object-matching book. Pocket on one page of book contains given shape. Object to be matched is selected from shapes on facing page.

5. Set up three beanbag frames around the room. One has circular-shape hole, one triangular, one square. Teacher holds up cutout. Child is to go to correct frame to toss his beanbag.

---

5. Makes circle out of two half circles

Materials for Activities

1. *Wooden puzzles with different geometric shapes*

2. *Picture of complete circle; two half circles*

3. *Doughnuts*

1. Provide an array of simple shape puzzles. For example, a wooden puzzle of two half circles or a wooden puzzle containing one or more whole geometric shapes.

2. Give each child two half circles. He places them over picture of complete circle.

3. At snack time use snacks such as doughnuts. Cut them in two or have the children cut them in two and then put them back together.

---

6. Matches to sample pictures of animals

Materials for Activities

1. *Animal pictures; sorting box*

2. *Animal pictures*

3. *Four sets of animal pictures*

1. Sort pictures of animals by animal.

2. Several animal pictures are placed around the room. The teacher holds up one animal picture and asks child to find an identical picture in the room.

3. Four children are chosen as leaders, and each is given a different animal picture. Additional pictures of the four animals are distributed throughout the class. Children form groups according to animal picture. Children act out animals.

Developmental Objective (by task no.)	**Instructional Activities**

4. *Two sets of animal-picture cards*

5. *Picture lotto game*

6. *Construction paper; magazine pictures of animals*

4. Teacher puts one set of cards in a box, and deals the other set to the children. Children put their cards face up. A player draws a card from the box. If he has a matching card, he puts the two matching cards together.

5. Picture lotto. (There is a commercial animal lotto game.)

6. Animal scrapbooks.

---

7. Names picture of items removed from view

Materials for Activities

1. *Three objects*

2. *Two sets of identical pictures*

3. *Page from a catalog or magazine*

4. *Two sets of identical pictures; projector*

1. Teacher places three objects in front of child, and talks about each object. Child closes eyes, teacher removes an object. Child opens eyes and guesses which object is missing.

2. Pictures from one set are placed somewhere in the room. One picture from the other set is shown to the class, then turned over. A child finds the matching picture. Number of picture sets expanded with ability.

3. Expose a catalog or magazine page that contains a number of familiar items. Cover the page and have the child name as many items as he recalls.

4. Place a picture on an overhead projector for a few seconds. Cover picture. Child chooses the picture he saw from duplicate.

---

8. Selects two identical pictures out of a set of three

Materials for Activities

2. *Parquetry blocks*

3. *Three sets of pictures: two sets identical, one set different*

4. *Overhead projector*

5. *Picture pairs*

6. *Old Maid cards*

7. *Picture lotto*

1. See activities for task 5.

2. Use parquetry designs.

3. Picture cards are distributed to children. Teacher holds up a picture. Child with matching picture comes to front and matches.

4. Use overhead projector and proceed same as above.

5. Place a number of picture pairs randomly around the room. Children find identical pictures on a "Treasure Hunt."

6. Old Maid cards.

7. Picture lotto.

Developmental Objective *(by task no.)*	Instructional Activities
9. Adds two parts to an incomplete man.	1. Have the children put together puzzles of people. Start out with large two- or three-piece puzzles and then work up to puzzles with more pieces.
Materials for Activities	2. Sing songs that name body parts.
1. *Puzzles of people*	3. Have each child lie down on a large piece of butcher paper and draw around his body to make a silhouette.
3. *Butcher paper and crayons*	
4. *Flannel board; disassembled person*	4. Using a flannel board, create a picture of a person with several body parts missing. Children in the group take turns adding the missing parts.
5. *Picture of incomplete man*	5. Have each child in the group draw in a missing part. The rest of the group has to name the part that has just been drawn.
10. Copies three designs	1. Have children match cards with different designs. Start out with geometric shapes and work up to more complicated designs.
Materials for Activities	2. Make simple yarn designs and have the children copy them.
1. *Design cards*	3. Use colored blocks (only a few at first) to make simple designs. Have the children copy the designs with their set of blocks.
2. *Yarn; paper*	
3. *Colored blocks*	
4. *Masking tape*	4. Put large tape designs on the floor, and have the children walk on the tape. They might even pretend it is a road and drive a truck on it.
11. Puts together a large four- to six-piece puzzle	1. As child watches, spread jam and peanut butter on a piece of bread (paper can be used for make-believe sandwich). Cut in half diagonally. Have child place bread back together to form original square.
Materials for Activities	2. Cut the sandwich into quarters and have child put the pieces back together to form a whole sandwich.
1. *Bread; jam; peanut butter; knife*	
2. *Sandwich; knife*	3. Draw a large circular face on construction paper. Cut out face in four unequal pieces. Have child arrange pieces to make a whole face.
3. *Construction paper; scissors*	
4. *Picture; paste; crayon; scissors*	4. Have child make his own puzzle by taking a drawing or a colored picture and pasting it on cardboard. Guiding the child's hand, let him draw the dividing lines on top of the picture. Keep the number of puzzle pieces small—four or five. Then have the child cut out the sections and put "his" puzzle back together.
5. *Old ceramic object; glue*	

5. Have a "pretend accident" with an object made from hardened clay or plaster of paris (attempt to break object in several large pieces). Children watch and help find the "right" piece in the project of gluing it back together. Stress how the edges look and how certain edges fit together.

---

12. Arranges coins from smallest to largest (dime, nickel, quarter, half dollar)

Materials for Activities

1. *Blocks, picture cards of blocks drawn to scale*

2. *Beads; two cups*

3. *Beads or blocks*

4. *Six cards with a different train car on each card*

5. *Button; mustard-jar top; mayonnaise-jar top; plastic lids from a margarine and shortening container*

1. Give child three or four blocks of varying sizes. Show child picture cards that are illustrated to match the size of the block. Ask the child, "Find the picture that goes with the block."

2. Give the child beads or buttons that are distinctly small or large. Ask the child to sort the beads and "put the big ones in this cup and the small ones in that cup."

3. Show the child an arrangement of three to five beads. Ask the child to duplicate the arrangement ("Make one like this one"), starting by placing a bead like the one furthest to the left first and proceeding left to right.

4. Give the child a picture of a train divided into six cards with a car on each card. Ask the child to arrange the train starting with engine on left and ending with caboose on the right.

5. Give the child a (medium size) button, a mustard-jar top, a mayonnaise-jar top, and plastic lids from a soft-margarine container, and a solid shortening can (or salted peanut can). Ask the child to select the smallest one and place the items in the proper sequence, small to large. Example: "Make them go from littlest to biggest."

Checkpoint

What Have You Learned?

1. Visual perception can be defined as a _____ process of attaching _____   **Facts**
   or order to _____ stimuli.

2. Which of the following tasks are *primarily* visual perceptual in nature?

   a) Catches a large ball
   b) "Put these pieces together to make a circle"
   c) "Pick the one that is different"
   d) "Put the ball in the box"
   e) Matching to sample
   f) "Point to the *big* dog"

3. Describe a lesson activity that would promote perceptual flexibility.

4. The _____ factor refers to the ability to differentiate perceptually
   between figures representing foreground and background visual stimuli.

5. Recognizing likenesses and differences between pictures is called the
   _____ factor.

6. The perceptual-structuring factor is commonly referred to as "visual
   closure." This deals with the child's ability to draw visual _____ based
   on incoming visual _____.

7. Describe a lesson activity that will promote perceptual structuring.

8. List two prepared (published) curriculum programs for visual-perception
   development.

9. Name two important factors to consider when planning cognitive
   curriculum activities for children under four.

10. Cite an illustration of an activity that would incorporate two elements of
    number 9 above.

1. You have a group of five four-and-one-half-year-olds that need   **Simulation**
   strengthening in "visual closure." Develop a method of presenting
   structural acquisition tasks that motivate and teach effectively.

2. Utilizing the cognitive cubes, design a perceptual-discrimination
   activity involving perceptual speed and accuracy for children at a
   two-year-old developmental level.

Administer the perceptual section of the *Carolina Developmental*   **Application**
Profile to a four- or five-year-old child. Then present the child with tasks
representing each of the perceptual factor areas (perceptual speed,
perceptual structuring, perceptual flexibility, and perceptual selection).
Compare how the child does on specific items on the profile with his
ability to engage in the lesson activity. Which perceptual factor areas do
the profile items primarily represent?

Chapter 7   Developing Reasoning Processes

Objectives

After you have completed this chapter, you should be able to:

1. Define and explain the differences between *reasoning*, *conceptual*, and *cognition*.

2. Describe how instruction for the development of reasoning processes in children under the age of four differs from that for children over four.

3. Define and give examples of lessons in classification, association, picture sequencing, bead sequencing, part-whole relationships, figure grouping, and analogies.

It's Saturday morning. Jonathan and Bruce, two six-year-olds, are intently watching the television screen. A buccaneer movie is just ending. The hero, having defeated a band of villainous pirates and freed their captive (a fair young maiden), is sailing away into the sunset. The rescued maiden clings gratefully—and seductively—to our young hero as he steadfastly mans the wheel. Impatiently Bruce says, "Doesn't she know that he has more important things to do, like steer the ship?" "Yeah," responds Jonathan. "He probably wishes he never rescued her now." Using their own background of information, or prior learning, Bruce and Jonathan have arrived at conclusions that are consistent with the information available to them. In other words, they have been involved in a reasoning process.

There is often a great deal of confusion, especially at the applied level, between the terms *cognition*, *conceptual*, and *reasoning*. We view "cognition" as an all-inclusive term that could be used to describe most of the curriculum activities presented in this text. Cognition refers to an awareness, a discovery or rediscovery, a recognition of information in various forms: comprehension or understanding (Guilford, 1967). Often cognition is used to refer to the entire realm of formal academic learning. (Formal language development programs are often thought of as cognitive in nature.) Bloom (1966), in his taxonomy of educational objectives, divides all curriculum activities into three major categories: cognitive, affective, and psychomotor.

We regard "reasoning" as a subset of cognition, defining it as the process by which several pieces of prior learning are combined to produce a solution to a newly encountered problem. This definition is supported by the findings of the primary mental abilities studies discussed earlier. Often reasoning, perception, and language are grouped together as "cognitive" processes; we view them as separate, but interacting, ability areas. The term *conceptual activities* is generally used to refer to a subset of reasoning or language. A "concept" is a smaller, more precise unit of information, such as "big," "little," "under," and "first."

Thurstone and Thurstone (1944) identified reasoning as one of the specific mental abilities present at the five-year-old level. Tasks that reflect reasoning process more than any of the other primary mental abilities can be grouped under the following major headings: classification, associations, part-whole relationships, sequencing, and analogies.

Guilford (1967), using a factor-analysis approach to the study of intelligence, came up with a somewhat different set of terms. He broke all intellectual functioning into five categories: evaluation, convergent production, divergent production, memory, and cognition. Traditionally, in American education, emphasis has been placed on convergent production, or thinking; that is, the identification of relevant information from given information, with the emphasis on the selection of one precise correct answer. With an educational emphasis on skill development in areas such as reading, mathematics, spelling, and writing, it is easy to see why convergent thinking is important.

In the last few years, educational programs stressing divergent thinking have captured the imagination of many educators. Divergent thinking refers to the generation of new information from given information with an emphasis on variety and quantity of output.

We believe that there is a very close interaction between convergent and divergent thinking, and that the development of abilities in one area leads to the development of abilities in the other.

Curriculum research on the development of reasoning ability in young children is practically nonexistent. In spite of various efforts to investigate the development of specific cognitive and reasoning skills in this age group, researchers have discovered very little information

Research and Development of Reasoning Curriculum

that is directly useful in designing instructional sequences for young children.

A few curriculum programs for young children have been developed that address the area of reasoning, such as *Let's Look at Children* (1965) developed by Educational Testing Service for the Board of Education of the City of New York. However, this program, like so many other published programs, did not report research or field-test findings on the effectiveness of the curriculum materials.

A major contribution to the development and research on reasoning curriculum is the work of Weikart (1971), cited in chapter 1. Although Weikart refers to his program as a cognitively oriented curriculum, his curriculum concentrates, for the most part, on the development of processes that we would label reasoning. Weikart's curriculum is based on Piaget's developmental theory and is designed to help children develop an awareness of their world and to see relationships between objects and events. This program provides four major content areas for curriculum planning: classification, seriation, temporal relations, and spatial relations.

Classification is broken down into three subgroups: (1) relational, that is, grouping items on the basis of common function or by association; (2) descriptive, that is, grouping items on the basis of common attributes; and (3) generic, that is, grouping items on the basis of general classes or categories.

Seriation activities are also subdivided into three areas for curriculum construction: (1) ordinary sizes, (2) ordinary quantities, and (3) ordinary qualities. In the *Learning to Think* program initially developed in the late 1940s, we referred to similar activities as "sequencing." Both time sequences (for example, sequences over a period of time such as a flower growing) and shape sequences (for example, beads strung or sequenced in a specific pattern) were built into our program. Examples of some of these reasoning lessons can be found later in this chapter.

Spatial relations, as Weikart employs the term, refers to four subgroups of curriculum activities. (1) Body awareness and body concepts; for example, naming and identifying parts of the body, developing body coordination, and understanding of the functions of various parts of the body. Many of the activities discussed in chapter 5 (motor development) are also included in this subgroup. (2) Position; this subgroup includes position concepts that we have placed in language development. Here curriculum activities are designed to develop concepts such as "on," "off," "in," "out," "first," and "last." (3) Direction; this area of spatial relations deals with directional concepts such as "up," "down," "forward," and "backward." (4) Distance; a subgroup that refers to the development of concepts dealing with an understanding of distance such as "close to," "far from," "near," and "far."

The last major content area in the cognitively oriented curriculum is labeled temporal relations. This area is divided into three subgroups: (1) beginning and end of time intervals, which includes development of such concepts as "now," "start," "stop," and "end";

(2) ordering of events, which refers to planning and evaluation activities as well as the development of concepts like "first," "last," "next," and "again"; and (3) different lengths of time, which includes development of such concepts as "a short time," "a long time," and "a longer time."

As we discussed in chapter 1, the curriculum devised by Weikart has proven to be successful over a period of years. Weikart's attempts, however, to prove the superiority of his curriculum approach over other well-planned and well-supervised general approaches to early childhood curriculum were unsuccessful. He concludes that "broad curricula are equivalent . . . . In short, no specific curriculum has the corner on effective stimuli, and children are powerful enough consumers to avail themselves of what the market offers." (1972, p. 40.)

Recently we have been engaged in field testing a reasoning curriculum program aimed at four-and-one-half to six-year-old children. During the spring semester of 1971, approximately 100 five- and six-year-old children enrolled in an ungraded public school program in Saxapahaw, North Carolina, were involved in the reasoning program. During a three-month period, these children received daily 20-minute lessons designed to develop reasoning processes and skills. The *Primary Mental Abilities* test was used in a pre- and post-test manner to determine the extent of gains. It was found that the children enrolled in the program made, on the average, significantly greater gains than the similar-age children whose scores provided the normative data for the P.M.A.

Reasoning Curriculum Activities for Two- and Three-Years-Olds

When planning curriculum activities in reasoning skills for children under four it is necessary to adjust the specific content of the tasks (classification, associations, and sequencing) to fit the ability level of the younger child. Also extremely important is a presentation format that is stimulating to the child and not beyond his level of manipulative and organizational skills.

Two formats for curriculum presentation discussed in the last chapter, Katy the Kangaroo and the Cognitive Cubes, have been used extensively—and successfully—for the presentation of reasoning lessons. Presented below are two curriculum activities used with Katy. The lessons are designed to develop a simple level of classification ability.

Lesson 1   Note figure 7-1 (page 112). The top row of pictures, which are placed in the top row of Katy's pockets, show a girl, a man, a woman, and a boy. Then a pack of 20 cards containing five pictures each of men, women, boys, and girls, all different and none identical to the four pictures in the top row, are randomly placed in the single top pocket. The child's task is to sort the pictures by placing each in the appropriate pocket; that is, the one directly under the picture which represents that classification category. As you can see, the thinking involved goes beyond perceptual accuracy to a simple form of classification reasoning.

Figure 7-1 Lesson 1

Figure 7-2 Lesson 2

Lesson 2 Note figure 7-2. The four cards presented in Katy's top row of pockets show pictures of four classes of animals: animals that can fly, wild animals, animals that live in the water, and farm animals. The single top pocket contains five pictures that correspond to each class. Again, the children place the cards, one by one, into the appropriate pockets.

Katy can also be used in conjunction with other types of reasoning activities: associations, part-whole relationships, and sequencing.

Many early childhood programs concentrate on the development of reasoning processes in a child-oriented, non-teacher-directed manner. For reasoning learning to take place this way, the teacher must plan the learning environment carefully. An abundance of objects and playthings will enable the child to make classification and association groupings: for example, farm animals, wild animals, trucks, and automobiles. We believe that an open learning environment is more likely to be successful in fostering the development of reasoning processes if the children have first been introduced to these processes through a teacher-planned and teacher-directed activity. (Remember our earlier discussion of the two primary stages of learning: acquisition and practice/generalization.)

Most of the reasoning activities used at the early childhood level emphasize convergent rather than divergent thinking. Because of the academic demands of elementary school programs, we stress convergent problem-solving skills. The development of reading skills, writing skills, spelling skills, and math skills calls for convergent problem solving. There is only one correct response for $5 + 7 + 6 = $ ____.

In emphasizing convergent thinking at the early childhood level, we are not suggesting that divergent thinking is not important and should not be developed or encouraged. On the contrary, there should be many opportunities each day for children to find out that in some situations a variety of responses are correct. Many of the lessons we present here have several correct responses. If a child offers a unique response to a reasoning task, you should evaluate its appropriateness by asking the child to tell you why he chose that response.

Reasoning Curriculum Activities for Four- and Five-Year-Olds

Perhaps the most interesting and gratifying curriculum development activity that we have engaged in over the last several years has been the development and field testing of a series of reasoning lessons for four- and five-year olds. (See the figures on pages 115-22.) Watching children discover and grasp the processes of classifying, associating, and sequencing is deeply rewarding.

We developed eight basic kinds of reasoning exercises for four- and five-year-olds: classification, associations, picture grouping, bead sequencing, part-whole relationships, figure grouping, time sequencing, and analogies. Each reasoning curriculum area is explained in more detail below.

Classification. These tasks require the child to arrange objects into groups according to a definite concept or plan. A typical task, shown in figure 7-3, asks the child to select from a group of four pictures those that represent animals.

Association. These tasks require the child to use previously acquired knowledge to establish a relationship between two objects. The association tasks in figure 7-4 call for the child to select from three pictures the one that has a direct, strong relationship with the picture to be matched.

Picture grouping. Here the child is asked to group objects together on the basis of a characteristic (or principle) that is common to three of the objects but not to the fourth. Figure 7-5 demonstrates this activity well. Although all the pictures in the top illustration are articles of clothing, the common principle that relates three and excludes one is number.

Bead sequencing. In these lessons the child is asked to determine the principle underlying the sequence in which beads are placed on a string, and to apply that principle by following the sequence. As you can see in figure 7-6, the child must choose the bead which, according to the system, comes next.

Part-whole relationships. This activity is closely related to association activities, but with a diferent dimension. Here the child learns to relate parts of an object to the object itself. As the sample in figure 7-7 shows, the pedals are part of the bicycle, and the foot is part of the boy. The child's task is to select and mark the one picture that represents the "whole" which the first object is a part of.

Figure grouping. These activities are the same as picture grouping with one important difference: in picture grouping the child is dealing with familiar concrete objects; whereas in figure grouping he is dealing with unfamiliar abstract symbols or figures. As before, the child learns to discover the principle that relates three of the symbols and excludes the fourth. Samples of this type of reasoning lesson are shown in figure 7-8.

Time sequencing. Here the task is to place in proper time sequence four pictured events. Note the examples shown in figure 7-9. In our lessons for the development of this kind of sequential reasoning, the child's task is to mark the picture that occurs last.

Analogies. These activities are the most difficult for the child to perform (as well as for us to construct). The child must learn or recognize the relationship between two objects or situations, and then identify a similar relationship between another set of objects or situations. In the first sample activity shown in figure 7-10, the child is presented with a pair of pictures: a horn and an ear. Then, given a picture of a flower, he must determine which of the three remaining pictures bears the same relationship to the flower as the ear does to the horn. The correct analogy, of course, is the nose.

Figure 7-3 A Classification Task

Figure 7-4 An Association Task

Figure 7-5 A Picture Grouping Task

117

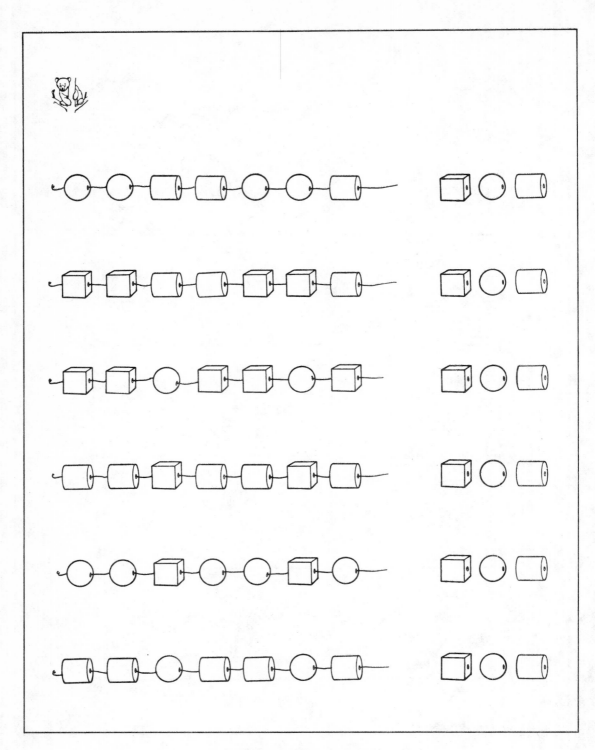

Figure 7-6 A Bead Sequencing Task

118

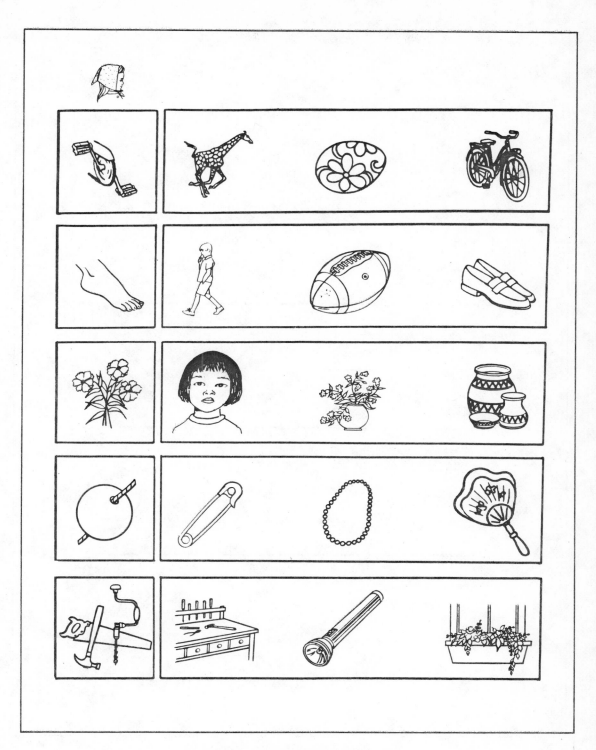

Figure 7-7 A Part-Whole Relationship Task

119

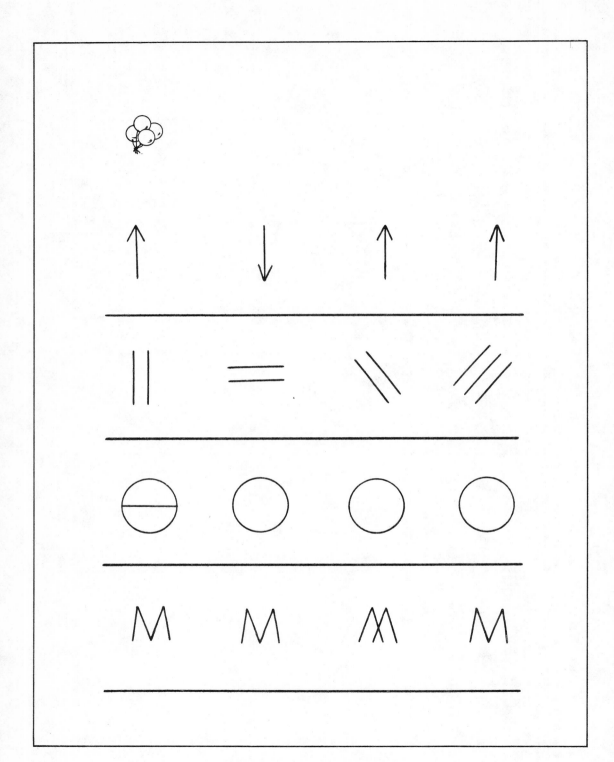

Figure 7-8 A Figure Grouping Task

Figure 7-9 A Time Sequencing Task

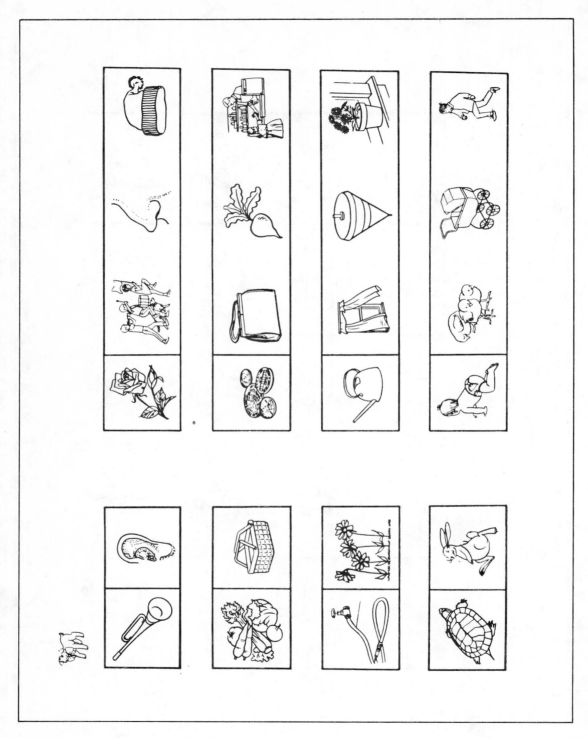

Figure 7-10 An Analogies Task

We have found that, in general, the difficulty order of these activities follows the sequence in which they are listed above, with classification the simplest type of reasoning activity, and analogies the most difficult. To ensure acquisition of the eight kinds of reasoning processes, we developed a series of daily lessons for each area. Again, each lesson within each area has been sequenced for difficulty level. These lessons, like the perceptual curriculum lessons, provide for multi-level instruction which can be managed by one teacher with a large group of preschool children.

Generalization of Reasoning Processes

Almost all interest centers in an early education program will have some elements and activities to facilitate the generalization and practice of basic reasoning processes. When a child is involved in any problem-solving activity, he will be engaged in such processes as classification, grouping, associations, sequencing, and analogies.

Therefore, as you select materials for the various interest centers, it is important to keep these various reasoning processes in mind.

There are three types of interest centers that are particularly suitable for the generalization of reasoning processes: the math center, the science center, and the social studies center.

Math Center

The math center facilitates various kinds of quantitative thinking. As the child sorts, counts, weighs, and measures the materials provided, he will indeed be involved in classifying, sequencing, grouping, and associating. In a math center, the child can take part in: (1) weighing and measuring activities with scales, balances, measuring tape, and rulers; (2) exploration of time measurement with stop watches, clocks, and calendars; (3) various counting, sorting, comparing, and grouping activities through the use of such objects as marbles, buttons, small cube blocks, and peg boards; (4) comparing, classifying, and associating through the use of such materials as blocks, geometric shapes, marbles, dominoes, and beads.

Science Center

The science center may be combined with the math center, or it can be established as a separate center. Some examples of the activities that children can engage in in a science center are: (1) exploration play with various kinds of prisms; (2) using a compass to explore the concept of direction; (3) monitoring thermometers and barometers, and comparing the readings of these instruments with the actual weather; and (4) exploration play with such objects as magnifying glasses, magnets, and mirrors. A number of other activities can be integrated into the science center such as handling and feeding small pets (for example, hamsters or rabbits) and planting and caring for various types of plants.

Social Studies Center

In a social studies center problem-solving activities can be set up to encourage reasoning processess dealing with geographical concepts. For example, children can become involved in comparing various societies and peoples of the world—an excellent means for facilitating such reasoning processes as classification, grouping, association, and analogies. Materials appropriate for this center are picture reference books; posters; large pictures showing living styles of various peoples; maps; model ships, planes, and trains; and objects from different cultures. Such materials encourage play activities in which the children simulate the dress and customs of people from other countries, manipulate dolls and objects, and discuss similarities and differences based on such concepts as geographical regions, climate, language spoken, and primary means of making a living.

Developmental Activity Guide
Reasoning Processes

In this guide, the task number refers to the corresponding item on the *Carolina Developmental Profile.* The objective defines the behavior to be learned. In the instructional activities column, we suggest several activities that will give your children the experience necessary to accomplish the stated objective. As you gain experience working with children, you will no doubt want to add other activities that will increase the usefulness of the guide.

Developmental Objective *(by task no.)*	Instructional Activities
1. Discriminates between big and little	1. The teacher builds two or three towers of widely ranging heights. The size gradations should be random. Ask child to "Point to the big (biggest, smallest) tower." Then change the heights by adding or removing cubes and repeat directions.
Materials for Activities	
1. Blocks	2. Have child close his eyes and then give him a large block and a small block. Let him give you the big one; the little one.
2. Blocks	
3. Pictures	3. Use pictures of objects and have child point to big object, little object.
4. Clay	
5. Cookies	4. When child is playing with clay, ask him to roll some clay to make a big ball and some to make a little ball.

Developmental Objective *(by task no.)*	Instructional Activities
	5. At snack time have some big and some little cookies.

2. Chooses one and then one more

Materials for Activities

1. *Flannel board and cutouts*
2. *Cookies or crackers*
3. *Blocks*
4. *Container; small objects*

1. Teacher initiates several different flannel-board stories which start out with duck, truck, cookie, dog, postman, etc., and then asks the child to help by adding one more.

2. At snack time give children one cookie or cracker apiece, and then tell them each to take one more.

3. When the child is building with blocks, have him add one more to the tower.

4. Game. Give each child a container and several small items such as beads or blocks. Have each child put one item in container. Teacher hides her eyes and tells everyone to put in one more. She opens her eyes and each child who has put in one more gets a point.

3. Discriminates between long and short

Materials for Activities

1. *Cuisenaire rods*
2. *Cuisenaire rods*
3. *Paper plates; yarn*
4. *Blocks*

1. Teacher asks child to "find a rod that is longer (shorter) than this rod."

2. Place two rods of different lengths in front of the child. Have him point to long one, short one.

3. Paper plates are used to make a face. Long pieces of yarn are stapled on for long hair. Child then cuts to make short hair.

4. Blocks should be stacked in proper places on shelves. Have individual children go to the shelves and bring longest and shortest block; or hold up a block and have child bring a block that is same length or a longer or shorter one.

4. Uses bigger, slower, and heavier correctly on request

Materials for Activities

1. *Books or blocks*
2. *Pictures; books*
3. *Equal-arm balance; blocks*
4. *Scales*

1. Use concrete objects for experience (small and large book). Ask child to point to bigger one.

2. Use members of same category (animals, people, plants) to represent the task. Make discrimination gross in the beginning. "Which is bigger: man or baby?"

3. Let children experiment with an equal-arm balance, placing groups of blocks on each end of arm to see which combinations are equal in weight.

4. Use scales in same manner.

Developmental Objective (by task no.)	**Instructional Activities**

5. *Bag; blocks*

6. *Bricks; blocks; box*

8. *Wheel toys*

9. *Pictures*

5. Ask children to lift an empty bag. "The bag is light when it is empty. Put some blocks in it. It is heavier now. Put in more blocks. It is much heavier now." Then remove the blocks gradually and let children observe how the bag becomes lighter.

6. Use a brick, a hardwood and softwood block about the same size, and an empty two-pound cheese box to give the children experience in judging the weight of an object.

7. Put an object in each of a child's hands and let him decide which is heavier. Then change one of the objects and ask, "Now which one is heavier." Try this with the children blindfolded.

8. Using wheeled objects, have the children guess which one goes slower. Have children move objects and discuss which one is slower and why.

9. Game. Have pictures of cars, trucks, trains, bicycles, tricycles, airplanes, etc. Hold up two pictures and ask which one is slower. Whoever gets it right gets a point.

---

5. Completes opposite analogy statements

Materials for Activities

1. *Wagon; record player; record*

2. *Pictures*

4. *Container of cold and warm water*

5. *Wet and dry cloths*

6. *Sandpaper; block*

7. *Pillow*

8. *Drum*

1. Have children participate in activities that involve opposites. Examples: running both fast and slow, listening to both loud and soft music.

2. In pictures talk about whether it is day or night, about men, women, boys, and girls.

3. Play a guessing game. Name some characteristic of day or night, and then children must guess which it is. Same can be done with other opposite analogies.

4. As child dips his hands into cold or warm water, the teacher says, "This water feels cold; this water feels hot."

5. As child feels each cloth teacher says, "This cloth is wet; this cloth is dry."

6. As child touches each surface, teacher says, "The sandpaper is rough; the block is smooth."

7. As child pats or feels the pillow and then the floor, say, "The pillow is soft; the floor is hard."

8. Tell the children to "clap their hands the way the drum tells them. Now the drum says 'clap fast.' Now the drum says 'clap slowly'."

9. Act out lowering and raising arms with children. Say "My arms go up, my arms come down."

Developmental Objective (by task no.)	**Instructional Activities**

6. Counts four objects

Materials for Activities

2. *Fruit*
3. *Chairs; music*
4. *Pennies; piggy bank*
5. *Flannel board and pictures*
6. *Beanbags; basket*

1. See activities for task 2.

2. Divide apples, oranges, etc., into four pieces. Give pieces to a child. Have him count the pieces.

3. When playing musical chairs, the teacher and children count the number of chairs. They recount as one is taken away.

4. Drop pennies in a piggy bank to teach children to count by rote to five or more.

5. Teacher illustrates the story of "The Three Bears" with flannel-board pictures. At the appropriate time the children count the bears' bowls, chairs, etc.

6. Beanbags are thrown into a basket. The teacher requests children to throw one or two.

---

7. Uses softly and loudly correctly

Materials for Activities

1. *Objects that make noise: records; noisemakers; etc.*

1. Game. Play both loud and soft music or use different noisemakers and other sounds within environment. Children must decide (discriminate) which noises are loud and which are soft.

2. Have children take role of the teacher in activity 1, and let them control loudness and softness of noises.

---

8. States number of wheels a bicycle has

Materials for Activities

1. *Toy bicycle, pictures of bicycle, or bicycle*
2. *Wheel cutouts or crayons*
3. *Flannel board and cutouts*

1. Teacher has child look at a small toy bicycle, a picture of a bicycle, or a life-sized bicycle, and asks him to count the number of wheels.

2. Have the children add wheels to a predrawn picture of a bicycle, either by drawing them in or pasting them on.

3. Have a child add wheels to a bicycle on a flannel board.

Developmental Objective *(by task no.)*	Instructional Activities
9. Touches the middle in a row of five blocks on request *Materials for Activities* *1. Train cars* *2. Flannel board and cutouts*	1. Teacher makes a train of three cars. Hides a surprise in the middle car, and asks children to see if they can find it. 2. Put series of cutouts on flannel board. Hide a surprise behind the middle object. 3. Have five children stand in a line and have another child pick the child who is in the middle. Continue this activity until all children have been involved in some way.
10. States number of wheels a car has *Materials for Activities* *2. Blocks* *3. Blocks; cardboard boxes*	1. See activities for task 8. 2. When children are building toys with blocks and other manipulative equipment, ask them, "How many wheels does your truck have?" 3. Have the children make a car out of large blocks or large cardboard boxes. Ask them how many wheels does a car have? 4. Activities that encourage children to count sets of four.
11. Touches first, then last, block in row of five on request *Materials for Activities* *2. Flannel board and cutouts* *3. Snacks*	1. Have children line up and decide who is first and who is last. 2. Using flannel board, have children put up cutouts of animals, shapes, etc., and then decide which is first and last. 3. During snack discuss who is first and last to receive such items as napkins, cups, juice, and cookies.
12. Names composition of three items on request *Materials for Activities* *2. Feely bag* *3. Small screen; objects*	1. When possible take items apart or cut into them to see what they are made of. 2. Have a feely bag. Child must reach in, feel items, name them, describe them, and tell what they are made of. 3. Behind a small screen, strike an object so that it makes a noise. Children must then tell the name of the object. Ask them how they knew, and why wood sounds different from metal, etc.

Checkpoint

What Have You Learned?

Facts

1. The process whereby an individual makes use of prior knowledge to produce a solution to a newly encountered problem is referred to as _____

2. Small units of information (big, little, over, under, etc.) are labeled _____

3. _____ refers to an awareness, discovery, or recognition of information in various forms.

4. The author suggests that reasoning activities for children under four years be reduced to three specific content areas. Name them.

5. Children over the developmental age of four years have been found to possess five additional specific reasoning skills to those identified in younger children. Name those additional skills.

6. Grouping a frog and a raccoon in a series of pictured objects that also contains a tree and a rock is known as _____

7. _____ may be exemplified by pairing a water faucet with a glass rather than with a coke bottle or a cup of coffee.

8. Arranging four pictures to represent the chronology of events in a well-known fairy tale is an example of _____

9. The skill of _____ is used when a stamp is matched with an addressed envelope rather than a cash register or a dozen eggs.

10. When a child matches a nose to a flower (rejecting a hat and a purse) after having been given a model of an ear and a horn, he is using the process of _____

Simulation

1. You have been assigned to demonstrate to an educational-methods class activities or lessons that could be used to teach the kinds of reasoning skills identified in children below the age of four and those identified in children over four. Briefly discuss what kinds of activities you would use in each of the eight skill areas.

2. Explain how concepts, reasoning, and cognition are related to one another in the mental makeup of an individual.

Application

1. Although few early education programs attempt to teach specific reasoning skills to young children, find some that do and identify what specific skills they are learning.

2. Visit several preschool programs and observe what reasoning skills are most frequently taught, and whether or not the teacher is aware that these skills are being taught.

3. Review some of the most recently published books on preschool curriculum and assess the extent to which each deals with teaching reasoning skills and what skill areas they have identified.

Chapter 8

Developing Language Skills

Objectives

After you have completed this chapter, you should be able to:

1. Present the sequence of normal expressive- and receptive-language development in terms of a child's language abilities.
2. Define *word meaning* and *verbal fluency.*
3. Describe the three major models or approaches to language intervention presented in this chapter.
4. Identify and describe commercial programs that represent each of the three major approaches to language intervention.
5. List the six types of receptive-language exercises in the *Learning to Think Series.*
6. List the three types of expressive-language exercises in the *Learning to Think Series.*

The child who cannot communicate his needs or understand the needs of others will find it almost impossible to cope with the simplest academic task. This is why language development receives a great deal of attention in early childhood education.

Language interacts constantly with the other areas of development that we have discussed here. For example, an interaction with fine-motor development takes place when a child tells about the picture he is coloring. Language must have content to it. That is, there must be a precise purpose for expressing thoughts to another.

The development of language in infants and young children is an extremely complicated process. There are numerous theories explaining how language capabilities are acquired, but at this point in time, there does not appear to be a specific, widely accepted theoretical foundation on which to base the development of instructional content and methodology for early childhood programs. Therefore, we will offer here a plan organizing educational experiences that foster language development, not a theory about *how* language develops.

As with the other areas of development that have been discussed, a great deal of research has been done on the sequence of language development. In general, all children follow the same sequence. The chart on page 133 describes the normal pattern of development for both expressive and receptive language in children from one to six years of age.

Our approach to the development of a language curriculum reflects many years of actual work with young children in early education programs. The rationale for our language development program is consistent with the rationale for all our preschool programs. You will recall the frequently mentioned Thurstone studies on the intellect of young children. Two of the intellectual factors that were isolated dealt with language. At that time, these factors were labeled "word meaning" and "verbal fluency." *Word meaning* refers to comprehension abilities, including listening behavior, following directions, auditory discrimination, attaching meaning to vocabulary, and attaching meaning to longer verbal units or sequences. Today, the more popular label for this intellectual factor is *receptive language.*

Verbal fluency was the term used to label language skills that reflect the ability to express one's thoughts in a meaningful way. These abilities include quantity and quality of spoken vocabulary, ease and frequency of expressing thoughts, ability to construct word sequences to express complex thought verbally, and the use of proper syntax. This factor is more commonly known today as *expressive language.* Although receptive and expressive language were found to be separate factors, and are treated separately here for discussion purposes, in actual practice educational experiences should be organized so that there is an interaction between these two types of language to ensure the appropriate development of each.

Language Curriculum Research

As we mentioned earlier, language development has been receiving wide attention from theorists and researchers. However, when the number of studies are narrowed down to ones specifically dealing with the effectiveness of early education language intervention programs, the amount of information available is considerably reduced.

Relevant studies leave little doubt that language abilities can be significantly improved through intervention, even though some professionals might challenge this statement. Willa Gupta and Carolyn Stern (1969) studied the effects of different language activities on Black preschool children. They found that children who echo and produce sentences in response to instruction showed greater gains in verbal skills than children who only listened to correct responses during instruction.

Another project demonstrating the positive effects of language intervention was reported by Freeman McConnell, director of the Bill Wilkerson Speech and Hearing Center in Nashville, Tennessee (McConnell et al., 1969). A long-term program for approximately 100 two- to five-year-old "culturally" disadvantaged children was conducted in day-care-center settings. For five half days a week, children were placed in small groups for language instruction. A variety of lessons in receptive and expressive language were used, with the focus on face-to-face conversation between teachers and children. Each child was required to use appropriate sentence structures, verb forms, and word endings. A large increase in I.Q. (which is heavily loaded with language abilities) was noted over a period of nine months. This was not the case, however, in a control group of comparable children.

These two studies are typical of the research activities in this area. A number of other studies can also be cited to support our position that language acquisition can be accelerated through early educational intervention. (See Lindstrom and Tanenbaum, 1970; Mann, 1970; and Moore, 1970.)

Many different language intervention approaches are being successfully used in current early education programs. Most of these, however, will fit into three major categories: developmental models, behavioral models, and information-processing models.

Developmental Models

As we mentioned in chapter 2, the curriculum advocated in this text is based on a developmental model, that is, a model constructed from normative data on child growth and development. To some extent, the other two major models for language intervention programs, behavioral and information processing, also call upon normative data to establish the sequence and content of their curricula. Therefore, both content and methodology have to be considered before we place a particular approach into one of these broad categories.

For the most part, programs that use experience methods to develop language skills can be classified as developmental. One example of an experience is the Show and Tell story exchange used in kindergarten programs. Broader experiences, such as field trips and topically oriented discussion in the classroom, are other examples of the "experience broadening" method. Within this framework, the teacher and aides, as well as other children, act as language models. A developmental model can be very informal or very structured. For example, a teacher who presents several objects for a child to label is providing a structured experience activity.

Examples of programs that can be considered developmental in nature are Tina Bangs's program at the Houston Speech Hearing Center (Bangs, 1968), the New Nursery School program (Nimnicht, 1969), and the Bank Street program.

Pattern of Normal Language Development

Age Yr.	Expressive Language	Receptive Language
1-2	Uses 1 to 3 words at 12 mo., 10 to 15 at 15 mo., 15 to 20 at 18 mo., about 100–200 by 2 yr. Knows names of most objects he uses. Names few people, uses verbs but not correctly with subjects. Jargon and echolalia. Names 1 to 3 pictures.	Begins to relate symbol and object meaning. Adjusts to comments. Inhibits on command. Responds correctly to "give me that," "sit down," "stand up," with gestures. Puts watch to ear on command. Understands simple questions. Recognizes 120–275 words.
2-3	Vocabulary increases to 300–500 words. Says "where kitty," "ball all gone," "want cookie," "go bye bye car." Jargon mostly gone. Vocalizing increases, has fluency trouble. Speeach not adequate for communication needs.	Rapid increase in comprehension vocabulary to 400 at 2½, 800 at 3. Responds to commands using "on," "under," "up," "down," "over there," "by," "run," "walk," "jump up," "throw," "run fast," "be quiet," and commands containing two related actions.
3-4	Uses 600–1000 words, becomes conscious of speech. 3–4 words per speech response. Personal pronouns, some adjectives, adverbs, and prepositions appear. Mostly simple sentences, but some complex. Speech more useful.	Understands up to 1500 words at age 4. Recognizes plurals, sex difference, complex and compound sentences. Answers simple questions.
4-5	Increase in vocabulary to 1000–1600 words. More 3–4 syllable words. More adjectives, adverbs, prepositions, and conjunctions. Articles appear. 4, 5, 6, word sentences, syntax quite good. Uses plurals. Fluency improves. Proper nouns decrease, pronouns increase.	Comprehends from 1500 to 2000 words. Carries out more complex commands, with 2–3 actions. Understands dependent clause, "if," "because," "when," "why."
5-6	Increase in vocabulary to 1500–2100 words. Complete 5–6 word sentences, compound, complex, and with some dependent clauses. Syntax near normal. Quite fluent. More multisyllable words.	Understands vocabulary of 2500 to 2800 words. Responds correctly to more complicated sentences, but is still confused at times by involved sentences.

Reprinted from: "Doctor's Manual for Speech Disorders" by Herold Lillywhite, *J.A.M.A.*, June 14, 1958, Vol. 167.

Bank Street Program One of the primary goals of the *Bank Street Early Childhood Discovery Materials* (1969) is to encourage development of language skills by helping the child express his thoughts and understand what others are saying to him. The program consists of a variety of interrelated materials organized around themes; for example, On the Farm, In the Supermarket, At School, and In the City. The materials are used to stimulate dialogue between the teacher and children, as well as among the children themselves. Each theme program contains the following materials:

Folding Pictures. Large, busy pictures that provide a wide spectrum of people, places, and situations to stimulate the children's questions and discussions.

Children's Books. "Name and Know" books which show detailed closeup pictures of the characters in the folding pictures. The child names the character, object, or situation pictured, and tells about qualities and uses. "Turn the Page" books tell simple stories in pictures, stimulating the children to tell the story in their own words.

Puzzle and Sequence Boards. For problem solving and manual dexterity. The children use the sequence boards to place pictures in the correct time sequence.

The teacher's manual for the Bank Street program describes the skills the program is designed to develop. These skills are broken down across developmental areas that correspond very closely to the areas presented in this text: language skills, conceptual skills, perceptual skills, and motor skills.

Behavioral Models

When classifying a behavioral-model program we place more emphasis on the methodology used to acquire language than on the actual content of language acquired. This is not to say that the proponents and users of this approach are not concerned about content. It is only that they are recognized more by their methods than by their content. Behavioral programs stress the management of the learning situation through use of systematic observations of children's language performance. Through stringent application of the operant conditioning learning theory initiated by Skinner (1953), users of the behavioral approach stress the scientific application of reinforcement principles.

Distar An excellent example of the application of this approach is the *Distar* language program developed by Englemann (1969). Englemann's purpose was to develop a functional "school language" so that any child who completed the program successfully would be able to understand the language used by his teachers in explaining and discussing concepts students are expected to learn. In this sense, the *Distar* program may not be appropriate for the acquisition of a social language.

The *Distar* language program attempts to teach a logical language that will serve as a communication system between child and teacher. For example, a direction implies many operations. To perform the tasks required by the direction, the child must first understand and be able to act upon the operational implications of the words contained in the statement. This concept of language is narrow in that it does not directly concern itself with the social and expressive use of language.

A basic and simple presentation is consistently used. Only when the children have mastered a skeleton language, and have used it as a vehicle for acquiring some new concepts, are the statements and patterns altered. Teaching tasks are broken into logically sequenced subtasks. For each subtask, the teacher gives instructions, the children respond, and the teacher corrects or praises the response. The teacher sits in a circle with several children, leading them in a pattern drill of alternating statements, questions, and responses.

The pattern drill is based on statements and the questions and answers that are implied by the statements. The child learns that statements have parts, by combining a set of words into a statement that describes a reality.

The children learn to speak rhythmically and in unison. The teacher changes tasks frequently and, by moving at a very fast pace, keeps the children working in a highly disciplined manner.

For correct responses, the children are firmly praised, and in terms directly related to what they are doing: "That's good talking"; "You said that just right"; "You said the whole statement that time—good for you." Corrections are made in a clear and forthright manner: "John, you haven't said it right. I want to hear every word." Or "No, you're wrong," followed by the correction. Englemann points out that a child's mistake is a signal to the teacher either that she must go back several steps and repeat the teaching sequence, or that she must provide clearer demonstrations, or that something is wrong with her presentation.

The *Distar* language program is divided into five books, each treating a different aspect of the language curriculum. Book IV consists of stories written not only to amuse and interest the children but also to give them practice in hearing and saying the language they have been learning in a more formal way in the first three books. Book V consists of teacher directions for Take Home pages. These pictures are discussed by the teacher and the children, and then sent home with the children to encourage them to tell their families what they are learning in school.

Information-Processing Models

Programs in this category are characterized by their heavy reliance on both Osgood's original statement of learning theory (1957) and its subsequent adaptations and translations (Kirk, 1966; Dunn, 1967). In brief, information-processing models view language as a sequence of decoding (or receiving), association (or processing), and encoding (or expressing). When such a system is applied to an early childhood language curriculum, the acquisition of the skills making up the component parts of the system is stressed. One example of an application is the diagnostic use of the *Illinois Test of Psycho-linguistic Abilities* (Kirk, McGarthy, and Kirk, 1968). Language sub-areas in the ITPA consist of auditory reception, visual reception, auditory association, visual association, auditory closure, sound blending, verbal expression, manual expression, grammatic closure, visual closure, auditory sequential memory, and visual sequential memory. If a child is found to be deficient in a specific ITPA sub-area, the teacher may stress remedial activities dealing specifically with that area.

Information-processing models also focus on developing an awareness of the rules for generating language. Thus the curriculum intent is to improve the child's knowledge of how language works as well as his ability to use words more effectively.

Classroom application of the information-processing model can be seen in the use of the *Peabody Language Development Kits* (Dunn, 1967) and the Ameliorative Preschool program operated by Merle Karnes at the University of Illinois.

The Peabody Language Development Kits are made up of a series of lessons; a teacher may follow the suggested program or structure his own in a number of different ways. The Peabody program stresses all three major areas of the information-processing system: expression, reception, and conceptualization of language.

Goal: Language Development

The *Goal: Language Development* program* (Karnes, 1972) is one major result of the Ameliorative Preschool program. This language program contains 337 short lesson activities for use with children from three to five years of age. Although, as the title implies, language development is stressed, a number of other areas of activities based on the ITPA model are included. The activity areas and examples of a lesson in each are presented below.

Area	Sample Activity
Auditory Reception	I am going to say something I want you to do and I will ask one of you to do it. Ready? . . . Make a sad face. Touch your nose. Stick out your tongue. Smile. Pretend to cough. Pull your ear . . ."
Visual Reception	Review body parts with the children by saying, "Watch me. I will point to a part of my body. You are to tell me its name." Point to your head, nose, toes.
Auditory Association	Review the six emotions one at a time, looking at the caricature in each picture. Encourage each child to label each caricature.

*Permission to reproduce the following material from *Goal: Language Development Program* has been granted by Milton Bradley Company, Springfield, Mass. © 1972, Milton Bradley.

Visual Association	"Now I am going to show you another picture. What looks funny about this picture? That's right; lions don't wear glasses. Who does wear glasses? That's right; people wear glasses."
Verbal Expression	Depending on the picture, call attention to the time of year. Why the child thinks it is that time of year. Stress action in the picture. Why the people are doing what they are doing. If there are any animals, what are they and what are they doing. What would you do if you were they?
Manual Expression	"Now I wonder if you can show me what the picture tells about. I will show you a picture and I want you to show me what the child is doing in the picture. Here is the first picture."
Auditory Sequential Memory	"I woke up this morning with some of the silliest words running through my head. Do silly words ever run through your head? Try to say them in the same order I do."
Visual Sequential Memory	"Look at this picture. Now, look at the other picture. I will cover both pictures." Cover the pictures with the sheet of construction paper. "_____, tell me the names of the pictures in the order you saw them."
Grammatic Closure	"I want you to step on the black paper and the red paper." (You may name two colors which are adjacent and can be stepped on simultaneously.) If the child steps on only one paper, say, "Step on the black paper and step on the red paper at the same time." . . . Emphasize the connective *and* in giving these directions.
Auditory Closure	"A big black bear sat on a _____. What could he sit on that would rhyme with bear? Can anyone help me? _____? Chair! Of course! A big black bear sat on a chair. Why didn't I think of that? Here's another one. A little grey mouse ran into the _____."
Visual Closure	"These pictures are different than most pictures because in every picture something is missing. Here, let's look at one of the pictures and you'll see what I mean." Show the picture of the house with the door missing.

The *Learning to Think Series* (Thurstone, 1972) contains many specific lessons for acquisition of language. Each of the books in the series contains lessons to build receptive-language (verbal meaning) and expressive-language (word fluency) skills. Receptive-language skills are emphasized, not only because they are easily acquired by young children but also because of their importance in future learning situations. Students with large vocabularies typically make better grades in school than those with small ones. In addition, we have found that lack of adequate receptive-language skills often creates difficulty in learning to read.

Learning to Think

Receptive-language exercises   Six types of exercises that have proven to be especially effective in developing receptive-language skills are included in the *Learning to Think Series.*

Vocabulary. Every lesson adds new words directly or indirectly to the child's receptive vocabulary. A large auditory vocabulary makes the acquisition of a visual vocabulary easier when the child begins to read.

Auditory Discrimination. This is the ability to discriminate between similar sounds. It is an important receptive-language skill, and one that is vital in learning to read. Remedial-reading experts have found that many reading failures can be prevented by teaching very young children to hear words accurately. Spelling difficulties can also be prevented by a clear understanding of the sound of words. One of our graduate students in psychology once wrote the word *wheelbarrel* on a term paper. When asked about the spelling of *wheelbarrow*, he replied, "I can never remember whether there is one *l* or two on the end of it." Such errors are not uncommon and show that many adults have only a fuzzy conception of the exact sound of even relatively familiar words.

Most children acquire the ability to discriminate between sounds by random and incidental practice. But many youngsters have difficulty discriminating between similar sounds, or tend to pronounce words inaccurately. Training in listening closely to the sound of words will lead to better understanding, more precise speech, and improvement in spelling ability. To accomplish this, *Learning to Think* contains lessons to teach children to listen carefully for small differences in words that sound much alike. For example, the teacher reads the names for a pair of pictured objects, say, "coat" and "colt," and tells the children to "mark the colt." This procedure also overcomes differences in size and content of children's vocabularies, and is particularly useful in adding new words to the vocabularies of pupils who have not had adequate verbal experiences in the home.

Recognizing initial, middle, and ending sounds. As the child gains the maturity necessary to learn to read, he becomes aware that many words sound alike. Although nursery rhymes have taught him that many words have identical final sounds, it is the recognition of similar initial sounds that is more immediately significant for reading. The explosive initial *b* sound is one of the first lessons in sound recognition. In the *Learning to Think Series*, later exercises give the child practice in hearing and responding to several important initial sounds.

Understanding verbal units. The total meaning of a sentence is more than the meaning of those same words taken individually. A typical comprehension exercise asks, "Which is used to clean the floor?" and presents the pupil with four pictures from which to choose his answer: a mop, a washing machine, a scrubbing board, and a faucet.

All the alternatives relate in some way to the cleaning process, but only one clearly answers the question.

Superficially it may appear that a child's ability to do these exercises will depend mainly on prior knowledge. But, in fact, the prior knowledge factor is minimized by assuming a level of experience that virtually all kindergarten and first-grade children are known to possess. Thus, the child's essential task here is to pay close attention and understand the question. The wording of the questions begins at a relatively easy level of difficulty and as the lessons progress, the vocabulary becomes more difficult and the sentences more complicated.

Verbal precision. Many children make unnecessary errors because, although they have a general idea of what a particular word means, they fail to discriminate between that word and others that recall similar events or associations. A typical exercise in this area shows a Christmas tree, a Santa Claus, a fireplace, and a holly wreath. The child is asked to mark the picture that corresponds to the phrase "the one that hangs in the window at Christmas time." Only one picture fits this concept precisely, although all the others are related to the same concept or to the words used in the question.

Such lessons teach the child to listen carefully and to grasp the precise meaning of a phrase several words long. This type of training is of great value in teaching children to understand and follow all kinds of instructions.

Verbal judgment. These are the most difficult receptive-language exercises for young children. They consist of a series of sentences from which the last word is missing. For example: "When the electric lights went out, Father lit a _____." The children complete the sentence by marking one of the four pictures, in this case, a light bulb, a pipe, a lamp, and a candle. The right answer is chosen from among distractors in meaning or sound. As you can see, these tasks require close and sustained attention, precise comprehension of the part of the sentence read aloud, and verbal memory while examining the four pictures for an acceptable answer. This type of exercise is a good indication of receptive-language ability at all age levels.

Usually such lessons are presented in written form. In the *Learning to Think Series*, however, lessons have been adapted to an oral and pictured format for children who cannot read.

Examples of some of the different types of receptive-language activities discussed above are shown on pages 140–44.

Expressive-language exercises Expressive-language acquisition lessons should concentrate on the development of fluency in the use of words. In spite of the fact that there is a strong relationship between expressive- and receptive-language ability, many children who have good verbal comprehension do not speak fluently, while others with quite limited vocabularies speak very fluently.

The *Learning to Think Series* uses pictures of familiar things to develop word fluency. It is suggested that children be allowed to

GROUP LESSON Look at these two pictures. Here is a peddler *(point)*, and here are some pedals *(point)*. These names sound alike, but you can tell the difference. I am going to mark only one of these pictures. I am going to mark the peddler. *(Make a diagonal mark on the picture of the peddler.)*

Here is another pair of pictures—a cradle *(point)* and a ladle *(point)*. Will someone put a mark on the ladle? *(Have a child mark the picture of the ladle.)*

In this pair of pictures are a picture *(point)* and a pitcher *(point)*. Will someone mark the pitcher? *(Have a child mark the correct picture.)*

Here are four more pairs of pictures. I will tell you what they show, and then I will tell you which one to mark. Mark only one picture in each box, the one I tell you to. Don't mark a picture until I tell you which one to mark.

Here are the names for the pictures:

PUDDLE and POODLE	Mark the poodle.
CANDLE and KENNEL	Mark the kennel.
BUCK and BUCKET	Mark the buck.
HAND and HAM	Mark the ham.

GOLD BOOK LESSON Now you will mark some pictures in the same way in your Gold Book.

Open your book to page 14, with the picture of the toy elephant at the top. Put a mark on the picture of the toy elephant.

Read the names of each pair of pictures and tell the children which of the pair to mark. The names of the pictures and the directions to mark are summarized below.

BERRIES and BARREL	Mark the barrel.
COCK and CLOCK	Mark the cock.
RADIATOR and AVIATOR	Mark the aviator.
BLOOM and BROOM	Mark the bloom.
CARD and CART	Mark the cart.
TOP and POP	Mark the pop.
COMB and CONE	Mark the comb.
TRUCK and TRUNK	Mark the truck.
PLANE and PANE	Mark the plane.
BEES and BEADS	Mark the bees.
BLOCKS and BOX	Mark the box.
PUMPS and PUP	Mark the pup.

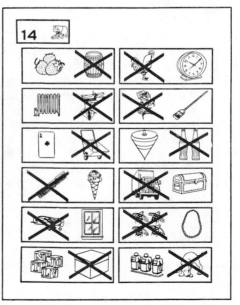

Figure 8-1 Auditory Discrimination

34 VERBAL MEANING—P-WORDS

GROUP LESSON Listen carefully while I name the pictures in the first row of this chart. *(Pronounce the words with exaggerated emphasis on the initial "puh" sound.)*

PIANO   PALETTE   PEAS   PARROT   PIXIE

There is a "puh" sound at the beginning of each word. Listen again. *(Point to the pictures and pronounce the words again.)* You are to mark every picture in which the name of what you see begins with this sound. Here in the first row, I'm going to mark every picture, because the name for each one begins with "puh." *(Name and mark each picture.)*

I am going to name the pictures in the second row:

PEACH   MILK   PAIL   LANTERN   PADLOCK

Who would like to mark all the pictures that have a name beginning with "puh"? *(Let a child mark the pictures.)*

Proceed in the same way with the next two rows. Read the words one at a time. The names for the pictures are:

MAN   PRESENT   MONKEY   MUSHROOM   TIRE
PAINTS   TOY   PADDLE   BUNNY   PINS

GOLD BOOK LESSON Open your Gold Book to page 34, with picture of the dog at the top. Mark the dog.

Read the names for the pictures one at a time and ask the children to mark every picture with a name that begins with the "puh" sound. The names are:

BRIDE	PAPER SACK	DUCK	CHAIN	PAJAMAS
PENGUIN	VEST	PITCHER	PENCIL	WHEELCHAIR
BATTER	PUMPS	PROFILE	PEPPERS	BULB
PAINTER	JAR	DOG	CARD	PANDA
CHAIR	PAINTBRUSH	PURSE	CONE	CAR
SCISSORS	PARADE	NAIL	PILLOW	PAIL

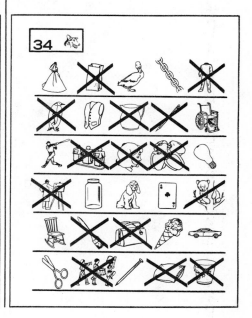

Figure 8-2   Recognizing Initial, Middle, and Ending Sounds

GROUP LESSON I am going to read you a short story about one of the pictures in the first row of the chart. When I have finished reading the story, I want you to tell me which of the pictures goes with the story. The story is:

Row 1: Sally is buying a gift to give her friend for her birthday.

(Read the story a second time if necessary and then have a child mark the right answer.)

Present the stories for the other rows of pictures in the same way:

Row 2: Polly's Christmas present can say "Ma-ma" but it cannot run or eat.

Row 3: Many children think the most exciting part of the circus is the acrobats.

Row 4: While the little children play on the shore, Carol takes a swim.

GOLD BOOK LESSON Now we are going to mark some pictures in the same way in your Gold Book.

Turn to page 47, with the picture of the ice-cream soda at the top. Mark the picture.

Present the sentences as you did in the group lesson. Read a sentence more than once if necessary:

Row 1: Father and Mother enjoy taking the train when they go on a vacation.

Row 2: Tom is mussing his hair as he takes off his sweater.

Row 3: We like to sit by the fire with no light except a candle.

Row 4: Father is running with his suitcase to catch the train.

Row 5: We are having a picnic with the pie Mother made this morning.

Row 6: The big ship is steaming fast across the ocean.

Go on to the next page.

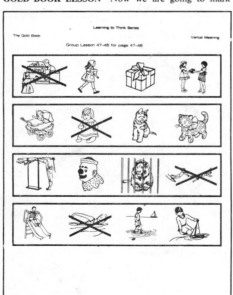

Figure 8-3 Understanding Verbal Units

7-8 VERBAL MEANING—QUESTIONS

GROUP LESSON *For each row of pictures on this chart, read a question and ask the children to find the answer in the corresponding row of pictures. The children should discuss and mark the pictures on the chart..*
   The questions are:
   Row 1: Which boy is making the most noise?
   Row 2: Which is delivered to your house every day?
   Row 3: Which of these toys is made of wood?
   Row 4: Which is the bird's home?
GOLD BOOK LESSON Open your Gold Book to page 7, with the picture of the flowers at the top. Mark the picture.

Read a question and have the children mark the answer for each row of pictures on the pages.
   Row 1: Which one do you need when it is raining even if it is not cold?
   Row 2: Which one of these do you most often see on your way to school?
   Row 3: Which one does Father wear around his neck?
   Row 4: Which one do you think is talking?
   Row 5: John likes to make a lot of noise. Which of these presents does he like best?
   Row 6: Which fruit grows in a bunch?
   Go on to the next page.

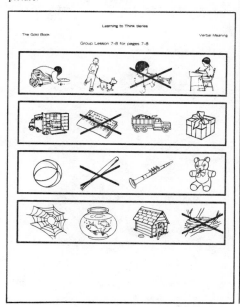 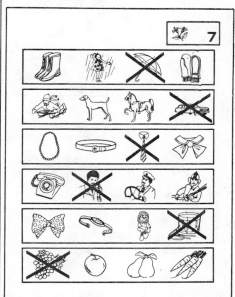

Figure 8-4   Verbal Precision

GROUP LESSON Listen closely to what I read to you.

1. When we moved to our new home we traveled by automobile, but our furniture went in a _____.

Can you finish what I read? One of the pictures in this row (*the first row*) will finish this little story. Which is the picture? (*Children will answer "truck."*) That's right: it's the truck. The whole story would say:

"When we moved to our new home we traveled by automobile, but our furniture went in a truck." (*Give further explanation if necessary.*)

Will someone mark the truck to show that it is the answer? (*Have a child do that.*)

The other three sentences are presented similarly:

2. Jack's big brother plays football. So that his head won't get hurt, he uses a _____.

3. "I'm sorry I can't fix your broken chair," said Father, "but I will as soon as I get my _____."

4. A baby who is learning to walk can't wear bootees anymore. He needs _____.

GOLD BOOK LESSON Open your Gold Book to page 17, with the picture of the children's parade at the top. Mark the picture.

Read the sentences as in the group lesson:

1. Father is going to plant a tree. To dig the hole he must have a _____.

2. Jane is learning to help Mother in the kitchen. She peels potatoes and strings _____.

3. John saw that he would be late for school when he looked at the _____.

4. Jane had a Halloween party. In the center of the table was a _____.

5. My mother likes to read. For her birthday we are going to give her a _____.

6. Marjorie is hoping for a letter. She stands at the window watching for the _____.

Go on to the next page.

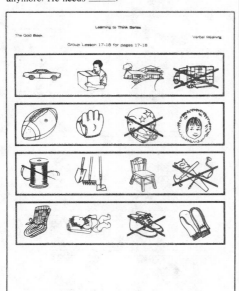

Figure 8-5 Verbal Judgment

use their own names for objects, and not be corrected for poor pronunciation or baby talk. Otherwise, the teacher may stifle rather than encourage their attempts at fluent speaking.

It is a good practice to encourage children to talk at length about the pictures in a lesson. They frequently want to relate personal experiences that are connected in some way with a pictured object or objects—precisely the situation in which they are likely to become most fluent.

The *Learning to Think* exercises to develop fluency are divided into three groups.

Picture naming. Nearly all kindergarten and first-grade children know the names of the objects shown in the early lessons. They are presented not to teach new words but to provide practice in using the names of things that are already familiar: umbrella, clock, button, and so on. For purposes of developing fluency, any appropriate name a child uses to identify a picture is correct. He may say "lamb," "sheep," or give the name of his own toy lamb.

Later exercises ask children to name the action shown in pictures (driving a bus, mowing a lawn) or to tell what one does with the object shown (brushing teeth, for a drawing of a tube of toothpaste; painting, for a picture of a paint brush).

Oral communication. In these activities children are shown pictures and encouraged to discuss them freely. Some pictures show amusing absurdities, such as a fisherman catching a bird, to add interest and encourage response. The teacher might also bring in other pictures and make use of situations in the classroom to stimulate spontaneous discussions.

Rhyming words. Young children are intrigued by words that sound alike: in their play they frequently invent nonsense words that rhyme. The invention and recognition of rhymes is a function of the word-fluency factor of intelligence. The recognition of similar final sounds is also helpful in learning to read. In rhyming word lessons, children are given groups of two or four pictures and asked to think of rhyming names for the pictures in each group: key, tree, hog, dog, log, frog, and so on.

Several times we have been asked, "Don't you have a cultural bias built into your worksheets? For example, how many culturally different children would recognize a Christmas wreath?" The pictures we use represent the predominant cultural bias in the country today. Education itself is culturally biased, depending on the culture in which the educational institution is functioning. Therefore, some of these materials may be inappropriate for some minority-group children, particularly Spanish-American. In this event, we suggest that you replace them with materials more appropriate.

On pages 146–49 you will find several sample lessons from the *Learning to Think Series* that we have used successfully in developing expressive-language skills.

1 WORD FLUENCY–PICTURE NAMING

GROUP LESSON I am going to read you the names of the animals pictured in the first row on the chart:

COLT   DUCK   ALLIGATOR   PANDA

(Don't point to the pictures in this lesson. That might discourage fluency.)

Now I want you to tell me the names of the animals in the first row. *(Have several children give the names.)*

The other rows of pictures are presented in the same way. The names are:

REINDEER	LAMB	APE	DOG
BIRD	MOOSE	PIG	CAT
ELEPHANT	EAGLE	BUTTERFLY	MOUSE

All the pictures used in this lesson represent familiar animals. It is possible, however, that some children are not familiar with them. New words should be taught to them, and they should be given practice in saying them.

Don't insist that the children say exactly the words listed above. "Deer" is as good as "reindeer," and "rat" is as good as "mouse."

GOLD BOOK LESSON Now you will name some pictures in your Gold Book.

Open your book to page 1, with the picture of the teddy bear at the top. Put a mark on the picture.

The pictures are presented in the same way as in the group lesson. At first the children should give names for the pictures a row at a time, and then practice with a longer list, up to the whole page. All the children should have an opportunity to practice.

The children may not all give the same names for the pictures. No set word is required, since the purpose of the lesson is to encourage fluency.

This page can be used in the same way a second day if you feel that more practice will be helpful.

Figure 8-6 Picture Naming

GROUP LESSON All the pictures on this chart show a person or an animal doing something. The name of each picture is what is happening. I will read to you the names for the pictures in the first row on the chart:

CLEANING   CRYING   SLIDING   HOEING

(Do not point to the pictures in this lesson. That might discourage fluency.)

Now I want you to give me names for the pictures in the first row. *(Have several children name the action in the pictures of the row.)*

The other rows of pictures are presented in the same way. The words are:

HAMMERING	CARRYING	DIVING	MARCHING
WASHING	BURNING	SKIPPING	SITTING
BUILDING	HANGING	KNITTING	RUNNING

Don't insist that the children say exactly these words. "Sweeping" is as good as "cleaning," "pounding" is as good as "hammering," and so on. Remember that the lesson is planned to develop fluency.

GOLD BOOK LESSON Now you will name some pictures in your Gold Book.

Open your book to page 19, with the picture of the cowboy at the top. Put a mark on the picture.

The pictures are presented in the same way as in the group lesson. At first the children should name what is happening in the pictures a row at a time, and then practice with a longer list, up to the whole page. All the children should have an opportunity to practice.

The children may not all give the same names for the pictures. No set word is required, since the purpose of the lesson is to encourage fluency.

This page can be used in the same way a second day if you feel that more practice will be helpful.

Figure 8-7 Picture Naming

GROUP LESSON Look at the first picture on this chart. I want you to tell me as many things as you can about this picture. *Present the second picture in the same way.*

The principal purpose of the lesson is not so much to see whether the children can find the absurdities as to give them practice in presenting their ideas orally to the class. The pictures serve to stimulate oral composition.

Some children may talk about things that may not be very closely related to the pictures. Although the pictures and the absurdities in the situations presented are the central themes around which the discussions should revolve, don't discourage the children from going further. The lesson is intended to encourage fluent speech. Encourage as many children as possible to participate.

GOLD BOOK LESSON Now we are going to talk about some pictures in your Gold Book in the same way.

Open your book to page 30, with the picture of the boy and girl dancing at the top. Put a mark on the boy and girl.

The pictures on this page should be discussed fully. The children will probably think these pictures are funny. If the point of a picture is not clear, lead them to discover it.

Keep in mind that this is an exercise in speaking fluently and encourage the children to talk freely about any experience suggested by the pictures.

Figure 8-8 Oral Communication

GROUP LESSON We can give all the pictures in the first row of the chart names that sound alike, names that rhyme. Listen while I name them:

CAT   BAT   HAT   RAT

Who else would like to name the pictures? *(Let a pupil name and point to the pictures.)*

Now let's all look at the next row and see who can give all the pictures names that sound alike. *(If no one can name all the pictures, give whatever help is necessary. Have several pupils name the pictures in each row, so that all will be able to hear the similar sounds of the endings.*

The other rhymes in the group lesson are:

TREES	PEAS	KEYS	BEES
PAIL	NAIL	MAIL	SAIL
ROSE	HOSE	TOES	BOWS

GOLD BOOK LESSON We can do the same thing with a page of pictures in your Gold Book.

Turn to page 24, with the picture of the farmer at the top. Mark the farmer.

Look at the first row of pictures *(pause)*. Who can give all the pictures names that rhyme? *(Give help only when no pupil can provide the correct name for any given picture. The naming can be repeated several times; give as many pupils as possible the opportunity to participate.)*

The rhymes on page 24 of the Gold Book are:

STAG	BAG	FLAG	TAG
GATE	SKATE	PLATE	GRATE
FROCK	CLOCK	SOCK	LOCK
EYES	PRIZE	TIES	PIES
TREE	KNEE	KEY	TEA
COAT	BOAT	NOTE	GOAT

For added practice, children can be asked to give other words that rhyme with those in the lesson or with other words you suggest.

Some good words are HAND, POST, HOP, DOOR. You can provide as much practice in this task as you like.

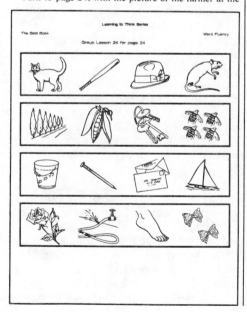

Figure 8-9 Rhyming Words

As mentioned earlier, every activity in a program should be consciously used as an opportunity to develop language capabilities in your young children. The types of lesson activities found in programs like the *Learning to Think Series* should help you organize your thoughts on how to make the best use of all verbal interactions.

Many of the suggestions for language development activities provided here are rather didactic in nature. Nevertheless, we believe that such an approach is necessary in any program that attempts to accelerate development. We are, of course, aware of the fact that language is not used in a vacuum. Although we have focused on developing the tools that will enable the child to receive information and to express himself, we know that what the child talks about will be increasingly important in his life. We can only hope that in a well-rounded comprehensive curriculum, language will interact with reasoning, perception, motor, and social activities to provide the child not only with the proper language tools, but with something worth talking about.

Generalization of Language Skills

Interest centers for language should be set up in such a manner that the children are free to explore and talk with one another as well as with the teacher. There are several centers that are appropriate for language development: (1) the housekeeping center; (2) the store; (3) the cooking center; and (4) the language-arts center.

The Housekeeping Center

This center should be set up to encourage two or more children to interact verbally as they simulate the various activities that go on in the home. Dress-up clothes encourage role characterizations such as mother, father, postman, fireman, nurse, policeman, and doctor. Other materials appropriate for this type of center are table and chairs, mops and brooms, and kitchen equipment.

The Store Center

Although store centers are usually set up for older children, there are many activities that will also facilitate language development in younger children. Such activities might include: (1) simulation of selection and purchase of groceries; (2) simulation of bagging and checking out of groceries; (3) grouping various kinds of food items together; (4) reordering and stacking grocery shelves; and (5) making up shopping lists based on children's likes and dislikes in foods.

Cooking Center

A cooking center can be set up as part of the housekeeping center, or it can be established as a separate center. Within this center, materials and supplies can be arranged to provide for the simulation of cooking activities as well as some very simple real cooking activities. For the most part, activities in this area would revolve around the use of verbal recipes, measurements of various amounts of foods, the use of pots and pans and other utensils, the use of various kinds of cooking and baking supplies, and the use of stove, ovens, and refrigerators.

Language-Arts Center

A language-arts interest center contains an array of materials that are intended to stimulate the kinds of activities that involve language usage. This center might contain various kinds of listening devices: tape recorders, tape recordings, record players, records, and Listening Posts. Picture books and storybooks can be used to stimulate discussions and verbal interaction among children. Picture-sequence stories are often used to stimulate language.

Developmental Activity Guide
Language Skills

In this guide, the task number refers to the corresponding item on the *Carolina Developmental Profile.* The objective defines the behavior to be learned. In the instructional activities column, we suggest several activities that will give your children the experience necessary to accomplish the stated objective. As you gain experience working with children, you will no doubt want to add other activities that will increase the usefulness of the guide.

RECEPTIVE LANGUAGE

Developmental Objective (by task no.)	Instructional Activities
1. Follows simple directions *Materials for Activities* *1. An object for each child* *2. Puppet; an object for each child* *3. Puppet; an object for each child* *4. Puppet; ball or block*	1. Game. Divide the children into two groups. Give them each an object. Teacher then calls a child's name in group one to gain his attention, and then says, "Take the _____ to (another child's name)." Continue until each child has had a turn to take his object to another child. 2. Game. Give each child a different object. The teacher uses a puppet, who does not call the child by name, but does say, "Bring the _____ to me." This activity should be done in small groups. 3. Game. Give each child an object. The puppet calls each child by name and says, "Put the (name of object) on the (table, chair, box, stove, sink etc.)."

4. Game. "Do what the puppet says." The puppet gives the child an object (block or ball). The puppet then gives four directions, each separately. "Give me the ball. Put the ball down. Throw the ball. Go get the ball." If the child does not understand a direction, the puppet can demonstrate.

5. Give the child simple directions at snack time. "Give a napkin to _____. Give a cup to _____. Put the cup on the table," etc.

---

2. Touches objects designated by name on request

Materials for Activities

1. *Common objects*
2. *Classroom objects*
3. *Common objects*
4. *Common objects*
5. *Mystery box; objects*

1. Give child known or common objects one at a time. Say, "Here is a ball. What do you have?" Child says "Ball."

2. When using objects in the classroom, name them often. Refer to objects by name rather than by pronoun.

3. Teacher hides a common object. "I will hide the car. Find the car. What did you find?" Child says "Car."

4 Give child common objects. Say, "Give me the spoon. Give me the ball."

5. Have several objects in a mystery box. Take two objects out of the mystery box and say, "Touch the _____." More advanced variation: Leave all the items in the mystery box. Tell the child to "reach in the box and touch the _____." Begin with no more than four objects in the box and increase the number of objects gradually.

---

3. Touches objects designated by function on request

Materials for Activities

1. *Puppet; common objects*
3. *Pictures of people using common objects in appropriate and inappropriate way*

1. Puppet has several objects around him, and asks child to give him object by designating the function of the object and not the name. Example: "Give me what we color with. Give me what we throw."

2. Show and Tell. During Show and Tell the teacher also has a turn. He or she names the object, describes its characteristics, and gives its function. Talks about objects at other times as well.

3. Game. Pictures of people using common objects in appropriate and inappropriate ways. Examples: girl using a fork to eat; a girl using a fork to throw. Ask the children, "Which girl knows how to use the fork the right way?"

---

4. Touches three pictures designated by action on request

1. Put action pictures on bulletin board. Designate an action like running or riding, and have the child point to the appropriate picture.

Developmental Objective *(by task no.)*	Instructional Activities

Materials for Activities

1. *Action pictures: riding, running, eating, sleeping, etc.*

4. *Action pictures of Peter Rabbit*

2. Show Me game (simple). Teacher says to child, "Show me a boy running." Child must then run. Use familiar action words such as running, riding, falling, eating, sleeping, sitting.

3. A Show Me game. The leader asks the child to pantomime the requested action. "Show me something your mother does at home. Show me something a cowboy does."

4. Teacher shows picture of action; teacher says, "Peter Rabbit is jumping. Show me jumping."

---

5. Follows simple directions (each containing a different preposition)

Materials for Activities

1. *Table; chair*

2. *Doll*

4. *Obstacle course made up of tables, chairs, blocks, etc.*

7. *Different colored blocks*

1. Place a small table in front of the child; direct the child to sit *under* the table, then *on* the table. Chair could also be used for *behind* and *on*.

2. Variation of activity 1 above. Child makes doll follow directions.

3. Sing the songs "Put Your Finger in the Air" and "Put Your Hands in the Air."

4. Set up an obstacle course. Have children go through the course as you, the teacher, give them directions such as "Go over the chair; under the bridge; through the tunnel."

5. Simplified version of Simon Says. Always precede direction with "Simon says." This allows the children to focus attention on the direction itself and not whether they are supposed to follow it.

6. I Spy game. "I see a red ball under the table. Can you find it?"

7. Teacher says, "Let's make a line with the blocks. The black block is in front of the red block. Watch me. I'm going to put the blue block in front of the black block. You put the red block in front of the blue block."

---

6. Touches picture of nighttime when asked, "Which picture tells you it is nighttime?"

Materials for Activities

1. *Pictures of daily activities*

2. *Pictures of moon and sun*

1. Show picture sequences of child getting up, getting dressed, eating, going to school, playing, getting ready for bed. Have child tell or point to pictures of activities that happen during the day and those that happen at night.

2. Picture game. Give each child a picture of the moon and of the sun. Then children take turns drawing pictures from a stack in the middle of the table. They must decide if the picture goes under the sun (day) or moon (night). Everytime the child gets three cards in the same category (example: day), he gets a point.

Developmental Objective *(by task no.)*	Instructional Activities
3. *Two boxes; magazine pictures depicting day and night activities*	3. Sorting box. Children place pictures cut from magazines into the appropriate box— day or night.
7. Touches blocks designated by color on request *Materials for Activities* 3. *Colored objects* 5. *Three boxes: one red, one blue, one yellow*	1. First check to see if the child knows three color names. This is not the same as matching the color name with the correct color. 2. The Yellow game. "There are lots of things in our room that are yellow. I will name some of them. Then I will stop and point to one of you. Then, it will be your turn to tell me something you see that is yellow." You may play this game using any color. 3. Look and See game. "Look and see. If yours is red like mine, give it to me." Both children and teacher should have objects of different colors. 4. Teacher says, "I am thinking of the color red (etc.). If you are wearing anything red, raise your hand." She then asks each child who has raised his hand to show what he is wearing that is red. If a child has on something that is red but has not raised his hand, the teacher points out his omission in a tactful manner. For example: "John, did you forget that your socks are red?" 5. Teacher fills a magic box with about 20 small items of three different colors. The rules of the game are then stated: "we will make three different piles of things. Yellow things go in this yellow box, blue things go in this blue box, and red things in this red box."
8. See receptive-language task 5	1. See activities for task 5.
9. Touches pictures designated by distinctive characteristics on request	1. See activities for tasks 2, 3, and 4. Tasks should be similar, but more emphasis should be put on descriptive adjectives. For example: "Point to the tall girl; show me the red ball."

Developmental **Objective** (by task no.)	**Instructional Activities**
10. Touches the pictures with the knives on request *Materials for Activities* *1. Two long pieces of yarn; common objects* *2. Flannel board and cutouts* *3. Pictures of single objects; pictures of multiple objects*	1. Using yarn, mark off on a table two areas approximately 6 x 6 inches square. In one area put two or more forks. Then ask the children to show you the forks. Be sure that you do not always put the single object in the same place. 2. Follow the same procedure as activity 1 above except use the flannel board. 3. Have several pictures that show each object as a single unit in one picture and as a multiple unit in a second picture (one boat, two or more boats). The teacher says, ''Point to the boat; point to the boats; point to the knives; point to the knife.''
11. Touches the one that is dark but not little on request *Materials for Activities* *3. Sets of objects (objects in set should be the same color but different sizes)*	1. Child must be able to discriminate between big and little, between dark and light, and know the meaning of *not* before he can pass this objective. 2. Play altered version of Simon Says. Use familiar objects in the room. "Simon says touch the chair but not the table." 3. Gather sets of several objects. Examples: Two red apples, one very big and one little. Say to the children, "Show me the one that is [color] but not big [or little]."
12. Touches the picture of the one who will be hurt, on request (is able to understand the concept of "will") *Materials for Activities* *1. Calendar* *2. Pictures that indicate a future event* *3. Pictures of objects in the process of being made; pictures of the completed objects*	1. During the opening activities many teachers discuss the days of the week. "Yesterday was _____; today is ____; tomorrow will be _____." 2. Show the children a set of three pictures: a boy swimming, an apple, and a Christmas tree. Ask the child to show you which picture tells us that Santa will come. You can use the same procedure with other holidays. 3. Present the children with pairs of pictures such as cookie dough and finished cookies, cake batter and finished cake. Ask the children which picture will be cookies.

Developmental Objective *(by task no.)*	Instructional Activities
1. Repeats two digits correctly in given order after practice *Materials for Activities* *1. Sound-effects records; pictures to accompany sounds* *2. Ball* *4. Records*	1. To teach or improve auditory memory, listen to sound-effects records; use an accompanying picture. Tell what is making each sound. 2. Blindfold child. Bounce ball and ask child to tell how many times the ball bounced. (Also can clap hands, beat drum.) 3. Play simple finger games and recite nursery rhymes. 4. Listen to simple music records.
2. Names pictured objects on request *Materials for Activities* *1. Shoe box; pictures* *2. Objects and matching pictures: shoe, comb, block, egg, etc.* *3. Large storybook*	1. Put pictures to be named inside a shoe box and cut a hole in the box to simulate a "peepshow." Ask "What do you see?" 2. Have children name concrete objects and then match them to pictures. 3. Read simple stories with large pictures and say, "What is this?" Also reread familiar stories. Teacher says, "This is a _____." Child fills in blank.

3. Tells first and last name on request
 	
Materials for Activities
 	
3. Record
 	
8. Language Master card
	1. Mention the child's name often during activities. "Mary can hop. I like the way you can hop, Mary."
	
	2. Games like Who Has Gone? and Hide and Seek provide opportunities to call children by name and for them to call each other by name.
	
	3. Use the record *Learning Basic Skills Through Music* (volume 1), and play the song: "What Is Your Name?"
	
	4. A rhythm game. Clap hands as each child says name in rhythm with beat:
	    "Jane"—one beat
	    "Rox-ie"—two beats
	    "Hel-en"—two beats
	
	5. Responds to teacher's question "What's your name?"

6. When teacher distributes materials with child's name on it, she asks, "Whose is this?" Child must respond with first and last name.

7. Singing game for circle activity: "Do you know what your name is? Yes, I know what my name is; it is ———."

8. Language Master card has recording "What is your name?" Child's response is recorded on same card and he can hear finished card (teacher assistance).

9. Make an attractive chart at children's eye level. Paste a picture of each child on the chart and write his or her name underneath. Game: Teacher points to a picture of child who must then say his first and last name. Variation: Teacher begins by pointing to a picture. If child says name correctly he may point to picture.

4. Answers comprehension questions

Materials for Activities

1. *Two bowls; ice cream, ice cubes, etc.*

2. *Pictures of what to wear when it is cold*

3. *Articles of clothing or pictures of such articles*

4. *Dolls*

5. *Slide projector; slides*

6. *Flannel board*

8. *Slide projector; slides*

1. Have a bowl of ice cubes and a bowl of hot water. Let the children touch the ice cubes and talk about how cold they are. Give the children many experiences with items that are cold. Other examples: ice cream, refrigerator, cold soft drink, snowball.

2. Have children help pin pictures of cold-weather clothing on bulletin board.

3. Use articles or pictures of clothing. Have children indicate which ones should be worn in cold weather.

4. Provide an opportunity for children to play with dolls. Suggest to them that the doll is sleepy and ask them what should be done about it.

5. Show slides of a sleepy child and what happens to him. Make up a story to go along with the slides.

6. Make up flannel-board stories about hungry animals and children.

7. At snack and lunch ask who is hungry. Then initiate talk about why people eat when they are hungry.

8. Take slides of children's daily activities. Include getting up, dressing, eating, preparing to go outside (whether it's hot or cold), playing, washing, and preparing for bed. Discuss the slides with the children. Ask what (and why) the child in the slide is doing.

Developmental Objective (by task no.)	Instructional Activities
5. Talks about pictures *Materials for Activities* *1. Bag; objects from room* *4. Pictures of various objects* *5. Stimulus cards* *6. Stimulus cards* *7. Lotto cards* *8. Flannel board*	1. Have child select three or more objects from grab bag and identify. 2. Same as activity 1 above, but must also give some description: red, big, little, fat, etc. 3. Child points to three objects in room and names. Next step: identifies an object and gives some description. 4. Same procedure as activity 3 above, but with pictured objects. 5. Present individual "stimulus" or story cards and encourage children to tell about what they see in the picture. 6. Present pictures depicting simple actions. Teacher asks, "What is this boy doing?" 7. Lotto. Teacher holds up cue card. "Do you have a picture like this one on your card? Tell me what it is." Child receives card for correct response. 8. Flannel-board story. Child identifies by name each "piece" of the story.
6. Uses two-or three-word phrases, some of which must include personal pronouns and/or ask questions	1. Encourage children to express themselves in free play. 2. Use short functional phrases. Repeat the phrases many times under different circumstances. 3. When the child has learned one phrase, say it in a different way. "Sit down" becomes "Sit in the chair." 4. When modeling short phrases, call the child's name before he is to respond: Say, "Big ball. John . . . ." 5. At snack ask the child, "Do you want a cookie?" Child must respond, "I want (a) cookie." He should be encouraged to use the carrier phrase "I want" at other times during the day.
7. See expressive-language task 2	1. See activities for tasks 2 and 5.

Developmental Objective *(by task no.)*	Instructional Activities
8. Repeats twelve- or thirteen-syllable sentences *Materials for Activities* *1. Puppet* *3. Suitcase; small items: shoe, sock, comb, cup, toothbrush, etc.*	1. Use a puppet. Have the puppet begin talking in three- or four-syllable sentences. The child repeats what the puppet says. After the child masters four syllables, begin with five-syllable sentences, etc. 2. Very simple songs, finger games, and nursery rhymes. 3. Suitcase packing. Use a small suitcase and actual items. Teacher puts shoes into the suitcase. The child then says the model sentence and puts the shoes in the suitcase. To make more difficult, have child put in objects and say, "I put in black shoes and red socks." 4. Encourage child to answer teacher's questions in complete sentences.
9. Gives purpose for having beds and television(s) on request *Materials for Activities* *1. Puppet; objects or pictures of objects such as cup, glass, crayon, block* *3. Pictures of people using beds, T.V.s, etc.* *4. Housekeeping corner; beds and cardboard T.V.* *5. Lotto game* *6. Two large pockets made out of cardboard; picture cards of things found inside and outside* *7. Cardboard box; paint; costumes* *8. Flannel-board pictures of car, bed, store, and person sleeping*	1. Make sure children are familiar with and can respond to questions using why. They might know the purpose of beds and televisions but be unable to respond to the question because they are unfamiliar with the structure. A game to help with this is the "why" game. Have several objects or pictures. Have a puppet hold up the object or picture and ask the child, "Why do we have _____?" 2. Unit on furniture where you identify and give the function of each—include beds and television. 3. Show children pictures of beds and televisions (along with other furniture) and have them make up stories about them. 4. Provide beds and, if possible, cardboard television in housekeeping corner. 5. Play lotto games using furniture. 6. Pocket game. Have two large pockets—one for things found outside and one for things found inside. Have children then place picture cards in the appropriate pockets. Use bed and television. 7. Make a large television screen out of cardboard box (or use classroom puppet show). Let the children act out their favorite television show. 8. Use a flannel board. At the top of the board put a picture of a person sleeping. Underneath put three pictures:(1) an automobile, (2) a bed, (3) a store. Then ask the children, "Where does this person belong? And why does he belong there?" Have them put the person in bed. Do the same with other articles such as television, table, chair.

Developmental Objective (by task no.)	Instructional Activities
10. Gives function of eyes and ears on request	1. Simple songs and finger games about body parts and functions.
	2. Ask children to identify body parts by function. "What do we see with?"
Materials for Activities	3. Nonsense game. Teacher gives sentences; some are correct and some are nonsensical, such as "Ears can chew." The child has to say whether a sentence is "silly" and if it is, he must correct it.
4. *Poster board; fabrics of various textures*	
5. *Perfume; bacon; clay; paint; onions; chocolate; soap; etc.*	4. Feely board. Glue different textured fabrics on a board and let children feel them.
	5. Blindfold the child or have him close his eyes. Have him identify objects with familiar odors.
6. *Carrot; chocolate; sugar; apple; banana*	6. Have the children close their eyes, taste, and guess what the food is.
7. *Records; record player*	7. Children listen to records and name the sounds.

11. Uses four- to six-word phrases	1. See activities for tasks 5, 6, 8, and 9.

12. Uses regular plurals correctly most of the time	1. "Here is one dog." (Show one dog.) "Here are two dogs. Tell me how many dogs there are." (Child should answer "Two.") The teacher should say, "These are two _____" Child should say "dogs." Then proceed in this manner: "Here is a house. Here are two _____. Here are even more _____," etc.
Materials for Activities	2. Tell the child a story leaving out plural and single words for him to complete.
1. *Pictures or objects*	
4. *Picture cards of animals, some containing only one animal and some containing two*	3. When a child begins to name what he has drawn, pick something he has drawn and ask him to tell about it. Then say, "Draw me some more of these _____, so that the dog [whatever] can play with them." Incorporate his story in the motivation. Then have him tell about it.
	4. Deal picture cards of one or two animals. The child then names his cards. Example: cow, pigs.

Checkpoint
What Have You Learned?

1. *Word meaning,* or _____, refers to the _____ of spoken words.

2. *Verbal fluency,* or_____, refers to the ability to express thoughts in a _____ way.

3. Normative data on language development provides the basis for the content in a _____ model or approach to language instruction.

4. The information-processing model or approach relies primarily on the theoretical concepts of _____ and their translation into application tools like _____ by Kirk.

5. Match these exercises in the *Learning to Think Series* with the activities listed below.

   1. Auditory discrimination
   2. Understanding verbal units
   3. Verbal precision
   4. Verbal judgment
   5. Picture naming
   6. Oral communication
   7. Rhyming words

   a) Given a picture of a toothbrush, tells what it is.

   b) Given a Christmas tree, a Santa Claus, a fireplace, and a holly wreath, marks the picture that best corresponds to the phrase "the one that hangs in the window at Christmas time."

   c) Given a picture of a tree and a key, names a word that sounds like them.

   d) Given a picture of a mop, a washing machine, a scrub board, and a faucet, marks the one that is used to clean the floor.

   e) Child discusses given picture freely.

   f) The teacher first reads the names of a pair of similar pictured objects such as coat and colt, and then tells the children to "mark the coat."

   g) "When the electric lights went out, Father lit a _____." Mark one of these four pictures: a light bulb, a pipe, a lamp, a candle.

6. a) During what age range does a child use a two-word sentence such as "Where kitty?" and "Ball gone."

   b) By what age range is syntax near normal?

   c) At what age range does the child understand simple questions?

7. The *Distar* language programs are an example of the application of the _____ model or approach to language instruction.

1. Following is one example of language behavior displayed by three children. Discuss what other language behavior each child should be displaying and his appropriate functional age range.

> Child A: Can express herself in complete five-to-six-word complex sentences.

> Child B: Responds correctly to a few commands—"sit down," "come here," "don't touch."

> Child C: Uses around 750 words, three-to-four-word responses, but no complete sentences.

2. Compare and contrast the behavior model and the information-processing model in terms of the skills needed by the teacher.

1. Using old magazines, select pictures to cut out and make one exercise each for: rhyming words; understanding verbal units; and verbal judgment.

2. Obtain a copy of the *Illinois Test of Psycholinguistic Abilities* and give the test to yourself. Report on your observations of your own information-processing strengths and weaknesses.

Chapter 9   A Developmental Curriculum for Social and Emotional Growth

Objectives

After you have completed this chapter, you should be able to:

1. Cite and define the four areas of the social-emotional curriculum presented in this chapter.
2. Cite the relationship between cognitive, social-affective, and sensorimotor development in young children.
3. Cite characteristics of children at each level of the social-emotional developmental curriculum.

In the following treatment of emotional and social development, Dr. Wood* discusses the interrelationships between this and other areas of development, illustrating that social-emotional development does not occur in a vacuum. Dr. Wood's social and emotional developmental curriculum system corresponds very closely to the Development Task Instructional System: (1) it provides specific social-emotional behavior criteria that enable the child worker or teacher to assess a child's particular developmental level; (2) it provides a system for using significant social-emotional milestones as curriculum objectives; and (3) it outlines the activities, teacher behaviors, and teacher-child interactions necessary for the child to grow and develop emotionally.

---

* Mary Margaret Wood, associate professor of Special Education, University of Georgia, and director of the Technical Assistance Office for the Georgia Psychoeducational Center Network.

During the last several years I have been extensively involved in developing and refining a therapeutic system of educational intervention for young emotionally disturbed children. It is my belief that the resultant Developmental Therapy (Wood, 1975) can be used effectively in any early education program devoted to facilitating emotional growth in young children. This chapter presents a curriculum translation of that approach which can be used as a guideline for promoting emotional growth in all children, whether emotionally disturbed or not.

You may ask the question, "What is social and emotional development?" You might also ask, "If social and emotional growth are important, what can I do to help develop these qualities in my children?"

To answer the first question, social and emotional development appears to be the result of a combination of many forces. These forces may, on the one hand, produce a child who walks into a preschool or kindergarten class as a thinking, running, feeling, sharing, caring child; or they may, on the other hand, produce a child who is afraid to venture forth, distrusts himself and others, is unorganized, lonely, angry, and ill-prepared to meet challenges.

Mussen, Conger, and Kagan (1969, pp. 753-54) describe emotional maturity in the American culture in a way that seems applicable to all persons, regardless of background. The emotionally mature person has "learned to be reasonably independent and capable of foresightful planning . . . ." He is "motivated to gain satisfaction from fulfilling the roles he must play in his own society . . . ." He has "developed the skills necessary for performance of a vocation which is needed by the culture . . . ." He has "learned to compete and to cooperate, to assert himself when necessary and to gain satisfaction from being helpful to others . . . ." He has "learned to tolerate frustration and anxiety . . . ." He "must be flexible, able to try out new responses when old ones fail . . . ." He should have "a realistic knowledge of himself, his capabilities and limitations, his predominant needs, his fears, his sources of conflict."

A person who is not emotionally mature denies his own values and needs in the face of the demands of others, or presses his own demands and needs to the detriment of others. He may attempt goals that are unrealistic and are therefore inevitably failure producing. He may waste his energy on unrealistic activities. In short, emotional maturity seems to imply meeting the demands of life with a reasonable degree of balance between thinking, caring, and doing. One must balance one's own values, concerns, motivations, and ideas with one's effect on others within the cultural group. Any teacher who is concerned about a child's emotional development must therefore plan a curriculum that takes into account the impact of day-to-day experiences on a child's thinking, caring, and doing.

You may ask the obvious question: "Should childhood be a time of deliberate preparation for emotional maturity or does it happen spontaneously?" Although experts have differing opinions on this subject, most agree that children whose early experiences resulted in positive self-esteem and self-confidence are willing to encounter new

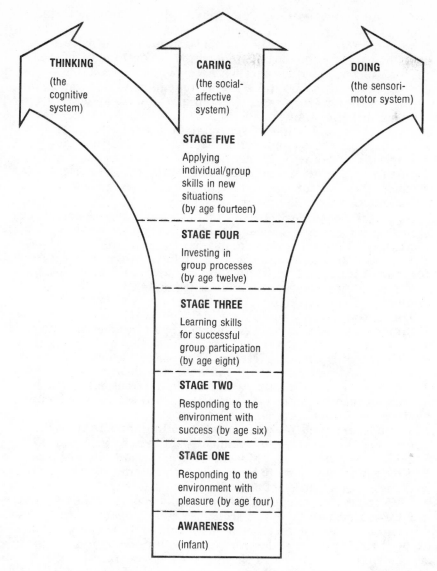

THINKING
(the cognitive system)

CARING
(the social-affective system)

DOING
(the sensori-motor system)

STAGE FIVE

Applying individual/group skills in new situations (by age fourteen)

STAGE FOUR

Investing in group processes (by age twelve)

STAGE THREE

Learning skills for successful group participation (by age eight)

STAGE TWO

Responding to the environment with success (by age six)

STAGE ONE

Responding to the environment with pleasure (by age four)

AWARENESS

(infant)

Figure 9-1   The Elements of Social-Emotional Development Shown in the Various Stages of the Developmental Curriculum

challenges or tasks. If a child's experiences convince him that it is painful or futile to venture out, he may resist new learning, and cling to older, less effective ways of responding (Keister, 1938; Baumrind, 1967).

Figure 9-1 shows how a teacher in a developmental curriculum program might look at the complex processes involved in the growth toward social and emotional maturity.

You will notice a series of horizontal lines delineating various stages of development and the approximate age at which each stage is mastered. It is important to understand that as the child matures, the functions of the prior stages do not stop, but continue to be used as the tools for success at the next stage. You will note that the systems emerge from a common trunk and become more differentiated and specific as they grow upward. The common trunk is used to convey the idea that the origins of social and emotional development are found in the combinations of several basic systems. These systems, which begin their development in the infant, increase in complexity and specificity as the child matures. These three systems, the *cognitive system,* the *social-affective system,* and the *sensorimotor system,* work together to produce the process we call social-emotional development.

The cognitive system (thinking) includes functions of intelligence, storage of information, concept building, and problem solving of an increasingly abstract, complex, and symbolic nature.

The social-affective system (caring) includes interpersonal (caring for others), intrapersonal (caring for self), and group attitudes, both positive (valuing, supporting, and caring) and negative (despising, rejecting, and alienating).

The sensorimotor system (doing) includes the reflexes, senses, and neuromusculature that provide the vehicle for interaction with the world; the sensorimotor system functions as the "enabler," the means by which the cognitive and social-affective systems can be expressed. Without considering the ways that these three processes work together, support each other, impede and reinforce each other, we cannot adequately consider what happens to a child as he acquires social and emotional responses and attitudes.

There is an abundance of research detailing the nature of these systems as they develop independently (Bruner, 1966; Hebb, 1949; Inhelder, 1957; Kagan and Moss, 1962; Macfarlane, 1943; Turiel, 1969). Unfortunately there have been fewer studies looking at the way these systems interact to produce social and emotional growth at various stages of development. However, if we consider the ways that the three systems develop in sequence, and compare what is happening across the systems at any given point in that sequence, we will notice a series of developmental milestones that can be used as guideposts for social and emotional development.

Traditionally, teachers have attempted to sequence learning within a given system; for example, they provide a series of graduated activities to help a child develop skill in handling materials. Using the idea of cross-system planning, a teacher might present activities that would develop a child's thinking and caring as well as his skill in handling materials. This kind of curriculum approach should also make it easier for the teacher to formulate sequential expectations: what happened before, what should be happening now, and what will happen next. Thus, the teacher is able to plan experiences, interactions, and learning situations that are important for a child's particular stage of development, avoiding the pitfalls of emphasizing experiences a child is either not ready for or has already mastered.

The developmental curriculum has four basic curriculum areas: *behavior, communication, socialization* and *preacademics/academics.* Following a sequence of specific objectives in each curriculum area can facilitate growth of cognitive, affective, and sensorimotor abilities, thereby ensuring that each major step toward emotional and social maturity is mastered. The teacher assists the child in mastering social-emotional developmental objectives by providing specific experiences designed to encourage the emergence of constructive behaviors. The teacher encourages particular social experiences and selects specific educational and play materials as the means to assist the child in the process of social-emotional growth.

The general goals and specific objectives for each area of the developmental curriculum follow established developmental sequences. Five distinct stages of development were shown in figure 9-1. Each stage requires a different emphasis, different techniques, and different materials and experiences. Progress through these five stages, in each area of the curriculum, results in an increasingly well-adjusted child. Goals for each stage of each curriculum area are presented in table 9-1. An individual child may be, at any given point in time, in different stages of development in each of the four curriculum areas and will progress at varying rates within each area. (A complete list of the specific curriculum objectives of developmental therapy for each curriculum area is given in Wood, 1975.)

Each curriculum goal for a specific stage of development focuses upon one particular aspect of the stage and represents a significant developmental milestone. It is important to make sure that a child has accomplished the general goal at one stage before you emphasize learning experiences for the next stage. The following sections provide a general description of how children behave at each stage, what kind of classroom experiences they need at each stage, and what they need from you, their teacher.

Stage one of the developmental curriculum is identified as the period in a child's life when he is learning to respond to the environment with pleasure. This process begins in infancy and continues until the child has mastered the stage-one curriculum goals, usually by age four. The stage-one curriculum involves helping the child to acquire the skills that will enable him to obtain satisfactory sensorimotor experiences. These are the sensorimotor-stage processes identified by Piaget (1967, pp. 3–17) as reflex, assimilation, and accommodation. Erickson (1959) and Wolff (1960) also describe this stage as the one in which autonomy and identity are formulated. It begins with the infant's seeking gratification and security. If he experiences pleasant

Table 9-1 The Developmental Therapy Curriculum Goals

	Curriculum Areas			
Stages	**Behavior**	**Communication**	**Socialization**	**Academic Skills**
One	To trust own body and skills	To use words to satisfy needs	To trust an adult sufficiently to respond to him	To respond to the environment with processes of classification, discrimination, basic receptive-language concepts, and body coordination
Two	To participate successfully in routines and activities	To use words to affect others in constructive ways	To participate in activities with others	To participate in classroom activities with language concepts of similarities and differences, labels, use, color; numerical processese of ordering and classifying; and body coordination
Three	To apply individual skills in group processes	To use words to express self in the group	To find satisfaction in group activities	To participate in the group with basic expressive-language concepts; symbolic representation of experiences and concepts; functional semiconcrete concepts of conservation; and body coordination
Four	To contribute individual effort to group success	To use words to express awareness of relationship between feelings and behavior in self and others	To participate spontaneously and successfully as a group member	To use successfully signs and symbols in formalized school work and in group experiences
Five	To respond to critical life experiences with adaptive-constructive behavior	To use words to establish and enrich relationships	To initiate and maintain effective peer-group relationships independently	To use successfully signs and symbols for formalized school experiences and personal enrichment

* Reprinted with permission from M. M. Wood, *The Rutland Center Model . . . ,* Athens, Georgia, Rutland Center Technical Assistance Office, 1972.

feelings and has his physical needs satisfied, he develops a sense of basic trust toward people and the world around him.

In stage one, then, the first important element is awareness of the environment and of various kinds of sensation. All future growth is based on these rudimentary processes. As the growth process continues, the young child increases body control, develops increasingly more accurate eye-hand skills, and acquires a memory of sensory and motor experiences that will increase his awareness of, and involvement in, the environment. Parents and nursery school teachers are often surprised to learn that very young children are involved in a basic form of social-emotional growth during the first year of life. When a young child discovers bright, attractive objects, he pursues these stimuli with his eyes and hands. The young child usually experiments with an object in a series of tasting, touching, and dropping activities. A parent or teacher might ask, "Is all of that dropping, tasting, and touching necessary?" The answer is definitely Yes. Repeated dropping, tasting, and touching are not in themselves particularly desirable goals, but these activities are the building blocks upon which the child will increase his capacity for future responses to his environment.

During this first stage the young child displays preferences for certain objects and pleasures in certain results. That is, very early the young child begins to show preferences for certain colors, toys, or people; and in these early preferences he shows a beginning ability to discriminate between things he likes and things he does not. It is important to recognize that such preferences indicate an emerging cognitive system; the child is able to distinguish qualities or characteristics of one stimulus from another, one person from another. The child responds to stimuli selectively: that is, he reacts to the preferred stimulus in a positive way.

These early choices and preferences are the forerunners of the process of valuing. Thus, we see that the first stage of the developmental curriculum involves recognizing some elements of the environment and responding positively to those elements that bring pleasure.

In order to ensure that the child's first experiences in the school environment are satisfying and pleasurable, the environment at stage one should be predictable and attractive rather than demanding and threatening. The teacher should see that the environment is also stimulating, arousing, comfortable, and that it satisfies such basic needs as warmth, food, and social and intellectual stimulation. Disorganization and subtle complexities have no place in the stage-one classroom. During this stage, activities that encourage active responding are essential for the young child's development.

You can use a number of techniques to ensure that the stage-one child is provided with the kinds of experiences which enhance growth. A few suggestions are presented below.

Stage-One Behavior Goal: *To Trust Own Body and Skills*   Vary the types of activities you make available for the stage-one child and the type of responses required of him. Singing, listening, talking, eating, looking, running, remembering, touching, exploring, coloring, climbing, cutting, pasting, smelling are appropriate activities at this stage.

Be certain that the child has the necessary skill to seek out and master the materials and toys in the classroom. Avoid toys that require complex fine-motor skills. The child's knowledge that an activity or material is pleasure-producing, not frustrating, will be the impetus for him to seek it again. A high level of performance or skill is definitely not necessary. Such expectations will generally produce hesitancy on the child's part. Each success will increase the child's interest and involvement, and help to produce a sense of trust in his own ability. Without this essential trust in himself, his emotional and social growth may lag.

Remember, at stage one the child needs to have simple choices, activities that evoke many different sensory and motor responses, and successful outcomes. He needs to learn to trust himself in a world that he sees as exhilarating and satisfying. When a child can respond independently to play materials and can participate in directed activities without assistance, the stage-one goal for behavior is accomplished.

Stage-One Communication Goal: *To Use Words to Satisfy Needs* Choose simple words when referring to specific objects and pro-cedures. Use the same words everytime you talk about a specific activity. When asking a child to perform some simple task, use the same words from your "controlled vocabulary." For example: Show me the _____ "; or "Bring me the _____ "

When a child spontaneously uses five to eight words which have functional value in the classroom, begin to link those words together in simplified sentence models for him: "I want a drink"; "I like big cookies"; "Johnny has a red shirt"; "Sally wants to play."

When a child begins to use a series of words spontaneously to seek what he wants from adults and other children, the communication goal for stage one is mastered.

Stage-One Socialization Goal: *To Trust an Adult Sufficiently to Respond to Him* Try to involve yourself with each child in the classroom every few minutes. This does not mean interrupting his activities. Rather, find some very personal and supportive way of contacting him: catching his glance; giving him a smile, a pat, or a hug; showing approval when you observe some activity he is involved in. It is important to develop a form of nonverbal contact that is appropriate for each child. It is also important to make this contact before the child has to ask for it; if you do not, he might act out or regress to more infantile behavior. It is difficult to make contact with each child in the group every few minutes, but because of its importance to the child's social-emotional growth, try very hard to develop a system that will work for you.

At stage one the child generally plays alone, and has only limited cognitive and communication skills for organizing his play. You may help him by initiating an activity (such as stacking blocks), or by providing a few additional toys and then using a "controlled vocabulary" to help define or extend the potential of the toys. Playing imitative games that include words and gestures is another means of helping a stage-one child learn to trust you.

When a child seeks contact with an adult spontaneously and is able to use a few simple words in the contact, he has mastered the socialization goal for stage one.

Stage-One Preacademic Goal: *To Respond to the Environment with Processes of Classification, Discrimination, Basic Receptive-Language Concepts, and Body Coordination* The preacademic processes at stage one grow from the interaction of processes in the other three curriculum areas: behavior, communication, and socialization. You will recall that in the area of behavior the child must discriminate before he can develop preferences; in communication he must put specific meaning to specific situations or objects before he can develop a functioning language system; and in socialization he must learn to trust and respond positively to adults. These skills and attitudes play a major role in preparing him to meet the preacademic goals of stage one.

You can assist a stage-one child in preacademics by providing the kind of activities that will stimulate these processes: stringing beads, recognizing details in pictures, playing simple memory games, matching objects that look alike. These activities have been discussed in greater detail in preceding chapters.

As in the other areas of the curriculum, remember that each instructional activity should be restricted to a brief time period, usually five minutes or less. If instruction periods are brief, it is possible to have several such periods every day. Provide sequential steps for each activity, beginning with the simplest and moving to more complex tasks as the child shows mastery. Try to have self-correcting materials, such as simple puzzles or peg boards, whenever possible. When a child can see for himself why he succeeds or fails, he tends to develop a sense of trust in himself. If he doesn't trust himself, he may hesitate to try something new.

The goal for preacademics at stage one is mastered when a child has a functioning receptive and expressive vocabulary; when he has mastered crayons, scissors, pasting; when he can listen to simple story sequences and respond with knowledge of events; and when he can perform eye-hand coordination activities such as buttoning and unbuttoning, copying a circle, and drawing a person with at least two parts.

In the second stage of the developmental curriculum, the child develops specific skills that enable him to respond to his environment with success.

During this stage the cognitive, social-affective, and sensorimotor

Stage Two: Responding to the Environment with Success

systems cannot be separated in function. For example, it would be impossible for a child to develop a preference for a particular activity if he is unable to sequence bits of information, differentiate characteristics, separate cause and effect, or relate these bits of information to a particular situation. When he is able to determine these differences, situations will take on meaning for him.

At stage two the cognitive system organizes meaningful bits of information by the process of discriminating, categorizing, classifying, and remembering (Piaget, 1967, pp. 29–33; Krathwohl et al., 1964). When this happens the child begins to recognize relationships that eventually merge into larger concepts. With a solid foundation of specific, reality based concepts relating to himself, his preferences, his body, and his behavior, the child at stage two will develop rapidly and enlarge his repertoire of concepts: the tools for continuing intellectual development.

In the emerging social-affective system the same processes are occurring simultaneously: preferences, investments, caring, and motivations are organized into a pattern which enables the child to satisfy himself in his own environment. This process should occur so that the interaction between a child's own needs and the requirements and demands of his environment is satisfying and supportive. Feelings of self-esteem will result. Erikson (1973) describes this phase as "autonomy versus shame," where experimentation and discovery of one's self in the environment result in successful control and feeling of mastery. If a child's needs and preferences are dissonant with the expectations of his environment, a sense of inadequacy develops. The child feels that he cannot control himself and is helpless in the face of pervasive overwhelming outside forces.

The early preferences shown by the child at stage one are elaborated and built upon during stage two. The child is beginning to grow from egocentricity and from initial self-esteem into an awareness of his own preferences and the values of others. It is important to note here that this is a discriminative function and can be linked directly to the discriminative functions that occur in the cognitive system.

The sensorimotor system has an essential role in the child's development during stage two. Sensory inputs are organized into motor and memory processes, and used extensively in cognitive and social-affective development. At stage two the child takes inputs, memory functions, and outputs, and connects and orders them: categorizing, classifying, discriminating, preferring, valuing, and mastering his own functions. The mobilization of the psychobiological processes that occurred during stage one provides the impetus for continued growth during stage two. The child is mastering his own body, and developing skills for organizing and challenging his environment. The young child during this second stage is so actively involved in himself, in emerging as a person, and in developing certain basic skills, that his awareness of others is limited except in direct reference to his own preferences and his own scheme of things (Parten, 1932). You might ask at this point, "Does this behavior suggest an antisocial child? Will this child remain so self-centered that he will not be able to make or maintain effective relationships with other people?" The answer is definitely No. At stage two, it is essential that the child develops tools and processes which make him a unique, organized, venturing person with a strong sense of self-esteem.

Stage two has also been described as the testing stage. It is seen as the time for the child to explore, organize, and master the new systems he encounters in his environment. For many children it may be a period of great discomfort. If inappropriate responses, preferences, and behaviors have been established at stage one, then the stage-two child may exhibit anxiety, regression, and acting-out behavior. Toward the end of stage two we see Erikson's concepts of initiative versus guilt emerging (Erikson, 1973). The adult must carefully sequence new experiences and new confrontations so that the child sees himself as an individual with the capacity to accomplish a task or master a situation. Therefore, the ideal experiences are those that help the child acquire basic skills which will lead him to new experiences, greater skill, and more success.

It is important to remember that children at this stage generally do not have a realistic value system. They may take seriously those things which are not important to you; or they may not consider something significant which you do. Therefore, it is important to sequence experiences so that children are able to handle these experiences comfortably, understanding the essential and non-essential elements.

The developmental curriculum must be organized so that the stage-two child masters his environment with success. Please note, however, that at this stage the focus is not on responding to others with success: that occurs at stage three. During stage two, the curriculum should emphasize situations and opportunities that will permit the child to develop successful skills in thinking, in feeling and caring, and in behavior. The learning environment at this stage should provide communication activities, free play, time for exploration and self-discovery, as well as structured learning activities, to help the child organize the more complex elements in his environment.

As a teacher, what can you do for children who are developmentally at stage two? You have an important role: you are probably one of the first persons outside of the family unit that the child has any significant contact with. He senses your significance, and through his relationship with you, he will learn more about himself and others. The stage-two teacher should be the provider of experiences and materials, the delineator of boundaries, the assister in organization, the reflector of reality, a helper in achieving success, a person to provide simple missing links between concepts, between cause and effect, between self and reality. It is often a temptation for teachers and parents at this phase to work hard to establish specific performance skills in children, but this is not necessarily a productive activity at this stage of development. Think of yourself as a significant motivator of the stage-two child, and remember that the major learning is occurring within the child himself. With this in mind, you will become aware of the situations in which you are needed to direct, instruct, and guide. You will also learn when to stand back and let the child explore his environment without help.

A few techniques to enhance the growth of stage-two children are described below. With these general techniques in mind, you will be able to select those activities suggested in other chapters that will facilitate appropriate social and emotional growth.

Stage-Two Behavior Goal: *To Participate Successfully in Routines and Activities* Consider how you define "successful participation" for children between the ages of four and six. You would expect an increasing attention span and sustained periods of concentration and involvement. You would also expect participation in planned activities as well as appropriate use of play materials. And re-membering the material discussed above, you would also consider exploration and successful outcome important prerequisites for "successful participation."

Among the most effective activities for stage-two children are storytelling, creative play, art, and music. With these activities, successful participation is almost assured. The stage-two child can try out his new sense of self and begin to explore solutions to critical issues from the safety of make-believe. Provide dress-up clothes, play materials, and toys that encourage role playing, such as a playhouse, housekeeping equipment, tools, trucks and roads, towns built out of blocks, dolls representing both sexes and various racial groups. Use stories in books, or on records, or make them up as you go along. Provide scrap styrofoam, toothpicks, scraps of materials and paste for collages. Explore with the children the wide range of sound they can get from various objects and instruments. Use rhythm as a way of putting together listening skills, concentration, and exploration.

When imagination or creative interest lags, the activity may have gone on too long, or the children may have lost interest in the potential of the materials. Perhaps they did not see ways to re-late their own concerns to the materials. Perhaps it was all too complicated. You can help in such a situation by seeking reasons for the lack of response. You also can redirect a child by showing him new possibilities in the material. Through your responses you can stimulate new ideas or help organize the activity into a manageable experience.

A child who participates will learn about his environment and feel good about the results. Such a child will continue to learn.

Stage-Two Communication Goal: *To Use Words to Affect Others in Constructive Ways* To have successful communication experiences at stage two, the child must learn to use word sequences to exchange information with other children and adults, and begin to organize his world around words and ideas. As his teacher, you will play a major role in facilitating his learning. In addition to enlarging his receptive and expressive vocabulary, building on processes begun in stage one, you will need to provide verbal links between what is happening and what a child is feeling or doing. Probably this is the greatest challenge for the stage-two teacher.

You should use simple word sequences and sentences to describe play; in time, your verbal patterns will become models for the children. In this way they learn appropriate words to describe experience, ideas, and feelings. As you become more aware of your impact as a communication model, begin to monitor your own language output. Are you specific in language structure? Do you respond to essential elements in an activity? Do your comments help clarify what is happening? Do you provide a model for expressing feelings appropriately?

In addition to your role as a communication model, you will find that you can redirect activities by describing the realities of a situation. Your communication activities will stimulate the child to rely more and more upon his own communication skills to help himself understand and be understood in the world around him.

A major resource for developing communication skills is children's literature. Select stories that have children involved with other children and their families. Try stories of children having adventures. Use favorite stories over and over. Let the children supply a key word, an important sentence, describe a character's feelings, or tell what could happen next. Children enjoy telling familiar stories to each other and dramatizing them during creative-play times.

Stage-Two Socialization Goal: *To Participate in Activities with Others* Because the stage-two child is so intensely involved with himself and the accumulation of the skills necessary to meet new physical challenges, he usually gives very little effort to social exchanges. His socialization can be described as a minimal movement toward others. During stage two, a child goes through a series of steps in socialization that take him from solitary play to the point where he plays cooperatively with others and begins to develop an awareness of the individual characteristics of his peers.

As a teacher of stage-two children, there is much you can do to move the socialization process along.

1. Each day discuss with the group who is present and who is missing.
2. Help children learn other children's first names.
3. Reflect feelings expressed by the children.
4. Help the group remember whose turn is next.
5. Encourage selection of partners.
6. Encourage one child to participate in some activity with another child at play time.

7. Provide opportunities for sharing supplies or materials.

8. Organize games such as Drop the Hanky, Cat and Mouse, or Musical Chairs, where all can participate.

9. Redesign games so that there are no losers (stage-three children are better able to cope with the experience of losing).

10. Use long strips of butcher paper for group murals; suggest a common theme and assign each child a section of the mural to complete.

11. Start a group story; have each child contribute an idea or a sentence to the story.

12. Use storytelling, creative play, and role playing to help children see their common concerns and interests.

If you will review the discussion of the teacher's role in the sections on stage-two behavior and communication, you will see that all those techniques can be used to facilitate the socialization process. Keep in mind the importance of including experiences for thinking, doing, and caring in every one of your activities.

Stage-Two Preacademic Goal: *To Participate in Classroom Activities with Language Concepts of Similarities and Differences, Labels, Use, Color; Numerical Processes of Ordering and Classifying; and Body Coordination* Preacademic activities for the stage-two child should follow the same sequence of growth mentioned in the previous curriculum discussions; that is, moving from simple concepts and limited language to a complex series of activities. You may have noticed that many of the activities discussed previously have preacademic importance. The more you weave preacademic goals and activities into the other curriculum areas, the more you facilitate the child's growth in each area.

Begin increasing the scope of the vocabulary you use with the child. Include words to describe how objects can be used in play. Teach opposites such as "up" and "down," "under" and "over," "big" and "little," "hot" and "cold," "first" and "last." These concepts do not have to be taught in formal instructional settings. They are easily woven into the fabric of play, music, or storytelling.

Remember the discussion of socialization activities? We mentioned that stage-two children can be helped to become aware of the individual characteristics and feelings of others. The preacademic counterpart to this is, first, to recognize details in pictures, then to identify feelings of people in pictures, and eventually sequence events in picture series.

During stage two most children become intrigued with counting, enumeration, and numerical grouping. When you plan numerical activities keep in mind the nature of the child at this stage. Remember his need to master his environment, to involve himself physically, and to succeed. Again, by including the developmental sequences of enumeration into all of the classroom experiences, you will facilitate the child's mastery of numbers, as well as his social and emotional growth.

Some teachers do not consider body coordination and eye-hand skill to be preacademic goals. However, others believe that competence in these areas is absolutely essential if learning disabilities are to be avoided when the child goes to school. From the standpoint of the developmental curriculum such skills are absolutely essential to the development of social and emotional growth. The activities planned for a stage-two child in body coordination and eye-hand tasks should reflect skills which were activated but not polished at stage one. These skills are the child's tools for growth. Without them he will fail, feel inadequate, and fear the consequences of involvement with others. With them, he can move toward new challenges with the confidence built upon previous successes.

Chapter 5 provides you with many suggestions to promote success in the areas of body coordination and eye-hand skills.

Entering stage three, the child has the basic intellectual, social, emotional, and physical skills he needs to enlarge his own experiences and his knowledge of himself in relation to others. Stage three is the period when the child learns to apply the skills he learned during the stage-two level of development to group processes and procedures.

Stage Three: Learning Skills for Successful Group Participation

During this stage of development the child's cognitive system, which formerly organized information into discrete categories, begins to sequence information into broader concepts. Ordinarily, the stage-three child is beginning first grade. In most cases, he has accomplished the goals for this stage by the time he has finished the third grade. Just as more complex concepts are forming in the cognitive system, caring and preferences are being organized into a system of values in relation to other people. In the sensorimotor system, awareness of his own body had developed sufficiently to enable a child to receive, integrate, and respond to increasingly complex situations.

The developmental curriculum at stage three must focus on social expectations (rules), on the child as a valued member of the group, on consequences of behavior, on the child's effect on others, and on adaptation to social situations. This is the stage when you as the teacher must be responsive to feelings; explore with children the boundaries of reality; help them learn to share with others, to control impulsivity, to participate in planning group rules and procedures, and, in general, to see that social cooperation and communication can be pleasurable and desirable. According to Piaget (1967, pp. 38–41) and Bobroff (1960), this is the time when group activity and team effort should emerge. This merging is most clearly seen in children's play, which begins with an emphasis on make-believe and magical solutions during the early phases of stage three, and moves in the later phases to problem solving by simple rules. Playing games and controlling social situations by rules signifies the emergence of a major developmental milestone for stage three. The child is now able to conform to rules established by the group.

Other significant processes occuring during stage three are the emergence of body concept, body image, and body schema. These terms are defined as follows.

Body Concept: knowledge of one's body, body parts, and functions of the body.

Body Image: the awareness of certain feelings and attitudes about oneself.

Body Schema: the organization of proprioceptive, affective, and kinesthetic senses nito a general integration and awareness of the capacities and limitations of one's own body.

As described by Erikson (1973, pp. 64–69) and Lowenfeld and Brittain (1970, pp. 145–52), body image and body schema seem to emerge during this period of "industry versus inferiority," where same-sex identification and an emerging sense of self are predominant. According to Koppetz (1968) a child's drawings of a person are an indicator of affective and social awareness at this stage, as well as eye-hand coordination and cognitive development. Such drawings reflect the interactive effect of these three systems upon each other.

In the organized sensorimotor system of stage three the child has developed the capacity to translate concepts and feelings into motor responses that express cognitive and affective processes through knowledge and preferences. At this stage a well-functioning body schema is an important factor in developing a positive body image. It is hard to separate the concept of body image and the concept of body schema. The way a child feels about himself as a worthwhile, successful person will be affected by his body schema (that is, how well his body is working for or against his motivations and drives). It is during this stage that physically or mentally handicapped children often show that they are aware of their limitations. This awareness may be directly due to a body concept of disability or difference and an attitude of self-denigration arising from a negative body image and an ineffective body schema.

Stage-Three Behavior Goal: *To Apply Individual Skills in Group Processes*   Three effective activities to help children master the stage-three behavior goal are group games, more complex toys, and group art projects. It is easy to understand the importance of these three types of activities in light of the preceding discussion about stage three.

Games bring children together. If the rules are simple, and there are opportunities for both success and failure, children at stage three gain the very important sense of "groupness." They learn that a feeling of individual success can result from participation in group success. They learn that they must wait their turn to participate, and that rules are necessary to hold both themselves and others in line.

Examples of games enjoyed by stage-three children are Beanbag Tag, Battling Tops, Kickball, Red Rover, Mother May I, School, Red Light, Store, relay races, Kick the Can, Picture Lotto, Bingo, and simple card games.

Toys preferred by stage-three children include miniature figures of people, soldiers, and animals; houses and toy cities; trucks, cars, and roadways; suction-dart guns; Lincoln Logs; erector sets; hand-puppets; adventure books which can be enjoyed without reading skills; and space and adventure toys. When selecting toys for stage-three children consider the processes they need to develop: participation in group activities (with rules) and recognition of the characteristics of others. Most important, the child should feel good about his own ability to share toys with others.

Art activities offer great possibilities for stimulating stage-three growth in behavior. Art activities also promote growth in self-concept, body image, and body concept. Unlined paper, pencils, crayons, paste, felt pens, and magic markers offer unlimited possibilities. You can extend a child's knowledge about the possibilities of these materials by varying the size, shape, and color of the paper he uses. The use of art materials should be preceded by a discussion about procedures in handling materials, the need for sharing, and cooperative planning. Cooperative cleanup is an important part of any activity planned for stage three.

Stage-Three Socialization Goal: *To Find Satisfaction in Group Activities*   Socialization is perhaps the most significant area of the developmental curriculum for the stage-three child. From a developmental standpoint, all his previous experiences and accomplishments are put to the test when he becomes involved in the group process. So often we expect a child to give up his newly developed sense of self to the demands of others. We forget that successful group participation requires certain skills that are probably not in the repertoire of the young stage-three child. He will need support and a model to learn such processes as taking turns, sharing materials, participating in group planning, accepting suggestions from other children, developing reciprocal friendships with other children, and recognizing the needs and characteristics of others. If you refer back to the list of socialization activities for stage two, you will see that such activities are designed to prepare the child to meet the socialization demands of stage three. If you find a child having difficulty at the stage-three level, lead him back to stage-two activities. You will very likely find that the child was not successful at that stage either. Begin where he was successful, and gradually introduce new activities he can successfully accomplish.

Stage-Three Academic Goal: *To Participate in the Group with Basic Expressive-Language Concepts; Symbolic Representation of Experiences and Concepts; Functional, Semiconcrete Concepts of Conservation; and Body Coordination*   The academic goals for stage three of the developmental curriculum are essentially identical with the goals for the primary grades. During stage three a child moves from the kindergarten readiness level to the mastery of basic learning processes.

It is easy to see how necessary the previous stages are in preparing a child for this task. To meet stage-three academic goals, a child must have eye-hand coordination; he must have acquired left-to-right reading and writing orientation; he must have a receptive vocabulary close to others his age; he must be able to reproduce forms and remember what the forms mean. During this stage the child also must learn to recognize numbers, know how to change numbers, and how to express numerical operations in symbolic form.

Success in such efforts depends, then, upon the skills the child brings from previous stages of development. He must feel that experiences are interesting enough to warrant translation into symbolic form. He must have enough confidence in himself to persist in learning difficult new tasks. If he is still struggling unsuccessfully to meet the demands of group participation, he will not be free to put his energies into mastery of the symbolic world.

Stage Four: Investing in Group Processes

In stage three a child learns skills necessary for successful group participation; in stage four he acquires an investment in group processes. Family groups, peer groups, and school groups are important forces for the stage-four child. In the process of becoming aware of the many different value systems of these groups, the stage-four child sifts through his own concerns and values. He seeks a comfortable balance between his inner and outer life. He has learned about himself and is involved in learning more about others. From this knowledge he will absorb and identify others' values as his own. This is the time of concrete operations, a time to generalize from experiences in order to perform mental operations.

In the social-affective system, we see the child begin to select value systems, identifying and assimilating them for his own. Erickson (1973, pp. 69–74) describes this as the emergence of identity. He describes the critical issue at this phase as "identity versus identity diffusion."

In the sensorimotor systems we see complete functioning sensory processes: visual, auditory, tactile, kinesthetic, and olfactory. Stage-four children rely on the completed sensory systems for all subsequent adolescent and adult activities.

Children who are at the stage-four level are usually between the ages of eight and twelve. Although this age span is beyond the scope of this book, I believe that an awareness of the sequence of maturation is essential for a teacher working with children of all ages and developmental stages.

If you agree that social-emotional development should be considered in planning a curriculum, then you will begin to look for ways to include such experiences in your teaching efforts. Remember that social and emotional development are not processes that can be isolated from other aspects of development. As a teacher concerned with social-emotional development, you should be aware of the ways in which every activity combines cognitive, social-affective and sensorimotor skills. The developmental curriculum suggests that every lesson you conduct should include elements each of four curriculum areas: *behavior, communication, socialization,* and *preacademics/academics.*

Finally, be sensitive to the sequential observable steps a child must go through in this process. Identify his stage of development in each of the four social-emotional curriculum areas. Recognize that your role is to assist him in achieving the goals that he has not accomplished. The results will be well worth the effort. You will see a child who has developed a level of emotional and social maturity commensurate with his age and the expectations of those around him. A socially and emotionally effective child is a productive child, able to meet the demands of life: thinking, caring, and doing.

Checkpoint
What Have You Learned?

1. Social-_____, _____, and sensorimotor processes are intricately **Facts**
   interlinked in the development of the young child.

2. The young child learns, grows, and develops through _____.

3. It is difficult if not impossible to separate the emotional and social development of the child from his _____ development.

4. The stage entitled "_____" is often described as the testing stage. It is seen as the time for the child to explore, organize, and master simple new systems that the environment is ready to offer.

5. What stage of the social-emotional developmental curriculum focuses upon the assimilation and adaptation of values of others in social groups?

6. Stage one of the developmental curriculum model is: Responding to the Environment with _____.

7. If the child has the intellectual, social, emotional, and sensorimotor skills necessary to enable him to enlarge his experiences, he is ready to be placed in a stage _____ environment. This stage is called _____.

Simulation
1. Discuss the emotional and social characteristics of a child who is (a) at the first stage of development in the developmental curriculum; (b) the third stage.

2. You are teaching a class of 20 kindergarten children and have been able to identify four children who are at the second stage of social-emotional development: responding to the environment with success. Discuss the kind of environment you might provide for these children and your role in interacting with them.

Application
Visit a preschool in your area and observe the children. Select three children and through your observation decide at which stage of the developmental curriculum they are functioning. List the behaviors you observed that characterized that stage of development.

Chapter 10   Adapting the Curriculum for the Developmentally Handicapped

Objectives

After you have completed this chapter, you should be able to:

1. Cite three goals of preschool education for handicapped children.
2. Define the term *developmentally handicapped.*
3. Cite the rationale for limiting the age range of the developmentally handicapped to children eight or below.
4. Cite at least three reasons why the Developmental Task Instructional System is ideal for use with developmentally handicapped children.
5. Cite and discuss at least three ways to adapt the Developmental Task Instructional System to developmentally handicapped children.

A little before nine on a Monday morning, Danny arrives at the preschool center for developmentally handicapped children. He climbs the steps with his mother, hanging back a step below her, clinging to her hand. Danny is five. He is a small child, with smooth brown hair, a narrow nose and chin, pale skin, and rather large low-set ears. His eyes are squeezed half-shut.

When Danny's mother opens the door to the classroom, he shrinks against her; when she tries to lift him over the threshold, he wraps his arms around her legs.

Mrs. Stanton, the preschool teacher, comes up to him. "Hey, Danny," she says. "It's good to see you this morning."

Danny huddles closer into himself and doesn't answer. His thumb creeps to his mouth.

"Let's get your coat off," she suggests.

"No." This "No," is probably the last word Danny will say until he is working with the teacher or the aide, safely screened off from everyone else.

Now Jimmy comes in. He lurches ahead of his mother, legs wide apart, knees scarcely bending, still as uncertain of his balance as a toddler. Jimmy is also five, taller than Danny, squarely built, with strawberry-blond curls. He doesn't seem to notice when his mother takes off his coat. His gaze wanders around the room, never really seeming to focus on any one spot or any one person.

"Good morning, Jimmy," says Mrs. Stanton. "Say 'Hi'."

Still looking around aimlessly, Jimmy opens his mouth and makes a long unarticulated sound. Then he trudges over to the tricycle.

Bob is next. A tall six-and-one-half-year-old, Bob bursts through the door grinning. His eyes are wide and alert behind the glasses that hold them in focus. His lips hang somewhat apart. A drop of moisture trails from the lower lip. He runs to the teacher, to the aide, to each child in turn, with a delighted, unintelligible greeting. Each person gets a hug or a pat. He then continues his trip around the room, touching everything, picking up everything that can be picked up. He uses his left hand; his thinner right arm remains slightly bent, the right hand hangs limp.

"Can you hang up your coat, Bob?" Mrs. Stanton asks. He nods vigorously, pulls the buttons apart one-handed and hangs the coat on the hook labeled with his name.

Alicia appears at the door, waves goodbye to her mother and looks about her with a confident elfish grin. Bob races up to hug her. She babbles happily and kisses him on the cheek. Alicia is a five-and-one-half-year old, smaller than any of the others, with bright oriental-looking eyes and thin flyaway hair. She lets Bob pull her over to the rocking boat, but she keeps looking around the room intently, studying the teacher, copying her gestures, watching the other children.

Jimmy has been riding the tricycle, not pedaling, but scooting it along backward with his feet. Now he has backed into the wall and sits there puzzled, whimpering. Bob leaps out of the boat, runs to him, hops onto the back of the tricycle and propels it to the middle of the room. Then he tears back to Alicia and gives her another enthusiastic hug as he climbs into the boat again. Alicia crows her pleasure.

Jimmy stops whimpering and resumes his stolid backward ride.

The aide, Miss Hauser, has removed Danny's coat. Danny stays huddled against the wall, his thumb in his mouth. When Miss Hauser speaks to him he squeezes his eyes shut, blotting her out. She kneels near him and talks to him softly. His eyes open gradually and his hand drops. Bob, who has given up the boat, gallops over and touches Miss Hauser for her attention. He talks rapidly, making exaggerated gestures with his good arm to illustrate the words his mouth will not pronounce.

Danny shields his face with his hands.

Alicia is charging back and forth with the doll carriage, jabbering to the dolls she has put in it. One by one the rest of the children arrive.

"All right, children," Mrs. Stanton says. "Let's find the hats and march."

Bob, Danny, Alicia, Jimmy, and their classmates are fortunate. They live in a school district that recognizes the need for preschool programs for handicapped children. For years the primary focus of educational efforts for handicapped children was centered on the late-elementary- and junior-high-age child. These are the ages when the child having academic difficulties usually comes to the attention of school officials: either because tests reveal that the child has dropped two or three years behind his classmates (usually sometime between the third and sixth grades) or because the onset of puberty has triggered extreme social-emotional problems (sometime during the sixth, seventh, or eighth grade).

The Need for Preschools for Handicapped Children

It is unfortunate that learning problems are not identified earlier because, as we have learned, educators and child-development experts agree that educational intervention has its greatest effect on children of preschool age. During this time span, learning interacts with maturation more intensely than at any other time in the individual's life. There have been numerous studies in recent years pointing out the effectiveness of early childhood educational programs in increasing the ability and potential of children with varying types of handicaps and problems (Gray et al, 1966; Guskin and Spicker, 1968). It is quite apparent from this evidence that the need for intervention at a very early age is more urgent for the handicapped child.

A structured preschool program for handicapped children should have at least three main goals for each child enrolled.

Goals of Preschool Education for the Handicapped

1. *Increase the rate of growth in each specific area of development.* Unless the child's rate of growth is increased substantially, he will always be behind in those particular areas. For example, if a child grows in language skills at a rate of only six months per year, each year he will fall further behind his chronological-age peers. The preschool's job is to maximize the rate of development for that particular child.

2. *Longitudinal assessment and diagnosis.* For educational as well as medical purposes, a formal objective assessment provides the information needed for planning an individual program. Continuing informal assessment provides specific information for establishing both treatment and educational objectives. Neurological and physical evaluations during the preschool years should provide additional diagnostic information for possible medical, nutritional, or therapeutic treatment, as well as for continued educational treatment.

3. *Specific skill training to provide readiness for the next educational placement.* This goal will naturally overlap with the first goal listed above. However, there are specific skills that are not necessarily within the province of one of the developmental curriculum areas which need to be learned as prerequisites for the next educational placement. Such skills might include sitting and attending for twenty minutes in a structured lesson situation; or, if the next placement is a regular

first-grade classroom, skills needed might include counting to ten, recall of the alphabet, and discrimination and identification of five colors.

Defining Developmentally Handicapped

The children described at the beginning of this chapter have one thing in common. Each came to the attention of his parents, physician, or social worker because he did not display normal signs of growth and development. This lack of development interfered with his ability to cope with environmental demands, and thus was recognized as a handicapping condition.

Similar children may be found in any section of the United States in any number of specialized or nonspecialized preschool classes. Visit a preschool for the mentally retarded, a preschool for neurologically impaired children, Mrs. Johnson's Play School, a preschool for disadvantaged children, or a public school kindergarten. You will see children similar to Bob, Danny, Alicia, and Jimmy.

Children are developmentally handicapped for a variety of reasons. If Bob or Jimmy had been placed in a program organized on the principle of homogeneous grouping according to etiology, or symptom, they would be in a preschool for brain-injured or neurologically impaired children. Alicia might be in a program for mongoloid (Down's syndrome) children. Danny could very well be in a preschool for maladjusted or disturbed children. On another classification dimension, the children discussed previously could be placed in a preschool for trainable mentally retarded or just mentally retarded.

In an educationally oriented preschool intervention program the focus should be on strengthening developmental abilities rather than identifying the reasons why a child is behind developmentally. This in contrast to focusing on academic topics, such as reading, writing, and number concepts. As we have discussed previously, developmental abilities are the prerequisites for academic-skill building. There will be plenty of time later in the child's school life for instruction in academic subjects.

A developmentally handicapped child, then, is a child of eight or under who has a one-third or greater deficiency in two or more of the following specific areas of development: perception, gross motor, fine motor, receptive language, expressive language, and reasoning.

We limit our definition of a developmentally handicapped child to children eight or under because we believe that, for older children, the focus of educational intervention should be on life and academic tasks. Rather than concentrating on language development with the ten-year-old child (unless there is a demonstrated language deficit), it is much more realistic to concentrate on the reading tasks he must cope with in school. Even though a child of ten has a two- or three-year deficit in language development, fine-motor development, or one of the other developmental areas, his developmental foundation is strong enough for the building of successful reading skills. In such a case, continuing to emphasize instruction for developmental abilities will retard the child further in academic skills.

We use a one-third or greater level of deficiency to define developmentally handicapped because this measure approximates two standard deviations below the mean on widely used intelligence tests. This is slightly below the cutoff point generally used in traditional definitions for handicapping conditions, but we take into consideration the fact that there is a greater range of normalcy in developmental abilities. Two standard deviations below the mean on the *Stanford-Binet Intelligence Scale* translates as an IQ of 70, which would indicate to many traditional diagnosticians that a child is mentally retarded and should be placed in a class for the educable mentally retarded.

We consider a child developmentally handicapped, a term which we believe is much more relevant to the educational needs of the young child, when he is one-third below the normal range in two developmental areas. We believe that at this point his deficiency is serious enough to call for specialized attention and specialized educational procedures.

As we mentioned earlier, a developmentally handicapped child is one who has a marked impairment in at least two areas of development. A developmental lag of this nature is of such magnitude that a regular preschool program will probably not meet the child's needs. A lag in only one area of development, however, should not be generalized as a handicap; it will not be as debilitating to the child, and can generally be handled in a regular program with some special attention.

Adapting the Developmental Task Instructional System for the Handicapped Child

The use of the concept of developmentally handicapped should be limited to preschool children who, because of the severity of their developmental lags, cannot be given the individualized attention they need when placed in a regular preschool program. The special needs of these children can be attended to more effectively individually or in small groups. Adaptation of the instructional system discussed in previous chapters to the developmentally handicapped child is a fairly uncomplicated procedure. Because the system is based on an individualized approach to early childhood education, it is not difficult for any teacher to apply it to children having developmental difficulties.

Not only can the Developmental Task Instructional System be used quite successfully with handicapped children in special programs, but it can also be used to provide effective instruction to mildly handicapped and high-risk children enrolled in regular day-care and preschool programs. Let's look briefly at the adaptations you will want to consider at each stage of the Developmental Task Instructional System.

Assessment

With many developmentally handicapped children an assessment instrument such as the *Carolina Developmental Profile* can be used effectively to gain the information you need to establish instructional objectives. With some handicapped children, however, you may find that the items are inappropriate because of the handicapping condition; for example, hearing loss, vision loss, or severe retardation. Although there are a few standardized tests available for specialized populations, in most instances you will probably need to rely on developmental checklists geared to the developmental tasks that you can realistically hope to see the child accomplish during the year. The danger, of course, is that you must avoid either over- or underestimating the child's present abilities and his capacity to learn new skills. To avoid these errors you should draw up your checklist on the basis of your observations of what the child can and cannot do. Do not try to generalize capabilities from the results of a standardized test or from a few checklist items.

As you assess a handicapped child, analyze carefully the tasks that he is requested to accomplish. For example, you might ask Charles to "take three blocks and build a bridge for me," and when Charles fails to make the bridge, you might chalk it up as an inability to complete a motor task. Perhaps the task with which he had difficulty was a receptive-language or reasoning one: not knowing the concepts of "three" or "bridge." Be careful to isolate the various aspects of a task so that you know specifically what the child is—or is not—able to do.

At the end of chapter 3 a number of assessment instruments were presented that can be adapted for use with handicapped children. One way of using these tests is to take only the items that fit in with your overall goals, and use them in a checklist procedure as observable criteria that the child meets or does not meet.

Establishing Objectives   In establishing your instructional objectives for the handicapped child you should proceed as you normally would, based on earlier discussion. However, you should give a great deal of thought to establishing the rate for achieving specified tasks. Observe the handicapped child's abilities closely early in the year, so that your estimates for the time required to achieve long-range objectives will be as accurate as possible.

A task-analysis approach is often used for setting short-range objectives for handicapped children. (You will remember from previous discussion that the task-analysis approach involves breaking a task down into smaller subtasks.) For example, your long-range objective might be to develop a child's skipping ability so that he can skip a minimum distance of 20 yards. In order to skip, however, the child must first be able to hop up and down on each foot, and then hop up and down on each foot while he is moving forward. Therefore you establish a series of short-range objectives: hopping up and down on the right foot; hopping up and down on the right foot while moving forward; hopping up and down on the left foot; and hopping up and down on the left foot while moving forward. Each of these objectives is a subobjective for the long-range objective of skipping.

Establishing Activities   The procedures used here are much the same as those used with so-called normal children. If the activities are selected with the instructional objectives in mind, they should be appropriate. Multilevel curriculum materials should be available so that the handicapped child can follow the same routine as other children in your program, but with simpler materials.

As you plan activities for the handicapped child, plan for more one-to-one relationships between teacher and child, either in smaller instructional groups or in tutoring situations. With handicapped children you will want to include more structured practice with plenty of opportunities for repetition of skills.

Although there are a number of different learning characteristics identified with certain handicapping conditions (for example, mental retardation), if you follow a precise system of assessing the child's abilities and establish realistic objectives you will minimize the need to focus on some of these characteristics. For example, a shorter attention span is often cited as a characteristic of the mentally retarded child. However, when you assess the child, attention span will be measured only as one component of the child's various abilities. In other words, attention span interacts with the task itself and becomes integrated with it. As you establish objectives, then, your objectives will reflect the attention span of the child.

More structure is needed for the handicapped child during both the acquisition of new skills and the practice/generalization of these skills. Often generalization may not take place unless you set up a structured instructional situation for that specific purpose. For example, during an acquisition-stage lesson you have concentrated on developing vocabulary dealing with various articles of clothing, and are satisfied with the child's ability to label various pictures of articles of clothing in a large picture dictionary. Rather than relying on the handicapped child to use these new vocabulary labels in other situations, you should set up appropriate practice/generalization activities. In this instance, it may be in a play situation where the child is dressing a doll. Encourage the child to tell another child what articles of clothing he or she is now placing on the doll. Setting up integrated-day activities around the classroom that call for the use of the skills learned in the more formal acquisition periods is essential for maximum generalization of abilities.

The Learning Situation

Checkpoint

What Have You Learned?

Facts

1. A developmentally handicapped child is a child of _____ or under who has a one-third or greater _____ in _____ or more developmental areas. Name the six developmental areas.

2. When considering the goals of preschool programs for the handicapped, increasing the rate of development will overlap to some extent with the goal of providing _____.

3. A one-third or greater deficiency is used in the definition for a developmentally handicapped child because it approximates _____ below the mean on widely used intelligence tests.

4. A ten-year-old child should not be considered developmentally handicapped because the educational focus must shift away from _____ tasks to _____ tasks or other life tasks that are appropriate for the child.

Simulation

1. Billy Anthony is a six-year-old child who demonstrates a three-and-one-half-year level of functioning in gross-motor development. All other development areas fall in the six-year-old range. Should he be classified as developmentally handicapped? Support your response with discussion.

2. Discuss the assessment adaptations you would need to make with (a) a blind child, (b) a hearing impaired child, and (c) a child who is confined to a wheelchair.

Application

1. Visit a class for preschool-age handicapped children in your vicinity. Using the *Carolina Developmental Profile* as a guide, observe and rate one child's developmental abilities. In how many areas, if any, does he or she demonstrate a one-third or greater deficiency?

2. Volunteer to tutor a child in a local program for preschool-age handicapped children. Select one objective for instruction and keep a record of your efforts, particularly noting the adaptations that are necessary as you proceed through the Developmental Task Instructional System.

Chapter 11 Planning a Parent Program

Objectives

After you have completed this chapter, you should be able to:

1. List five reasons for establishing parent programs.
2. Cite the two major purposes of parent programs.
3. List and describe the four major activity areas or dimensions of parent programs.
4. List and describe the three main parent-child interaction models in use today.
5. List six possible roles that parents can play in a preschool program.

It is eight o'clock, Tuesday evening. Mrs. McCready, head teacher at the East Side Head Start center, is anxiously counting the number of parents, almost all mothers, coming into the library. Tonight is the scheduled once-a-month parents' meeting. "I hope we have a better turnout than last time," Mrs. McCready says to herself. Miss Haywood, one of the center's teachers, listens with impatience to one mother as she explains why her husband was unable to come tonight. "Why should I have to put in this extra time after a hard day's work?" thinks Miss Haywood. "What's the purpose of this? Most of the parents don't come anyway. Why don't we forget this parent program business and concentrate on the children?"

There are a number of good reasons why early childhood educators attempt to involve parents in their programs. Research studies (Gray, 1970) point out that unless educational efforts in day-care centers,

Why Parent Programs?

nurseries, Head Start centers, and public schools are augmented by parent involvement these efforts will be only marginally successful.

During the early years of life, a large proportion of what the young and developing child learns occurs in the home environment. The parent, particularly the child's mother or mother surrogate, is the primary "teacher." This is true even if the child is enrolled in a substitute-care situation. Unless there is some correlation between the center's educational program and the experiences taking place in the home environment, the center program may not have as much effect on the child's development. Two-way communication between parents and program staff is essential, not only to coordinate training between home and center but also to give the staff valuable insight into the development of the child. For instance, if parents report their observations of the child's behavior in the home, the staff can plan more appropriate activities for the child at the center.

As consumers who are paying for a service, if not through fees then through public taxes, parents should participate in planning activities to make sure that they receive the type of services they want. The gap between parents' expectations and the services the center or school provides must become as narrow as possible. Then, too, many parents derive social value from the group activities that are part of the center's parent program. Meeting with other parents to work together for the common good of their children develops positive feelings in the parent. This is particularly true in the case of the modern housewife-mother. The mother who devotes all her time and energy to child-rearing receives little recognition in a society that is placing an increasingly higher value on the woman who works outside the home.

As we said earlier, the success of any preschool program is determined to a great extent by a partnership between parents and staff, a partnership that is based on mutual respect, honesty, and teamwork. You cannot produce such an atmosphere unless you are willing from the outset to be nonjudgmental toward parents. Although parents may have little formal knowledge of child development, they contribute a great deal to the child's development. Therefore, they must be encouraged to provide an emotionally warm, secure environment for their child, and to support and reinforce progress and positive behavior.

Very often parents tend to focus on problem behavior and to ignore the more positive aspects of the child's behavior. For instance, when parents note that their child is having difficulty accepting appropriate limits or discipline, they may feel that their youngster is not developing adequate respect for authority, and become convinced that this "lack of respect" will create serious problems during adolescence and later life. They may not notice the times when the child's behavior is quite appropriate, or they may not respond to that behavior. On the contrary, they may be constantly on guard for misbehavior and even set up artificial situations that encourage it.

Parents should be made aware of the fact that you share similar goals. Both of you are concerned with the optimal development of the child in all spheres—physical, emotional, intellectual, social, and interpersonal. Both want the child to reach the highest possible level of adaptation. The program needs the parents' cooperation and assistance in a variety of ways, and parents need support, advice, direction, and information from the program personnel. None of this can be accomplished unless there is a close, compatible working relationship between staff and family.

The major purposes for establishing parent programs in early childhood education are: (1) to improve the center's effectiveness in providing services to children through parent cooperation and feedback; and (2) to provide a supportive system for parents in accepting their role as parents and fulfilling their personal needs as individuals.

"O.K.! I understand the importance and need for providing services for parents, but what services should I provide?" Before you think in terms of providing specific services, you should first consider the four most important areas of a parent program: providing emotional support for parents, exchanging information with parents, improving parent-child interactions, and developing parent participation in your program.

Dimensions of Parent Programs

The purpose of activities in this area is: (1) to reduce anxieties caused by guilt feelings and feelings of inadequacy in the family; and (2) to provide socially stimulating activities that increase positive feelings about the family unit as well as the parents' feelings about themselves as competent parents.

Providing Social and Emotional Support

The birth of a child is in itself a potential crisis situation: the life-style of the present family members almost always changes as a result of the necessary changing of roles within the family. The ability of a family to welcome the arrival of a helpless infant depends on the maturity of the parents and their sense of self-esteem as persons and spouses. From early pregnancy on, the prospect of a new baby may cause frustration, even resentment, in parents (Enzer, 1972).

One of the most important ways you can help parents who are experiencing feelings of self-doubt, resentment, and inadequacy is to listen to what they have to say about their children. To be effective in this role, however, you must be able to listen in a calm, sympathetic, and nonjudgmental manner.

The ability to listen to the expression of feelings in a nonjudgmental way is only possible when the listener is sincerely convinced that feelings are always acceptable, even though the behavior engendered by such feelings may be detrimental to parent and child. A careful discrimination between feelings and actions is helpful both to the parent and to you as a teacher. Most parents will experience a great deal of relief at the opportunity to talk to someone who will listen. And most parents are willing to accept advice and helpful information from a sympathetic listener.

A few parents, because of prior emotional difficulties or lack of support, may be overwhelmed by their feelings. These parents may not experience a sense of relief by venting their feelings and may need additional professional help.

As you work with parents, be accepting, be understanding, and be yourself. Giving lip service to acceptance will be ineffective. All of us have learned to understand nonverbal language, and although you may say "I accept what you say," true attitudes will come through. Acceptance does not mean total approval of everything the parent says or does. It does mean that the teacher accepts the feelings that underlie the "unhealthy" attitudes of undesirable behavior, and helps the parent deal with feelings in a constructive fashion (Enzer, 1972).

Often the objective in this area is to help parents achieve a more positive attitude about their role as educators and—perhaps more important—to increase their feelings about their own importance as worthwhile human beings. There are many ways to meet the social-emotional needs of your parents, once you have identified what those needs are.

Often these needs can be met through meetings and activities with other parents in your program. Topics in these meetings may vary from a discussion of the various types of craft activities that parent and child can do together, to book reviews, to lectures by experts in the field. It is important, however, that the members of the group indicate to one another, through actions as well as words, that these meetings hold value for them.

On the facing page you will find a program outline for parent-involvement activities. As you can see, the first objective is primarily concerned with the emotional support of parents, centering around reducing anxiety in parents who are having difficulty coping with the stress of child rearing.

Exchanging Information

Activities established for parents in this area should lead to the following goals: (1) providing parents with an understanding of the rationale, objectives, and activities of the program in which their child is enrolled; (2) helping parents understand the processes involved in the growth and development of their child, and how these processes relate to the child's behavior and activities in the home; and (3) providing the project personnel with background information on the child to facilitate the effectiveness of the center program. This information should include descriptions of the child's activities in the home.

There are many different kinds of information you can and should be giving your parents about the program. Well-thought-out discussion or written information indicating what you hope to accomplish during the year is extremely important for the continuing support and interest of parents. What changes will they see in their children? What new accomplishments can they look forward to? When you have described your goals, your parents will then understand how the many things that go on during the year relate to your stated objectives. Periodically parents should be given a preview

Planning Outline For Parent Involvement

Goal: Involvement of parents in partnership arrangements stressing the needs, strengths, concerns, and special knowledge the parents have and utilizing the expertise of the professional.

Objective	Activities	Evaluation Plan
To reduce anxiety by the end of the second year of the project in 90 percent of the parents.	Parent group discussion in which parents discuss their efforts to help their child and the problems they have encountered in such effort. A social worker will be assigned and will be available to each parent two hours a week for individual counseling.	Records will be kept listing parents who participate and their time of involvement. Anxiety levels will be measured by a scale (the IPAT 8-Parallel Form Anxiety Battery) as the parents enter the program and at the end of the second year.
To increase in 80 percent of the parents an understanding of the program's objectives and strategies for their children six months after their child is enrolled.	One week after the child is accepted into the program a family conference will be held at which time the program objectives and strategies will be explained. Written reports of child's progress will be sent to parents monthly. Parents report the child's home progress to the staff in individual monthly conferences.	The Parent Program Evaluator will develop an instrument that will measure the parents' understanding of the strategies and objectives of their child's program. Each parent will respond to that instrument six months after their child enters the program, either in writing or in a parent interview, or both.
To increase the effectiveness of the parents as teachers of their children using homemade toys.	Home Visitor visits child's home weekly to demonstrate to parents how simple toys can be made in the home. During the visits parents learn to utilize toys as learning tools.	An anecdotal record is kept of each Home Visit. Parent keeps a record of use of toys during the week. Video tapes of parent-child interaction are taped in the home weekly and critiqued by the Home Visitor and parent.
To establish and implement three procedures that enable parents to give feedback to the project regarding their child's individual needs and the program in general.	A PARENT-FEED-BACK BOX will be installed at the entrance to the center. The parent group will elect two parent representatives to the advisory council. Individual conferences between parents and staff will be scheduled monthly.	Parent coordinator checks PARENT-FEEDBACK BOX Weekly. Two parent representatives serve on the advisory council. A record is kept by Parent Coordinator of individual conferences between parents and staff.

of the schedule of activities that lie ahead for their child; at this time point out the importance of the sequence of these events. You may want to involve parents in deciding what activities you will undertake during the year. This works especially well if you have several alternative and equally effective strategies in mind.

Routine information about the program—special events, parent conference schedules, fee schedules (if fees are collected)—can be transmitted by newsletter, form letter, or even by telephone.

There is a great deal of information that you should be receiving from the parents about the home and child. What does the child like and dislike in the way of toys, games, foods, pets, and people? What kinds of activities occupy his time at home? What toys are available in the home? What is his relationship with his brothers and sisters? Answers to these questions will help you understand the child's behavior while he is in your charge.

Many programs provide information to parents on child-rearing practices and child-development sequences. Often workshops are set up to assist parents in specific areas of child rearing such as "teaching your child to talk" or "disciplining your child." This kind of service, however, overlaps with activities recommended for the area we call parent-child interaction, which is discussed below.

Again, referring to the planning outline on page 195, we present a planning sequence for the area of information exchange. To meet the broad goal specified, we have established as one objective an exchange that provides parents with information about the activities of the program. The activities listed illustrate some of the ways you might accomplish this objective.

Improving Parent-Child Interactions

Activities in this area should be designed to improve the effectiveness of parents as teachers and nurturers. The parent, through the years, will be the child's primary source of information. Hence, he must be capable of interacting with his child in such a way as to stimulate cognitive, emotional, and social development.

To facilitate parent-child interaction, your program should provide opportunities for parents to learn more about (1) developing skills in general child-rearing practices, (2) promoting and fostering social and emotional development, (3) providing meaningful everyday experiences, (4) fostering and encouraging language growth, and (5) using available community resources for additional learning activities.

Although this may be an oversimplification, most parent-child interaction programs follow one of three models: (1) a behavior-modification model; (2) a psychological-insight model; and (3) an experience model.

The behavior-modification model is systematic and structured. The parents are first taught the basic terminology and rationale of reinforcement principles; then they learn how to observe and quantify, or count, the frequency with which various behaviors occur. The next step usually involves the parents' practicing, under observation and guidance, their newly learned skills in observing and counting frequency of behavior as well as in administering various types of positive reinforcement. After the parent has become sufficiently skilled at these tasks, he is asked to perform them in the home. Perhaps once a week, the parent will review with a program specialist the results of his interactions with the child by presenting and discussing the behavior frequency charts which he or she is using. As specific patterns of reinforcement become part of the parent's repertory, the charting of behavior is often discontinued.

A number of behavior-modification programs are available today. *Parents are Teachers: A Child Management Program* (1971) is designed to help parents become more effective teachers. *Living With Children* (Patterson and Gullion, 1968),* another popular book, gives detailed instructions for teaching children.

The psychological-insight model attempts to develop by an analysis of interaction between parent and child an understanding of why children behave the way they do. This approach, which was popularized by Haim Ginott (1965), often focuses on solving conflict situations by developing "insight" into the causes of the problem. Many psychological insight programs provide lectures and films on child development or personality development. Thomas Gordon's work in Parent Effectiveness Training (1970)* also falls into this category.

Programs following the experience model concentrate on teaching parents to provide developmental experiences for their children. These experiences may be highly focused on one area of development, such as the *Teach Your Child to Talk* program (Pushaw et al., 1969)* or on one stage of development, such as *Ways to Help Babies Grow and Learn* (Segner and Patterson, 1970)* Each of these programs provides activities and suggestions for developmental experiences.

A toy "lending library" can be used to help parents provide appropriate developmental experiences for their children. After a discussion of the developmental level and needs of the child, the parent is given an appropriate educational toy to take home to his child. Usually instructions are included to give the parent an understanding of how the toy can be used for learning. When the child is finished with the toy, the parent brings it back to the center and trades it for another geared to a slightly higher level of developmental learning.

Parents as Resources, a group in Illinois, has put together a series of activities aimed at increasing the quantity and quality of the interactions between parent and child in the home. Their book, *I Saw a Purple Cow* (Cole et al., 1972),* contains "recipes" for a variety of arts and crafts activities that parents and children can do together, using articles already available in most homes.

---

* References followed by asterisks are listed in the annotated bibliography at the end of this chapter.

Services in this area should involve parents in the ongoing activities of the program. The assumption is that by involving the parent in program activities, say, as a teacher's aide, the parent's feelings of self-worth will be strengthened, his understanding of children will increase, and his repertory of experiences and activities will be enlarged. Parent participation in your program will also provide the manpower needed for the successful functioning of ongoing activities.

Although the area of parent participation may overlap to some extent with other areas already discussed, there are a number of program objectives that you may want to pursue in this area alone. Parents can and should participate in your program in many ways. Parents need to be involved in some of the basic program decision making, perhaps as members of an advisory group. After all, the parent is one of the two main consumers of your services (the other, of course, is the child), and in one way or another, he is involved in financing the program.

This is not to say that parents should make program decisions unilaterally. On the contrary, you are the trained professional and should be able to provide alternatives for most aspects of your program. Parents will look to you for leadership in program decisions and will expect it. In return you should expect from them valuable assistance in program decision making.

Many professionals have found that parents make excellent volunteer aides. Under the direction of the teacher or child worker the parent aide can be involved in providing learning experiences for children, monitoring and assisting at lunch and snack time, assisting in taking off and putting on heavy outer clothing, constructing learning materials, and providing transportation.

Usually you will find in your group of parents some with special skills—carpentry, baking, or storytelling, for example. Some parents may have interesting jobs or have had interesting experiences, and you may want to use these as resources for your program activities from time to time.

Referring back to the sample program outline, you will note that the objective in the parent-participation area deals with parents providing feedback to the program in a systematic manner. Again, we have matched a few activities with the objective to demonstrate the need to think through the relationship between your objective and the activities you plan to use to reach it.

Annotated Bibliography*

Adair, Thelma, and Esther Eckstein. *Parents and the Day Care Center.* New York: Federation of Protestant Welfare Agencies, 281 Park Avenue South, 10010, 1969, 36 pp.

Scope: This guide offers suggestions to the director on how to develop and expand parent participation in a day-care setting.

Content: Parent participation is discussed in terms of parents as "actual and potential assets, capable of helping the center toward a mutual widening of horizons." (p. 7.) Attention is given to developing a parent group profile, a community profile, and channels of communication for more accurate assessment of parental needs for involvement. The last pages are devoted to evaluation questions.

Main Use: This booklet is a very useful, easy-to-follow, guide for planning parent involvement. It presents a format that could be used by most programs.

Caldwell, Bettye. *Home Teaching Activities.* Little Rock: Center for Early Development and Education, University of Arkansas, 814 Sherman, 72202.

Scope: This booklet contains enrichment activities that mothers can use with small children in the home.

Content: Each page contains one activity and a listing of: *materials* needed (the materials for every activity in the booklet cost only 75 cents); *instructions* for the mother; and *directions* for what the home visitor will expect next visit. Activities range from working with objects like cups and balls to drawing and making things. Each activity is age coded from 0 to 36 months.

Main Use: These activities would be very useful in a home-visitor program or as "take home" materials for parents. The format is easy to understand and could be used by most parents.

---

* This bibliography was prepared by Janet Grim, coordinator of parent programs for the Technical Assistance Development System, Chapel Hill, North Carolina.

Cole, Ann, et al. *I Saw a Purple Cow.* Boston: Little, Brown and Company, 1972, 96 pp.

Scope: This book, written as a "preschool curriculum for the home," emphasizes using articles already available in the home and learning by doing.

Content: These "learning recipes" are organized under the following subject categories: creating, pretending, exploring, music and rhythm, parties, and learning games. Each recipe contains a "you need" (a listing of materials) and a "you do" (instructions for the child) section.

Main Use: Both parents and professionals will find these ideas useful. The activities are simple for parents to organize and fun for children to do.

Forrester, Bettye J., et al. *Home Visiting with Mothers and Infants.* Nashville, Tennessee: DARCEE, George Peabody College, 1971, 100 pp.

Scope: Presents information about a home-visiting strategy for mothers and infants and about home-visitor practices to modify mothers' interactions with their infants.

Content: Ranges from general a priori considerations to specific empirical findings. Discusses considerations that underlie the home-visiting approach; overall process of planning, implementation, and evaluation; how home visiting proceeds; and suggestions, observations, and evaluation of home visits.

Main Use: Anyone interested in implementing a home-visitor program will find it useful. It is geared toward use with low-income families.

Gordon, Ira J. *Parent Involvement in Compensatory Education.* Urbana: University of Illinois Press (ERIC Clearinghouse on Early Childhood Education), 1968, 87 pp.

Scope: This monograph explores the role of parent involvement in compensatory education. Involvement is viewed at different levels, ranging from observation to control of school system and school board. Rights of parents are pointed out.

Content: The first section discusses the family as an agent of socialization and education. Examples are given of parent participation in university research programs and school and community programs. The final section discusses the implications of these findings for parent programs.

Main Use: This monograph would be useful to any person planning a parent program because it makes the reader aware of the parents' point of view. The emphasis is on planning with, not for, parents.

Gordon, Ira J., and Ronald Lally. *Intellectual Stimulation for Infants and Toddlers.* Gainesville: Institute for the Development of Human Resources, College of Education, University of Florida, 1969, 95 pp.

Scope: This manual contains learning games for mothers to use with infants and toddlers.

Content: A brief introduction discusses the value of "learning games" in nontechnical language. The major part of the manual presents eight series of "games," each series arranged according to developmental level. Each game is illustrated and is explained in the following categories: position of mother and baby; action (what mother is supposed to do); aim (what the baby is to do); and purpose (why is this game useful?). The appendix includes suggestions for making toys.

Main Use: This manual could be used in parent-education groups or any program that seeks to improve the quality of parent-child interaction. The format will appeal to parents of diverse educational levels.

Gordon, Thomas. *Parent Effectiveness Training: The "No-Lose" Program for Raising Responsible Children.* New York: Peter H. Wyden, Inc., 1970, 338 pp.

Scope: Book describes complete model for effective parent-child relationships. How to bring discipline into the home through effective management of conflict.

Content: Discusses such areas as: Parents as Persons, Active Listening, Putting "I Messages" to Work, Parental Power, "No-Lose" Method to Solve Conflicts, and exercises to facilitate using the model.

Main Use: Method of solving conflicts to be used by parents and children. Serves as a basis for an eight-week course in parent effectiveness training.

Instructional Technology Project. *A Mediated Training Program for Parents of Preschool Mentally Retarded Children.* Logan, Utah: Utah State University Special Education, 84321.

Scope: Mediated training package designed to equip parents of preschool mentally retarded children with the techniques necessary to train their children in self-help skills.

Content: The package contains four units; each unit has a participant's workbook and slide-tape program. The units are:
Unit I Behavior—analysis of complex behaviors and the synthesis of simple behaviors into an instructional sequence.
Unit II Cues
Unit III Reinforcement
Unit IV Programming and record keeping
A monitor's manual and script book are also included.

Main Use: This package could be very useful in teaching parents how to teach their children. It would require a skilled monitor and dedicated parents.

Lazar, Joyce, and Judith Chapman. "A Review of the Present Status and Future Research Needs of Programs to Develop Parenting Skills." Washington, D.C.: Social Research Group, George Washington University, 2401 Virginia Avenue., N.W., 1972, 203 pp.

Scope: This is a state-of-the-art paper on completed and ongoing research in parent education. It was prepared at the request of the Office of Child Development. It is based on a review of the literature of recent studies involving parent education.

Content: Abstracts of parent programs are presented in the following order: parent-oriented programs ("offer some kind of tutorial or group experience for parents"); child-oriented programs ("enrichment activities are presented almost exclusively to the child—parents may or may not observe and may be expected to carry out continuing activities with the child"); omnibus programs ("provide more than one pattern of service to children and families and may aim enrichment efforts simulateously"). (pp. 5,6) Studies are described and analyzed to identify available findings in the area of parent education. The final chapter contains an overall summary; issues, needs, and gaps are identified and recommendations made for future use.

Main Use: An excellent comprehensive source of information on parent-education research. Could be used to plan parent programs and to identify useful elements in other parent projects.

Lillie, David L. (ed.). *Parent Programs in Child Development Centers.* Chapel Hill, N.C.: Technical Assistance Development System, 1972, 87 pp.

Scope: This multi-author monograph explores various ways to plan programs for parents of young handicapped children.

Content: Chapter 1 presents an overview of the child-development triad: the roles of parent, child, and professional. Chapter 2 focuses on emotional support for parents; chapter 3 covers exchanging information; chapter 4 deals with parent-child interaction; and chapter 5 tells how to plan a parent program. An annotated bibliography is included.

Main Use: The focus of this document is on planning programs for parents of handicapped children, but the information is also useful for planning any parent program.

Marshall-Poweshiek Joint County Department of Special Education. *Home Stimulation of Handicapped Children.* Marshalltown, Iowa, 9 Westwood Drive, 40148, 331 pp.

Scope: This is a "how to" manual that contains many excellent suggestions for ways to stimulate a preschool child at home.

Content: Many areas are covered, including behavior modification, how parents can enhance creativity, discipline, toys vs. learning tools. Each chapter has a learning-episode evaluation for parents to complete.

Main Use: It is written in simple terms so that it can be used by parents of varying education backgrounds, either in groups or individually. There is an accompanying guide for use by professionals as they work with parents in groups. Shouldn't be limited to parents of handicapped children.

Patterson, Gerald R., and Elizabeth M. Gullion. *Living with Children: New Methods for Parents and Teachers.* Champaign, Illinois: Research Press, 1968, 120 pp.

Scope: Traces in detail the manner in which the parent teaches the child and the child teaches the parent. Social-learning approach. Introduction to behavior modification.

Content: First section deals with how parents and children learn— discusses reinforcers, accidental training and retraining. Second section deals with changing undesirable behavior in the child who fights too often, the overly active child, the dependent, frightened, or withdrawn child.

Main Use: Programmed-instruction approach is useful to teach behavior modification to parents in groups. Techniques applicable to parents of handicapped children.

Pushaw, D., et al. *Teach Your Child to Talk.* Cincinnati: CEBCO Standard Publishing Co., 1969.

Scope: This training package is designed to give parents of preschool children a better understanding of how they can help children learn to talk.

Content: The complete workshop kit contains: (1) a workshop manual—complete lesson plans for three workshops (152 pages); (2) 200 35mm color slides which augment the workshops; (3) 19-minute cassette tape recording—examples of child's speech; (4) A 16mm color movie that summarizes the major points made in the workshop; (5) a parent handbook which gives normal speech guidelines at age-appropriate levels (also included are suggested activities that parents can share with children and a suggested book list); and (6) a "Teach Me to Talk" booklet, a cartoon booklet designed for parents of newborn children.

Main Use: These materials could be used with any group of parents interested in language development. The workshops should not be difficult to organize and present. The parent handbook is a useful resource and could be used separately.

Rood, Larry A. *Parents and Teachers Together: A Training Manual for Parent Involvement in Head Start Centers.* Washington, D.C.: Gryphen House, 1971, 84pp.

Scope: This manual is designed to help parents and staff work together to develop the type of program they want for their center and to implement that program on a day-to-day basis.

Content: Provides training experiences for parents and teachers in the following areas of group interactions: building a relaxed, informal group; individual contributions; communication; problem solving; leadership styles; decision and policy making for the center. Also includes methods to evaluate the training.

Main Use: To be used in child-development programs by person responsible for parent involvement. Excellent ideas on helping parents and staff to become involved.

Schaefer, Earl S. "Parents as Educators: Evidence from Cross-sectional, Longitudinal, and Intervention Research." *The Young Child*, 1972, Vol. 2.

Scope: Rationale for parent-centered programs.

Content: Reports research results in the following areas: Conceptualization of parent behavior, intra-family resemblance, early emergence of levels of intelligence, studies of children in institutions and adoptive homes, cross-sectional studies, longitudinal studies, and intervention research.

Main Use: Reference for establishing a rationale for parent programs. It presents research findings on which to base the rationale.

Segner, Leslie, and Charlotte Patterson. *Ways to Help Babies Grow and Learn: Activities for Infant Education.* Denver, Colorado: World Press, 1970, 49 pp.

Scope: A guide to helping the infant and toddler learn skills which prepare them for successful school experiences.

Content: The material is divided into four learning areas: language development, personal-social development, fine-motor development, and gross-motor development. Activities are grouped separately for infants (to 12 months) and toddlers (to three years) and are arranged in order of difficulty. An appendix of toys and games is also included.

Main Use: This manual could be utilized by parents or teachers to develop and capitalize on parent-child interaction. The format is easy to follow. Activities could be used in a home-visitor program.

Checkpoint
What Have You Learned?

1. The psychological-insight approach to improving parent-child interactions stresses the manner of verbal _____ between the parent and child based on the parent's ability to _____ the child's feelings and actions.

2. Providing developmental experiences for children in the home, where the emphasis is placed on the quality and quantity of activities, is referred to as the _____ approach. The toy "lending library" is an example of this approach.

3. Name the four activity areas you should consider when planning a parent program.

4. Activities that are designed to improve the effectiveness of parents as teachers of their children are grouped under the heading of _____.

5. Providing _____ and _____ support for parents is becoming more and more important in our society because of the lack of reinforcement or support for the role of mother or parent.

6. The two main purposes for having parent programs are (1) to provide a supportive system for parents in accepting the role of parent, and (2) to _____ the center's effectiveness in providing services to children through _____.

You are asking your board of directors or school board for funds to start a parent program. Making your argument as strong as possible, discuss several reasons why a parent program is necessary.

1. Interview individually two or three mothers of preschool children, discussing their roles as child rearers. What are their feelings about this role? Rewarding? Restricting?

2. Attend a parent meeting, preferably a meeting of parents of preschool children, but a P.T.A. or other parent group will do. Make a list of the different topics discussed. Categorize the topics according to the four program areas discussed in this chapter. Where was the emphasis? Should the emphasis be different?

Chapter 12 Organizing an Instructional System

Objectives

After you have completed this chapter, you should be able to:

1. Cite and present the relationship between a short-range and long-range objective.
2. Cite and discuss the variations in the teacher's role in a skill-acquisition period as compared to a practice/generalization period.
3. Cite and discuss the variation in the child's role in a skill-acquisition period as compared to a practice/generalization period.
4. Cite the frequency of the teacher's engagement in (a) formal assessment, (b) informal assessment, (c) long-range objective setting, (d) short-range curriculum activity setting, and (e) instruction for the development of new skills.

By now, you are well acquainted with the various components of the Developmental Task Instructional System. Therefore, it should not be difficult to fit these parts together, and to see that each stage or step in the system is dependent on every other step or stage.

The chart on page 208 reviews three major aspects of the system used, and the frequency with which particular tasks are performed.

As you can see, the teacher's or child worker's role varies at each stage of the Developmental Task Instructional System. During the assessment stage you are primarily an observer, tester, and recorder. During the establishment of instructional objectives stage, you are a planner, developing individual objectives based on information received during the assessment stage. Next, your role changes to that of a curriculum materials and activities specialist. During the last stage, you are an instructor or facilitator of learning, the role that will occupy the major part of your time.

As we discussed in some detail in chapter 3, during the assessment stage you determine each child's level of development in the six developmental areas: fine motor, gross motor, perceptual, reasoning, receptive language, and expressive language. After you have established long- and short-range objectives for each child, it is helpful to maintain your records of objectives in a folder for periodic review and updating. Long-range objectives, which are based mainly on formal assessment findings, should be planned and reviewed at the beginning of each semester or approximately twice a year if you are not on a semester system.

Short-range objectives should be reviewed and updated or revised much more frequently. However, we have found that it is unwise to review short-range objectives more than once a week for each child. More frequent planning is often counterproductive because the teacher may use some of the time that should be spent on actual instruction to establish objectives.

Establishing curriculum activities also involves both long-range and short-range planning. Long-range decisions about the kind of instructional materials and equipment to acquire can be fairly general. After you have gathered your materials, you can then select the curriculum activities that will meet your short-range objectives. The suggested activities at the end of each curriculum chapter are examples of the kinds of activities that can be used for relatively short-range objectives.

Your role and the child's role vary greatly during the learning situation stage. As we discussed before, during the acquisition phase, you present structured activities that are designed to meet specified short-range objectives. The child's role in this situation is to attend and initiate appropriate responses to the instruction.

In contrast, during the practice/generalization stage, the child acts as the initiator, choosing the activities he wants to take part in. The child worker's role at this time is to facilitate the child's choice of activities. As a facilitator, your primary responsibility is to encourage (and guide when necessary) participation and to reward the child's accomplishments, especially when the child has reached closure on a particular activity.

Once you have established short-range objectives for each child, it should not be difficult to decide how to group children for instructional activities during the acquisition phase: children with similar objectives should be grouped together. You need to be careful, however, not to use instructional objectives as the only criterion for placing children in small or large groups. The learning characteristics of each child as well as his previous rate of development need to be considered also.

Unless you have a great deal of adult help, you may find it difficult to operate more than two or three formal learning groups at the same time. Adult leadership is essential during the acquisition stage; during the practice/generalization phase, however, one teacher may

Summary Chart The Developmental Task Instructional System

Steps in Each Stage	Teacher's Role	Procedures and Materials	Frequency
Assessment *Formal*	Assess each child with developmental assessment instrument.	Instruments like the *Carolina Developmental Profile* or P.M.A.	Every four months or beginning of each semester.
Informal	Observe and rate each child's abilities as he performs daily activities.	Keep instructional plan folder for each child. Insert observational notes on a routine basis.	Observe each child throughout the day at least once a week.
Establishment of Instructional Objectives *Long Range*	Based on child's performance on formal assessment instrument and teacher's observations of learning characteristics of the child. Write several long-range objectives for each child.	List long-range objectives in each child's instructional plan folder. Review each time short-range objectives are written.	Every four months or after each formal assessment.
Short Range	Based on long-range objectives, and informal observation of child's daily accomplishments. Write several short-range objectives.	Keep short-range objectives in each child's folder and update on a regular basis.	For each child, not more than once a week and not less than once a month.
Establishment of Curriculum Activities *Long Range*	Based on long-range objectives for all children. Decide on curriculum materials needed and room arrangement.	Purchase, make, or collect instructional materials for motor, perceptual, reasoning, social, and language development.	For each child, not more than once every four months and not less than once a year.
Short Range	Based on short-range objectives for each child, decide on instructional grouping and individual instructional needs.	Drawing from materials and resources available, select individual instructional activities.	For each child, not more than once a week and not less than once a month.
The Learning Situation *Acquisition*	Using a variety of methodologies, teach skills established as objectives.	Choice of large-group, small-group, or individual instruction using instructional materials.	Daily
Practice/ Generalization	Plan a variety of interest centers; facilitate child's choice of activities. Assure closure for child. Reinforce.	Child chooses to be involved in some activities. Make available appropriate games, practice materials, and simulation materials.	Daily

act as a facilitator and still supervise a fairly large number of children.

After curriculum activities have been decided upon, you can begin to work up a daily schedule. At first, of course, you will have to make a very general and temporary shedule. Later, when you have finished your initial assessment of the children, you can then fill in the details of the daily schedule in a more precise manner.

Below is a suggested daily schedule for a half-day program. There is probably not any "best" way to schedule a daily curriculum program. Certain elements, however, should be represented; for example, there should be learning experiences in each of the six developmental areas described earlier and enough time available for both the acquisition and the practice/generalization of skills. Also, two time-honored "rules" of scheduling should be followed: (1) a child has a longer attention span and learns more readily when he is not tired (which is usually the first part of the morning), and (2) gross-motor and other "exciting" activities should be followed by a "calming down" period before the child undertakes activities that require a certain degree of attention or quiet behavior.

Daily Instructional Schedule

Time	Content	Materials	Child's Role	Teacher's Role
8:15 – 8:40	Practice/ generalization of skills and processes. Social/emotional development.	Games; building materials; interest-center materials; simulation materials	Child chooses involvement; cooperates with others; does not interfere with others.	Facilitates child's choice. Encourages, reinforces, guides when necessary.
8:40 – 9:00	Language and reasoning development	Structured to facilitate skill development	Attends, initiates, responds.	Directs lesson activity in large group. Initiates, stimulates, reinforces.
9:00 – 9:20	Fine-motor development	Structured to facilitate skill development	Attends, initiates, responds.	Directs lesson activity in large or small groups or individually. Initiates, encourages, guides, reinforces.
9:20 – 9:40	Snack: self-help; social development; language development.	Juice, cookies, napkins, etc.	Routine, initiates, some choice, cooperation.	Directs and facilitates.

Time	Content	Materials	Child's Role	Teacher's Role
9:40 – 10:00	Perceptual development	Structured to facilitate skill development.	Attends, initiates, responds.	Directs lesson activity in large or small groups or individually. Initiates, stimulates, reinforces.
10:00 – 10:20	Gross-motor development	Large room or playground; gross-motor equipment	Initiates, participates, responds.	Directs activities in large group.
10:20 – 10:45	Practice/ generalization of skills and processes. Social/emotional development.	Various games. Building and simulation materials, practice materials, etc.	Child chooses involvement; cooperates with others; does not interfere with others.	Facilitates child's choice. Encourages, reinforces, guides when necessary.
10:45 – 11:20	Language, motor and social development through music and art	Rhythm instruments; arts and crafts materials.	Some choice in cooperation with teachers. Attends, initiates, cooperates with others.	Directs large group activities in music or art with some response to children's choice. Facilitates, initiates, reinforces.
11:20 – 11:30	Clean up. Social/emotional development	Cleaning materials; soap; etc.	Attends, cooperates, initiates, responds.	Directs and facilitates. Provides closure when needed.
11:30 – 12:00	Lunch: self-help. Social and language development	Standard.	Routine, initiates. Some choice; cooperation.	Directs and facilitates.

In our daily schedule we have briefly summarized the content of time periods during the day, materials that may be needed, the child's role, and the teacher's role during a specified activity.

The daily schedule deals only with the fourth stage of the Developmental Task Instructional System: the learning or instructional stage. As you can see, your role, as well as the child's, is going to vary according to the learning activity.

In our sample, we have included daily experiences in each of the developmental areas. However, you may want to organize your program so that some areas of development are treated on rotating or alternating days. For example, scheduling fine-motor development on Monday, Wednesday, and Friday, and perceptual development at the same time on Tuesday and Thursday. Another possibility would be to alternate by semesters, the first semester dedicated primarily to fine-motor skills and language skills, and the second semester to perceptual skills and reasoning development. Activities for the practice/generalization of all skills should be scheduled daily regardless of the skill acquisition areas you are concentrating on at that particular time.

Checkpoint
What Have You Learned?

1. During instructional periods for acquisition of new skills the teacher is considered a _____ of learning, whereas during instructional periods for generalization and practice of skills he is considered a _____ of learning. **Facts**

2. The child's major role during skill-acquisition instructional periods is to _____ and respond. Opportunities should be provided for the child to choose his involvement during _____ periods.

3. Long-range objectives should be re-established every few months or after each _____, whereas short-range objectives should be re-established no more than _____ and no less than once every _____.

4. Informal assessment occurs _____, whereas formal assessment should occur at the beginning of each _____.

1. Discuss the relationship between long-range and short-range objectives, and explain how they are interrelated with the tasks of planning short-range and long-range instructional activities. **Simulation**

2. Based on the frequency of a teacher's involvement in formal assessment, informal assessment, establishing long-range objectives, establishing short-range objectives, establishing short-range curriculum activities, establishing long-range curriculum activities, and actual instruction (both in direct instruction and in a facilitation role), draw a pie chart showing approximately how much of the teacher's total working time should be spent in each.

1. Visit a preschool program and spend the morning observing the instructional activities. What is the teacher's role in each activity? Does this role appear appropriate to the instructional task? **Application**

2. Ask for a copy of a preschool-program daily schedule. Rearrange the schedule so that it contains the elements of the Developmental Task Instructional System, at the same time retaining some of the elements now present in the schedule.

References

Bangs, T. *Language and Learning Disorders of the Pre-academic Child.* New York: Appleton-Century-Crofts, 1968.

Bank Street Early Childhood Discovery Materials. New York: Macmillan, 1969.

Baumrind, D. "Child Care Practices Anteceding Three Patterns of Preschool Behavior." *Genetic Psychology Monograph,* 1967, 75: 43–88.

Bayley, N. *The California Infant Scale of Motor Development.* Berkeley: University of California Press, 1936.

Becker, W. *Parents Are Teachers: A Child Management Program.* Champaign, Ill.: Research Press, 1971.

Bereiter, C., and S. Engelmann. "Observations on the Use of Direct Instruction with Young Disadvantaged Children." *Journal of School Psychology,* 1966a, 4: 55–62.

_____.*Teaching the Disadvantaged Child in the Preschool.* Englewood Cliffs, N.J.: Prentice-Hall, 1966b.

Bloom, B. *Taxonomy of Educational Objectives.* New York: Longmans, Green, 1956.

_____. *Stability and Change in Human Characteristics.* New York: John Wiley, 1964.

Bobroff, A. "The Stages of Maturation in Socialized Thinking and in the Ego Development of Two Groups of Children." *Child Development,* 1960, 31: 321–38.

Bruner, J. "On Cognitive Growth." In J. Bruner, R. Oliver, and P. Greenfield (eds.), *Studies in Cognitive Growth.* New York: John Wiley, 1966.

Caldwell, B. *Preschool Inventory.* Princeton: Educational Testing Service, 1967.

Corder, W. O. "Effects of Physical Education on the Intellectual, Physical, and Social Development of Educable Mentally Retarded Boys." *Exceptional Children,* 1966, 32:357–64.

Cratty, B. J. *Perceptual and Motor Development in Infants and Children.* London: Macmillan, 1970.

Cratty, B. J., and M. Martin. *Perceptual-Motor Efficiency in Children: The Measurement and Improvement of Movement Attributes.* Philadelphia: Lea and Febiger, 1969.

Distefano, M. K., Jr., N. Ellis, and W. Sloan. "Motor Proficiency in Mental Defectives." *Perceptual and Motor Skills,* 1958, *8:* 231–34.

Dunn, L. M. "Special Education for the Mildly Retarded—Is Much of It Justifiable?" *Exceptional Children,* 1968, *35:* 5–22.

Dunn, L. M., and J. O. Smith. *Peabody Language Development Kits.* Circle Pines, Minn.: American Guidance Service, 1967.

Engelmann, S., J. Osborn, and T. Engelmann. *Distar Language.* Chicago: Science Research Associates, 1969.

Enzer, N. "The Child Development Triad: An Overview of Parent-Child and Professional Interaction." In D. Lillie (ed.), *Parent Programs in Child Development Centers.* Chapel Hill, N.C.: Technical Assistance Development System, 1972.

Erikson, E. H. "Identity and the Life Cycle." *Psychological Issues,* 1959, *1:* 50–100.

————. "Growth and Crisis of the Healthy Personality." In S.G. Sapir and A. C. Nitzburg (eds.), *Children with Learning Problems.* New York: Brunner/Mazel, 1973.

Evans, E. D. *Contemporary Influences in Early Childhood Education.* New York: Holt, Rinehart & Winston, 1971.

Flavell, J. H. *The Developmental Psychology of Jean Piaget.* Princeton: Van Nostrand, 1963.

Francis, R. J., and G. L. Rarick. "Motor Characteristics of the Mentally Retarded." *American Journal of Mental Deficiency,* 1959, *63:* 293–311.

Froebel, F. W. *The Education of Man.* Translated by W. Hailmann. New York: Appleton, 1889.

————. *Pedogogics of the Kindergarten.* Translated by J. Jarvis. New York: Appleton, 1895.

————. *The Songs and Music of Friedrich Froebel's Mother Play (Mutter und Kose Lieder).* Prepared and arranged by S. Blow. New York: Appleton, 1905.

Frostig, M. *Developmental Test of Visual Perception.* Palo Alto, Calif.: Consulting Psychologist Press, 1964.

Gagne, R. *The Conditions of Learning.* New York: Holt, Rinehart & Winston, 1965.

Gesell, A., et al. *The First Five Years of Life.* New York: Harper and Brothers, 1940.

————. *The Child from 5 to 10.* New York: Schocken Books, 1964.

Gesell, A., and C. Amatruda. *Developmental Diagnosis.* New York: Hoeber, 1941.

Gill, N., T. Herdtner, and L. Lough. "Perceptual and Socioeconomic Variables, Instruction in Body-Orientation, and Predicted Academic Success in Young Children." *Perceptual and Motor Skills,* 1968, *26:* 1175–84.

Ginott, H. *Between Parent and Child.* New York: Avon, 1965.

Glaser, R. "Instructional Technology and the Measurement of Learning Outcomes: Some Questions." *American Psychologist*, 1963, *18*: 519–21.

Godfrey, B. "Motor Therapy and School Achievement." *Journal of Health, Physical Education and Recreation*, 1964, *35*: 65–66.

Goldstein, H., J. W. Moss, and L. J. Jordon. "The Efficacy of Special Training on the Development of Mentally Retarded Children." *Exceptional Children*, 1965, *19*: 247.

Gray, S. "Home Visiting Programs for Parents of Young Children." Paper presented at the meeting of the National Association for the Education of Young Children. Boston, 1970.

Gray, S., R. Klaus, J. Miller, and B. Forrester. *Before First Grade*. New York: Teachers College Press, 1966.

Guilford, J. P. "A System of Psychomotor Abilities." *American Journal of Psychology*, 1958, 71: 146–47.

———. *The Nature of Human Intelligence*. New York: McGraw-Hill, 1967.

Gupta, W., and C. Stern. "Comparative Effectiveness of Speaking vs. Listening in Improving Spoken Language of Disadvantaged Young Children." *Journal of Experimental Education*, 1969, *38*: 54–57.

Guskin, S., and H. Spicker. "Educational Research in Mental Retardation." In N. Ellis (ed.), *International Review of Research in Mental Retardation*, Vol. 3. New York: Academic Press, 1968.

Hall, G. S. *Educational Problems*. New York: Appleton, 1911.

Heath, S. R., Jr. "Railwalking Performance as Related to Mental Age and Etiological Types." *American Journal of Psychology*, 1942, 55: 240–47.

———. "The Relationship of Railwalking and Other Motor Performances of Mental Defectives to Mental Age and Etiological Types." *Training School Bulletin*, 1953, *50*: 110–27.

Hebb, D. *The Organization of Behavior*. London: Chapman and Hall, 1949.

Helman, P. "The Relationship Between General Mental Development and Manual Dexterity." *British Journal of Psychology*, 1932, *23*: 279–83.

Hodges, W. L., B. R. McCandless, and H. Spicker. *Diagnostic Teaching for Preschool Children*. Arlington, Va.: The Council for Exceptional Children, 1971.

Howe, C. E. "A Comparison of Motor Skills of Mentally Retarded and Normal Children." *Exceptional Children*, 1959, *23*: 352–54.

Hunt, J. McV. *Intelligence and Experience*. New York: Ronald, 1961.

———. "Revisiting Montessori." In Maria Montessori, *The Montessori Method*. New York: Schocken Books, 1964.

Inhelder, B. "Developmental Psychology." *Annual Review of Psychology*, 1957, *8*: 139–62.

Kagan, J., and H. Moss. *Birth to Maturity: A Study in Psychological Development*. New York: John Wiley, 1962.

Kahn, D., and H. Birch. "Development of Auditory/Visual Integration and Reading Achievement." *Perceptual and Motor Skills,* 1968, *27:* 459–68.

Karnes, M. *Goal: Language Development.* Springfield, Mass.: Milton Bradley, 1972.

Karnes, M., J. Teska, and A. Hodgins. *A Longitudinal Study of Disadvantaged Children Who Participated in Three Different Preschool Programs.* University of Illinois, Institute for Research on Exceptional Children, 1969.

Keister, M. "The Behavior of Young Children in Failure: An Experimental Attempt to Discover and to Modify Undesirable Responses of Preschool Children to Failure." *University of Iowa Studies in Child Welfare,* 1938, *14:* 27–82.

Kephart, N. C. *The Slow Learner in the Classroom.* Columbus, Ohio: Merrill, 1960.

Kilpatrick, W. H. *The Montessori System Examined.* Boston: Houghton Mifflin, 1914.

Kirk, S. A. *Early Education of the Mentally Retarded.* Urbana: University of Illinois Press, 1958.

_____. "Diagnostic, Cultural, and Remedial Factors in Mental Retardation." In S. F. Osler and R. E. Cooke, *The Bio-Social Basis of Mental Retardation.* Baltimore: Johns Hopkins Press, 1965.

_____. *Educating Exceptional Children* (second edition). Boston: Houghton Mifflin, 1972.

Kirk, S. A., J. J. McGarthy, and W. D. Kirk. *The Illinois Test of Psycholinguistic Abilities* (revised edition). Urbana: University of Illinois Press, 1968.

Koppetz, E. W. *Evaluation of Children's Human Figure Drawings.* New York: Grune & Stratton, 1968.

Krathwohl, D., B. Bloom, and B. Masia. *Taxonomy of Educational Objectives, Handbook II: Affective Domain.* New York: David McKay, 1964.

Langan, J. G. "A Comparison of Motor Proficiency in Middle and Lower Class Educable Mentally Retarded Children." Unpublished doctoral dissertation, Indiana University, 1965.

Let's Look at Children. Princeton: Educational Testing Service, 1965.

Lillie, D. L. "The Effects of Motor Development Lessons on the Motor Proficiency of Preschool Culturally Deprived Children." Unpublished doctoral dissertation, Indiana University, 1966.

_____. "The Effects of Motor Development Lessons on Mentally Retarded Children." *American Journal of Mental Deficiency,* 1968, *72:* 803–8.

Lillywhite, H. "Doctor's Manual for Speech Disorders." *Journal of the American Medical Association,* 1958, *167:* 852.

Lowenfeld, V., and W. L. Brittain. *Creative and Mental Growth* (fifth edition). New York: Macmillan, 1970.

Macfarlane, J. "Study of Personality Development." In R. Barker, J. Kounin, and H. Wright (eds.), *Child Behavior and Development.* New York: McGraw-Hill, 1943.

McConnell, F., K. Horton, and B. Smith. "Language Development and Cultural Disadvantagement." *Exceptional Children,* 1969, *35:* 597–606.

McMillan, M. *The Nursery School.* New York: Dutton, 1920.

Mager, R. *Preparing Instructional Objectives.* Belmont, Calif.: Fearon, 1962.

Malpass, L. F. "Motor Proficiency in Institutionalized and Noninstitutionalized Retarded Children and Normal Children." *American Journal of Mental Deficiency,* 1960, *64:* 1012–15.

Mayer, R. S. "A Comparative Analysis of Preschool Curriculum Models." In R. H. Anderson and H. G. Shane (eds.), *As the Twig Is Bent.* Boston: Houghton Mifflin, 1971.

Miller, L. B. *Experimental Variation of Head Start Curriculum: A Comparison of Current Approaches.* Louisville (Kentucky) University, 1970.

Montessori, M. *The Montessori Method.* New York: Schocken Books, 1964.

Mussen, P. H., J. J. Conger, and J. Kagan. *Child Development and Personality.* New York: Harper and Row, 1969.

NAEYC. *Play in Playgrounds.* New York: National Association for the Education of Young Children, 1970.

Nimnicht, G., O. McAfee, and J. Meier. *The New Nursery School.* New York: General Learning Corporation, 1969.

Oliver, J. N. "The Effects of Physical Conditioning Exercises and Activities on the Mental Characteristics of Educationally Subnormal Boys." *British Journal of Educational Psychology,* 1958. *28:* 155–65.

Osgood, C. E. "Motivational Dynamics of Language Behavior." In the *Nebraska Symposium on Motivation.* Lincoln: University of Nebraska Press, 1957.

Papp, H. "Visual Discrimination of Alphabetic Letters." *The Reading Teacher,* 1964, *17:* 221–25.

Parten, J. "Social Participation Among Preschool Children." *Journal of Abnormal and Social Psychology,* 1932, *27:* 243–69.

Piaget, J. *Six Psychological Studies.* New York: Random House, 1967.

Piaget, J., and B. Inhelder. *The Growth of Logical Thinking from Childhood to Adolescence: An Essay on the Construction of Formal Operational Structures.* Translated by A. Parsons and S. Milgram. New York: Basic Books, 1958.

Plowden, Lady B. (chairman). *Children and Their Primary Schools: A Report of the Central Advisory Council for Education,* Vol. 1. London: Her Majesty's Stationery Office, 1967.

Plowman, P. D. *Behavioral Objectives.* Chicago: Science Research Associates, 1971.

Roff, M. "A Factorial Study of Tests in the Perceptual Area." *Psychometric Monograph*, 1953, *41:* 8.

Schaefer, E. "Parents as Educators: Evidence from Cross-Sectional, Longitudinal, and Intervention Research. In W. Hartnup (ed.), *The Young Child*. Washington: National Association for the Education of Young Children, 1972.

Skeels, H. M. "Adult Status of Children with Contrasting Early Life Experiences." *Monographs of the Society for Research in Child Development*, 1966, *31:* No. 3.

Skeels, H. M., and H. B. Dye. "A Study of the Effects of Differential Stimulation of Children." *Proceedings of the American Association on Mental Deficiency*, 1939, *44:* 114–36.

Skinner, B. F. *The Behavior of Organisms: An Experimental Analysis* New York: Appleton, 1938.

———. *Science and Human Behavior*. New York: Macmillan, 1953.

Sloan, W. "Motor Proficiency and Intelligence." *American Journal of Mental Deficiency*, 1951, *55:* 394–406.

Thurstone, L. L. "A Factor Analysis Study of Perception." *Psychometric Monograph*, 1944, No. 4.

———. *Multiple-Factor Analysis: A Development and Expansion of the Vectors of Mind*. Chicago: University of Chicago Press, 1947.

Thurstone, L. L., and T. G. Thurstone. *Factorial Studies of Intelligence*. Chicago: University of Chicago Press, 1941.

Thurstone, T. G. *Primary Mental Abilities Test K-1*. Chicago: Science Research Associates, 1963.

———. *Learning to Think Series*. Chicago: Science Research Associates, 1972.

———. *P.M.A. Readiness Level*. Chicago: Science Research Associates, 1974.

Thurstone, T. G., and D. L. Lillie. *Beginning to Learn: Fine Motor Skills*. Chicago: Science Research Associates, 1970.

———. *Beginning to Learn: Perceptual Skills*. Chicago: Science Research Associates, 1972.

Turiel, E. "Developmental Processes in the Child's Moral Thinking." In P. Mussen, J. Longer, and M. Covington (eds.), *Trends and Issues in Developmental Psychology*. New York: Holt, Rinehart & Winston, 1969.

Weikart, D. P. "Preschool Programs: Preliminary Findings." *Journal of Special Education*, 1967, *1:* 163–81.

———. "A Comparative Study of Three Preschool Curricula." In J. Frost (ed.), *Disadvantaged Child*. New York: Houghton Mifflin, 1970.

———. "Relationship of Curriculum, Teaching, and Learning in Preschool Education." In J. C. Stanley (ed.), *Preschool Programs for the Disadvantaged*. Baltimore: Johns Hopkins Press, 1972.

Weikart, D. P., L. Rogers, C. Adcock, and D. McClelland. *The Cognitively Oriented Curriculum: A Framework for Preschool Teachers.* Washington, D.C.: National Association for the Education of Young Children, 1971.

Wolff, P. "The Developmental Psychologies of Jean Piaget and Psychoanalysis." *Psychological Issues,* 1960, 2.

Wood, M. M. *The Rutland Center Model for Treating Emotionally Disturbed Children.* Athens, Georgia: Rutland Center Technical Assistance Office, 1972.

———. *Developmental Therapy.* Baltimore: University Garden Press, 1975.

Carolina Developmental Profile*

The *Carolina Developmental Profile* is a criterion-referenced behavior checklist designed to be used with the Developmental Task Instructional System. In this system, the goal is to increase the child's developmental abilities to the maximum level of proficiency in order to prepare him for the formal academic tasks he will face in the early elementary school years. The *Profile* is designed to assist the teacher in establishing long-range objectives to increase developmental abilities in six areas: fine motor, gross motor, visual perception, reasoning, receptive language, and expressive language.

The items on the checklist were developed after a careful review of the literature (see facing page) and extensive testing on young children. In other instruments, similar items are standardized and age ranges are given. We have also included age designations, but care should be taken not to apply these age ranges precisely. The purpose of this checklist is not to compare or assess the child in terms of age normative data.

Instructions The items on the *Carolina Developmental Profile* are presented in sequence by area. A task number, a description of the task, and a developmental age are given for each item. If the child completes a task successfully, check the "Can do" column; if not, place a mark in the "Cannot do" column.

The checklist should be given to a child in a large room and in several different sessions. Start with the items on the gross-motor checklist, selecting the age level at which you believe the child will have success. If the items are easily passed, you may want to skip several age levels to find the child's base level of success. If all tasks at a particular age level are passed, it can be assumed that the child can do all tasks below that level in the specific developmental area.

The child's highest level of functioning is established by determining his Developmental Age Ceiling (DAC). The criteria for determining the DAC varies from one developmental area to another. For example, in the area of gross-motor abilities, the DAC is the highest age level at which the child can do three or more tasks. However, in the receptive-language area, the DAC is the highest age level at which the child can do two or more tasks. If you believe that the child might be able to accomplish some tasks at an even higher level, you should question him on those tasks. It is extremely important to keep in mind that the checklist is designed to determine what tasks the child can and cannot accomplish; it is not designed to be used as a standardized assessment instrument.

If you believe that a child could do a task if it were presented a little

---

*The *Profile*, in examiner's manual format, is available from the author, School of Education, University of North Carolina, Chapel Hill.

differently, try it and see. Remember, you are not comparing what the child can do with what other children of his age can do. Rather, the age levels should be used as a general sequential reference guide for the development of the child. To use the age levels as diagnostic labels (for example, fine-motor development at the four-year level) would be misleading. Instead, you want to find out if the child can do a particular task, how easy it was for him; or, if he cannot do it, how close he was to accomplishing the task.

The teacher should immediately translate his or her checklist findings into long-range instructional objectives. At the end of each developmental section, list on the appropriate line the numbers of those tasks that the child *cannot do* below and at his Developmental Age Ceiling. The remainder of your long-range objectives should be taken from the next highest DAC level. For example, if the child's DAC is three for reasoning skills, list the numbers of all the tasks at the four-year level in that area of development.

Summarize your findings in all six areas of development on the front of the *Profile*. First, draw a line through all the tasks the child completed successfully. Next, indicate the long-range objectives for each developmental area by circling those task numbers on the number chart. Finally, write in the area indicated your priority objectives — those objectives that you believe should receive the greatest amount of instructional time.

References

Alpern, Gerald D., and Thomas J. Boll. *Developmental Profile Manual.* Indianapolis: Psychological Development Publications, 1972.

Bayley, Nancy, *Bayley Scales of Infant Development.* New York: The Psychological Corporation, 1969.

Berry, Mildren. *Language Disorders of Children: The Bases and Diagnoses.* New York: Appleton-Century-Crofts, Educational Division, Meredith Corporation, 1969.

Boehm, Ann E. *Boehm Test of Basic Concepts.* New York: The Psychological Corporation, 1971.

Bzoch, Kenneth R., and Richard League. *Bzoch-League Receptive-Expressive Emergent Language Scale (REEL).* Gainesville, Florida: The Tree of Life Press, 1971.

Caldwell, Bettye M. *Preschool Inventory* (rev. ed.). Princeton: Educational Testing Service, 1970.

Doll, Edgar A. *The Oseretsky Tests of Motor Proficiency.* Circle Pines, Minn.: American Guidance Service, 1965.

————. *Vineland Social Maturity Scale.* Circle Pines, Minn.: American Guidance Service, 1965.

Frankenburg, W. K., J. B. Dodds, and A. W. Fandal. *Denver Developmental Screening Test.* Denver: University of Colorado Medical Center, 1970.

Gesell, Arnold, et. al. *The First Five Years of Life.* New York: Harper Brothers, 1940.

Haeussermann, Else. *Developmental Potential of Preschool Children.* New York: Grune & Stratton, 1958.

Jedrysek, Eleonora, Zelda Klapper, Lillie Pope, and Joseph Wortis. *Psychoeducational Evaluation of the Preschool Child.* New York: Grune & Stratton, 1972.

Lillywhite, Herold. "Doctor's Manual for Speech Disorders." *Journal of the American Medical Association,* 1958, *167:* 852.

Moss, Margaret H. *Tests of Basic Experiences (TOBE).* Monterey, Calif: CTB/McGraw-Hill, 1971.

Terman, Lewis M., and Maude A. Merrill. *Stanford-Binet Intelligence Scale.* Boston: Houghton Mifflin Company, 1960.

Thurstone, Thelma Gwinn. *P.M.A. Primary Mental Abilities* (experimental form). Chicago: Science Research Associates, 1970.

Thurstone, Thelma G., and David L. Lillie. *Beginning to Learn: Perceptual Skills.* Chicago: Science Research Associates, 1972.

Valett, Robert E. *Programming Learning Disabilities.* Belmont, Calif.: Fearon, 1969.

Carolina Developmental Profile

A Criterion-Referenced Checklist for
Planning Early Childhood Education

Name _____

Date of Birth _____

Date _____

Developmental Age Level	Gross Motor	Fine Motor	Visual Perception	Reasoning	Receptive Language	Expressive Language
5	20 19 18 17 16	15 14 13 12	12 11 10	12 11 10 9 8 7	12 11 10	12 11
4	15 14 13 12 11	11 10 9 8	9 8 7	6 5 4	9 8 7	10 9 8 7
3	10 9 8 7 6	7 6 5	6 5 4	3 2 1	6 5 4	6 5 4
2	5 4 3 2 1	4 3 2 1	3 2 1		3 2 1	3 2 1

Priority Long-Range Objectives (by area and task number): _____

_____

_____

GROSS MOTOR

Task Number	Description	Developmental Age	Can Do	Cannot Do
1	SEATS SELF IN SMALL CHAIR WITHOUT LOSS OF BALANCE.	2		
2	STANDS WITH HEELS TOGETHER WITHOUT FALLING FOR ABOUT FIVE SECONDS. Demonstrate and allow several trials if necessary	2		
3	TOSSES TENNIS BALL FORWARD. Demonstrate. Can be overhand or "push toss." Ball should travel around two feet or more.	2		
4	PICKS UP ONE-INCH CUBE FROM FLOOR WHILE STANDING, WITHOUT FALLING. Demonstrate. Allow several trials if necessary.	2		
5	WALKS UP AND DOWN THREE STEPS WITHOUT SUPPORT, USING ALTERNATING OR NONALTERNATING STEPS. Demonstrate.	2		
6	THROWS SIX-INCH TO TEN-INCH DIAMETER BALL AT LEAST FIVE FEET, WITHOUT LOSING BALANCE. Demonstrate and allow several trials.	3		
7	JUMPS FROM AN ELEVATION OF APPROXIMATELY SIX INCHES. BOTH FEET SHOULD BE IN AIR. Demonstrate.	3		
8	WALKS STRAIGHT LINE ONE INCH WIDE AND TEN FEET LONG WITHOUT STEPPING OFF MORE THAN THREE TIMES. Demonstrate.	3		
9	WALKS BACKWARD FOR TEN FEET ALONG LINE. Demonstrate. Feet need not stay on line, but general direction along tape should be maintained for pass.	3		
10	WALKS UP AND DOWN THREE STEPS WITHOUT SUPPORT, ALTERNATING THE FORWARD FOOT IN CLIMBING AND DESCENDING. Demonstrate.	3		
11	THROWS TENNIS BALL USING OVERHAND THROW WITH LITTLE TORSO PARTICIPATION. Demonstrate.	4		

Task Number	Description	Developmental Age	Can Do	Cannot Do
12	BALANCES ON ONE FOOT WITHOUT SUPPORT FOR FIVE SECONDS. Demonstrate. Allow three trials. Two successful trials for pass.	4		
13	HOPS AT LEAST TWICE ON ONE FOOT WITHOUT SUPPORT, EITHER IN PLACE OR NOT. Demonstrate.	4		
14	JUMPS AT LEAST TWO INCHES HIGH FROM CROUCHED POSITION. Demonstrate.	4		
15	MAKES RUNNING BROAD JUMP OF AT LEAST 23 INCHES FROM MARKED LINE. DISTANCE SHOULD BE MEASURED FROM POINT CHILD LEAVES GROUND TO POINT WHERE HE LANDS. Demonstrate.	4		
16	BALANCES ON ONE FOOT WITHOUT SUPPORT FOR TEN SECONDS. Demonstrate. Allow three trials. Two successful trials for pass.	5		
17	BALANCES ON TOES WITH FEET TOGETHER AND HEELS OFF THE GROUND FOR TEN SECONDS, WITHOUT SUPPORT. Demonstrate. Allow three trials.	5		
18	MAKES RUNNING BROAD JUMP OF AT LEAST 28 INCHES FROM MARKED LINE. DISTANCE SHOULD BE MEASURED FROM POINT CHILD LEAVES GROUND TO POINT WHERE HE LANDS. Demonstrate.	5		
19	KICKS AN EIGHT-INCH TO TEN-INCH DIAMETER BALL, EITHER FROM FLOOR OR USING DROP KICK, AT LEAST EIGHT FEET IN THE AIR. Demonstrate.	5		
20	SKIPS SMOOTHLY. Demonstrate if necessary.	5		

Developmental Age Ceiling (highest age level at which child can do three or more tasks): _____

Tasks that child cannot do *at* and *below* Developmental Age Ceiling: _____

_____

Long-Range Objectives (by task number): _____

Notes and Comments: _____

_____

FINE MOTOR

Task Number	Description	Developmental Age	Can Do	Cannot Do
1	TURNS A FEW PAGES IN A CHILD'S STORYBOOK, ONE AT A TIME WITH DEFINITE CONTROL AND EASE.	2		
2	BUILDS A STANDING TOWER OF SIX TO EIGHT ONE-INCH CUBES. Demonstrate, and leave tower in place as a model. Allow three trials.	2		
3	STRINGS AT LEAST TWO BEADS IN NO MORE THAN TWO MINUTES. Demonstrate. Count any bead put on string past plastic tip, even if it comes off later.	2		
4	UNWRAPS PIECE OF TWISTED-END WRAPPED CANDY WITHOUT ANY HELP. Demonstrate if necessary.	2		
5	BUILDS THREE-BLOCK BRIDGE. Demonstrate, and leave bridge in place as a model. For pass, base blocks should not touch each other. Allow two trials.	3		
6	COPIES CIRCLE FROM SAMPLE. Allow three trials. Pass any enclosed form. Ask child to "make one just like this." (See page 236.)	3		
7	CUTS PAPER IN TWO PIECES WITH SCISSORS. Match scissors to hand preference. Allow two trials.	3		
8	TRACES DIAMOND PATTERN WITH PRIMARY PENCIL OR CRAYON. (See page 236.) Demonstrate. Must begin at top, move on path counterclockwise, and stay within pathway for pass. Touching sides of pathway is permissible. Two trials.	4		
9	COPIES CROSS (+) FROM SAMPLE. Allow three trials. Pass any two crossing lines. Ask child to "make one just like this." (See page 236.)	4		
10	CATCHES AN EIGHT-INCH TO TEN-INCH BALL, THROWN FROM APPROXIMATELY FIVE FEET AWAY WITH ARMS FLEXED. Allow three trials. One catch for pass.	4		
11	PLACES TEN PENNIES IN BOX ONE AT A TIME (USING PREFERRED HAND) WITHIN FIFTEEN SECONDS. Demonstrate and then present pennies and box to child.	4		

Task Number	Description	Developmental Age	Can Do	Cannot Do
12	COPIES SQUARE FROM SAMPLE. Allow three trials. Pass only closed four-sided figures with sharp corners. Ask child to "make one just like this." (See page 236.)	5		
13	CRUMPLES PIECE OF TISSUE PAPER (4½ INCH BY 4½ INCH) TO FORM A BALL. Demonstrate.	5		
14	PLACES MATCHSTICKS IN BOX WITH BOTH HANDS SIMULTANEOUSLY. Put ten sticks in row on each side of box. Must pick up one stick at a time using thumb and index finger. Demonstrate. Pass: five sticks per hand within 20 seconds; two trials.	5		
15	FOLDS SIX-INCH PAPER SQUARE TO MAKE TRIANGLE. Demonstrate with separate sheet using same hand dominance as child's. Leave your model. Pass: any resemblance of a triangle; one trial.	5		

Developmental Age Ceiling (highest age level at which child can do three or more tasks): _____

_____

Tasks that child cannot do *at* and *below* Developmental Ceiling: _____

_____

Long-Range Objectives (by task number): _____

_____

Notes and Comments: _____ • _____

_____

VISUAL PERCEPTION

Task Number	Description	Developmental Age	Can Do	Cannot Do
1	MATCHES COLOR TO SAMPLE. Present child with six different colored cubes. Keep a matching set of six out of sight, presenting them one at a time and asking him to show you one just like it. Do not name the color, or ask child to do so. Demonstrate. Five correct for pass.	2		
2	GROUPS THINGS TOGETHER BY COLOR, FORM, OR SIZE. Examples: colored blocks, poker chips, or marbles; different size blocks, cups, or logs; different forms such as shapes, beads, or silverware (knives, forks, spoons). Does this during play.	2		
3	STACKS FIVE RINGS ON A PEG IN ORDER. Demonstrate. Rings should be of graduated sizes. Pass if the child is able to give you the rings in the correct order but has trouble stacking them on the peg. The objective of this item is to see whether the child can perceive (visually) differences in size — not the fine-motor ability to stack.	2		
4	MATCHES TO SAMPLE CIRCLE, SQUARE, AND TRIANGLE. Present child with templates (two each) for the above shapes. Pick up circle, asking child to find another like it. Return circle templates to the group. Repeat for square and triangle. Allow one trial for each shape. Three correct for pass.	3		
5	MAKES CIRCLE OUT OF TWO HALF CIRCLES AFTER DEMONSTRATION. Present halves to child with edges parallel to edge of table in front of child. Allow three trials.	3		
6	MATCHES TO SAMPLE PICTURES OF ANIMALS: DOG, HORSE, BEAR, AND CAT. Point to one of the pictures in the top row and ask child to "find one like this one."(See page 237.) Repeat for the three other pictures. Must get all correct.	3		
7	NAMES PICTURE OF ITEMS REMOVED FROM VIEW. Show child three culturally familiar pictures and name them. Hide pictures from view one at a time until each has been hidden once. Three correct for pass.	4		

Task Number	Description	Developmental Age	Can Do	Cannot Do
8	SELECTS TWO IDENTICAL PICTURES OUT OF SET OF THREE. Ask child to point to the two pictures that are exactly alike. Three correct for pass. (See page 237 for pictures.)	4		
9	ADDS TWO PARTS TO AN INCOMPLETE MAN. Tell child to draw in the parts that are missing. Pass anything that resembles an arm and leg.	4		
10	COPIES THREE DESIGNS. Allow two trials for each design. Ask child to "make one just like this one." Draw each of the following designs one at a time for the child. $$\mathrm{II} \quad + \quad L$$ He must copy the design using crayon or primary pencil. The objective of this item is to see if the child can visually perceive these designs not if he has the fine-motor ability to draw. Pass any design that perceptually resembles the one you drew.	5		
11	PUTS TOGETHER A LARGE FOUR-TO SIX-PIECE PUZZLE AFTER DEMONSTRATION.	5		
12	ARRANGES COINS FROM SMALLEST TO LARGEST (DIME, NICKLE, QUARTER, HALF DOLLAR.) Demonstrate and describe task. Allow two trials. One correct for pass.	5		

Developmental Age Ceiling (highest age level at which child can do two or more tasks): _____

Task that child cannot do *at* and *below* Developmental Age Ceiling: _____

_____

Long-Range Objectives (by task number): _____

Notes and Comments: _____

_____

REASONING (*= late range; x = early range)

Task Number	Description	Developmental Age	Can Do	Cannot Do
1	DISCRIMINATES BETWEEN BIG AND LITTLE: POINTS TO *BIG* DOG, THEN *LITTLE* BALL, THEN *LITTLE* DOG, THEN *BIG* BALL ON REQUEST. Allow one trial each. Four correct for pass. (See page 238 for picture.)	3*		
2	CHOOSES ONE AND THEN ONE MORE: FROM A GROUP OF TEN BLOCKS CHILD GIVES YOU ONE BLOCK ON REQUEST. THEN GIVES ONE MORE BLOCK ON REQUEST.	3*		
3	DISCRIMINATES BETWEEN LONG AND SHORT: POINTS TO THE LONGEST LINES WHEN ASKED TO DO SO. Draw two lines (two inches and two and one-half inches). Alternate position (one on top and one on bottom) by turning the paper. Three out of three, or five out of six, for a pass.	3*		
4	USES BIGGER, SLOWER, AND HEAVIER CORRECTLY ON REQUEST. Ask child: (a) "Which is *bigger*, a tree or a flower?" (b) "Which is *slower*, a car or a bicycle?" (c) "Which is *heavier*, a brick or a shoe?" One trial each. One correct for a pass.	4*		
5	COMPLETES OPPOSITE ANALOGY STATEMENTS AFTER EXPLANATION OF TASK. (a) "Brother is a boy; sister is a _____." (girl, woman, etc.) (b) "In daytime it is light; at night it is _____." (c) "Father is a man; mother is a _____." (d) "The snail is slow; the rabbit is _____" (e) "The sun shines during the day; the moon shines at _____." One trial each; two correct for a pass.	4*		
6	COUNTS FOUR OBJECTS (BLOCKS). Present blocks to child one inch apart in a row. For pass, must count blocks, and give correct total.	4*		
7	USES SOFTLY AND LOUDLY CORRECTLY. On request: claps hands softly; stomps feet softly; claps hands loudly; stomps feet loudly. One trial each.	5x		
8	STATES NUMBER OF WHEELS A BICYCLE HAS. Allow one response.	5		
9	TOUCHES THE MIDDLE IN A ROW OF FIVE BLOCKS ON REQUEST. Present blocks half an inch apart in a row. Allow one trial.	5		

Task Number	Description	Developmental Age	Can Do	Cannot Do
10	STATES NUMBER OF WHEELS A CAR HAS. Allow one response.	5½		
11	TOUCHES FIRST, THEN LAST, BLOCK IN ROW OF FIVE ON REQUEST. Allow one trial each. Pass regardless of which end block is selected for first and last if the two choices are consistent with each other.	5½		
12	NAMES COMPOSITION OF THREE ITEMS ON REQUEST. Ask child: (a) "What is a spoon made of?" (metal, silver, wood, or plastic) (b) "What is a shoe made of?" (leather, rubber, or cloth) (c) "What is a door made of?" (wood, metal, or glass) Allow one trial each, though each question may be repeated if necessary. Three correct for pass.	5½		

Developmental Age Ceiling (highest age level at which child can do two or more tasks): _____

Tasks that child cannot do *at* and *below* Developmental Age Ceiling: _____

_____

Long-Range Objectives (by task number): _____

Notes and Comments: _____

_____

RECEPTIVE LANGUAGE

Task Number	Description	Developmental Age	Can Do	Cannot Do
1	FOLLOWS SIMPLE DIRECTIONS. (a) "Put the block on the chair." (b) "Bring the block to me." (c) "Put the block on the table." Look at child while giving directions; do not accompany directions with gestures. Repeat directions, if necessary. Allow two tries for each direction.	2		
2	TOUCHES OBJECTS DESIGNATED BY NAME ON REQUEST. Ask child to give you or to touch the (a) cup, (b) crayon, (c) shoe, (d) ball, (e) scissors, (f) button. One trial per item; five correct for pass.	2		
3	TOUCHES OBJECTS DESIGNATED BY FUNCTION ON REQUEST. Ask child to give you or to touch what (a) we drink out of, (b) goes on our feet, (c) we can cut with, (d) we can color with, (e) we can throw, (f) we use to fasten our clothes. One trial per item; three correct for pass.	2		
4	TOUCHES THREE PICTURES DESIGNATED BY ACTION ON REQUEST. Ask child to touch the picture of the child (a) sleeping, (b) running, (c) eating. Pictures should be culturally familiar. Examples on page 238.	3		
5	FOLLOWS SIMPLE DIRECTIONS (EACH CONTAINING A DIFFERENT PREPOSITION). "Put the block: (a) on the chair, (b) under the chair, (c) behind the chair, (d) in front of the chair, (e) beside the chair." Look at child while giving directions; do not accompany directions with gestures. Repeat directions if necessary, but allow only one attempt per direction. Three correct for pass.	3		
6	TOUCHES PICTURE OF NIGHTTIME WHEN ASKED "WHICH PICTURE TELLS YOU THAT IT IS NIGHTTIME?" Allow one trial. Use culturally familiar pictures.	3		
7	TOUCHES BLOCKS DESIGNATED BY COLOR ON REQUEST. Present all four blocks together. Ask child to touch in turn the red, blue, yellow, and green block. One trial each color; three correct for pass.	4		
8	SAME AS RECEPTIVE LANGUAGE TASK 5. Four correct for pass.	4		

Task Number	Description	Developmental Age	Can Do	Cannot Do
9	TOUCHES PICTURES DESIGNATED BY DISTINCTIVE CHARACTERISTICS ON REQUEST. Ask child to show you the picture of what (a) we cook on, (b) we carry when it is raining, (c) gives us milk, (d) has the longest ears, (e) shines in the sky at night, (f) catches mice. One trial per item. Four correct for pass. (See page 239 for pictures.)	4		
10	TOUCHES THE PICTURES WITH THE KNIVES ON REQUEST. Ask the child to touch the pictures of the knives. This request may be repeated. Allow one trial. (See page 239 for pictures.)	5		
11	TOUCHES THE ONE THAT IS DARK BUT NOT LITTLE ON REQUEST. Tell the child to look at the different shapes. (See page 239.) Then ask him to *touch the one that is dark but not little.* Allow one trial.	5		
12	TOUCHES THE PICTURE OF THE ONE WHO WILL BE HURT, ON REQUEST. Tell the child to look at the pictures of the children. (See page 239.) Then ask him to touch the *picture of the one who will be hurt.* Allow one response.	5		

Developmental Age Ceiling (highest age level at which child can do two or more tasks): _____

Tasks that child cannot do *at* and *below* Developmental Age Ceiling: _____

_____

Long-Range Objectives (by task number): _____

Notes and Comments: _____

_____

EXPRESSIVE LANGUAGE

Task Number	Description	Developmental Age	Can Do	Cannot Do
1	REPEATS TWO DIGITS CORRECTLY IN GIVEN ORDER AFTER PRACTICE. Ask child to listen carefully and say "two." Do not proceed until child succeeds at this practice. Then ask him to say: (a) "4-7", (b) "6-3", (c) "5-8." Pronounce digits, one per second, clearly and with equal emphasis. Allow one trial per set of digits. One correct for pass.	2½		
2	NAMES PICTURED OBJECTS ON REQUEST. Point to one picture at a time. (See page 240.) Ask child what the picture is, or what he calls it. Allow one trial per picture. Eight correct for pass.	2½		
3	TELLS FIRST AND LAST NAME ON REQUEST. Ask child his name. Should he give only his first name, ask what the rest of his name is, or what his other name is.	2½		
4	ANSWERS COMPREHENSION QUESTIONS. Ask child: (a) "What should you do when you are hungry?" (b) "What should you do when you are sleepy?" (c) "What should you do when you are cold?" Examples of acceptable answers: (a) I eat. Candy. (b) I sleep. Go to bed. (c) Go in. I sick. (Question c may be understood by child to mean "When you have a cold.") One response per question. One correct for pass.	3		
5	TALKS ABOUT PICTURES. Present three culturally relevant pictures one at a time, asking the child to talk about the picture, but not asking him specific questions. All three pictures should contain several children participating in some event (party, picnic, parade, school, store). For a pass the child should be able to name at least three objects in each picture and describe some element (boy is wearing hat) or interpret some action (a party).	3½		
6	USES TWO- OR THREE-WORD PHRASES, SOME OF WHICH MUST INCLUDE PERSONAL PRONOUNS AND/OR ASK QUESTIONS. List some of these phrases used by child during the normal routine of the day. Typical examples are "Where kitty?" "Where kitty go?" "Ball gone." "Me want cookie."	3½		

Task Number	Description	Developmental Age	Can Do	Cannot Do
7	SAME AS EXPRESSIVE LANGUAGE TASK 2. Fourteen correct for pass.	4		
8	REPEATS TWELVE- OR THIRTEEN-SYLLABLE SENTENCES. Ask child to say "Spot is a good dog." Use this sample to make the task expectations clear to the child, then ask him to say: (a) "The boy's name is John. He is a very good boy." (b) "When a train passes, you will hear the whistle blow." (c) "We are going to have a good time in the country." Pronounce each word clearly, in a normal manner. One correctly repeated sentence for a pass.	4		
9	GIVES PURPOSE FOR HAVING BEDS AND TELEVISION(S) ON REQUEST. Ask child: (a) "Why do we have bed?" (b) "Why do we have television?" One trial for each question. For a pass, child must give one purposeful use or reason for each, or two uses or reasons for one.	4½		
10	GIVES FUNCTION OF EYES AND EARS ON REQUEST. Ask child: "What do we do with our (a) eyes, (b) ears?" One trial for each question. Must give the correct general function (see, hear), or accurate specific use (watch T.V., listen to songs).	4½		
11	USES FOUR- TO SIX-WORD PHRASES. List some of the phrases used by child during the normal routine of the day (similar to Expressive Language task 6).	5		
12	USES REGULAR PLURALS CORRECTLY MOST OF THE TIME. List some phrases (sentences) used by the child that include correct use of regular plurals. Typical examples are "two dogs," "flowers," "my hands."	5		

Developmental Age Ceiling (highest age level at which child can do two or more tasks): _____

Tasks that child cannot do *at* and *below* Developmental Age Ceiling: _____

Long-Range Objectives (by task number): _____

Notes and Comments: _____

Fine Motor*

6	
8	
9	
12	

*Material presented to child should be approximately twice the size shown here.

Reasoning

1

Receptive Language

4

2, 7

Answer Key

Chapter 1

1. (1) Social; (3) research; intervention/education
2. open-classroom
3. the child's
4. Bereiter and Engelmann's program/*Distar*
5. Skeels; intervention/education
6. supervision; planning (Use of systematic procedures is also acceptable.)
7. Weikart (1970); Bereiter and Engelmann (1966a); Hodges, McCandless, and Spicker (1971); Karnes, Teska, and Hodgins (1969); and Miller (1970)
8. treatment-comparison
9. The differences between (1) teachers; (2) groups of children; (3) prior learning experience of groups; and (4) classroom environments
10. Weikart's research shows that significant gains can occur in preschool programs if planning and supervision of the programs are effective (which indicates teachers should receive training in this area).

   The findings of the Karnes, Teska, and Hodgins study comparing five preschool curriculum approaches suggests that the more structured programs have greater effects on intellectual development (which indicates teachers should be trained in the skills of designing a structured program).

Chapter 2

1. growth; development; various research
2. Gross motor. The other areas are fine motor, perceptual, reasoning, receptive language, and expressive language.
3. practice/generalization; acquisition
4. first
5. establishing; objectives

Chapter 3

1. assessment
2. teacher or child worker; objectives
3. teacher or child worker
4. evaluation
5. normative
6. instructional objectives
7. gross motor, fine motor, visual perception, reasoning, receptive language, and expressive language

Chapter 4

1. goals/objectives
2. Individualized instruction
3. needs or set of needs
4. Cost of reducing teacher-child ratio; lack of instructional space; tradition; cost of materials and equipment; lack of training; disagreement on what is good individualized instruction
5. A teacher may overcome a space problem by using partitions to create small interest and learning centers; hallways and outdoor areas may also be used. He or she may also train aides and volunteers to work with children on an individual basis. Teachers may also set up learning situations where children can learn from each other. Individual needs can also be met by audio-visual equipment and (for older children) workbook materials.
6. Assessment, establishing instructional objectives, establishing curriculum activities, the learning situation
7. acquisition; practice
8. 85 to 90
9. By needs, abilities, or age

Chapter 5

1. Thurstone was the first to identify motor ability as a component of primary mental abilities. Guilford, also using factor analysis, isolated specific gross-motor factors (static balance, dynamic balance, gross-body coordination, agility, and endurance/strength).
2. fine-motor; finger dexterity, wrist flexibility; arm and hand steadiness, and finger speed
3. b, e, f, g, i, j
4. correlation/relationship
5. gross; fine

6. factor; participate

7. running, jumping, making snow angels, jumping jacks, sit-ups, trampoline activities, and tunnel crawling

8. task

Chapter 6

1. dynamic; meaning; incoming

2. b, c, e, f

3. Matching to sample; Katy the Kangaroo lesson

4. perceptual selection

5. speed and accuracy

6. conclusions; stimuli

7. Matching two halves of a circle; tracing geometric figures

8. *Beginning to Learn: Perceptual Skills; Learning to Think Series*

9. Breaking down large tasks into smaller, simpler tasks; presenting tasks in formats that are motivating and stimulating

10. In teaching children to write, for example, begin with a series of tasks such as tracing figures, imitating and copying figures, and then gradually introduce the copying of letters. A good example of a motivating "tracing" activity is giving the children toy cars, and having them follow "roads" drawn on large sheets of paper taped to the floor. The "roads" can be made increasingly more difficult.

Chapter 7

1. reasoning

2. concepts

3. cognition

4. classification, associations, and sequencing

5. part-whole relationships, analogies, figure relationships, bead sequencing, and time sequencing

6. classification

7. Association

8. time sequencing

9. part-whole relationship

10. analogy

Chapter 8

1. receptive language; comprehension

2. expressive language; meaningful

3. developmental

4. Osgood; *Illinois Test of Psycholinguistic Abilities*

5. 1(f); 2(d); 3(b); 4(g); 5(a); 6(e); 7(c)

6. (a) 2–3 years; (b) 5–6 years; (c) 1–2 years

7. behavioral

Chapter 9

1. affective, cognitive

2. sequential stages of development

3. cognitive, social-affective, and sensorimotor

4. Responding to the Environment with Success (stage two)

5. stage four

6. pleasure

7. three; Learning Skills for Successful Group Participation

Chapter 10

1. eight; deficiency; two; perception, gross motor, fine motor, receptive language, expressive language, and reasoning

2. specific skill training

3. two standard deviations

4. developmental; academic

Chapter 11

1. interaction; understand/develop insight into

2. experience

3. Providing emotional support for parents, exchanging information with parents, improving parent-child interactions, and developing parent participation in your program

4. the experience model

5. social; emotional

6. increase; information obtained from parents

Chapter 12

1. instructor; facilitator

2. attend; practice/generalization

3. formal assessment; once a week; month

4. at least once a week; semester or every four months

Early Childhood Education was set in Trump body type and Helvetica Condensed and Aurora Condensed display type by Graphic Typesetting Service, Los Angeles. George Banta Company was the printer. The book and cover were designed by Joseph di Chiarro; House of Graphics did the illustrations. Karl Schmidt was the sponsoring editor, and Sara Boyd the project editor.